D0932605

the series on school

Patricia A. Wasley
University of Washington

Ann Lieberman
Carnegie Foundation for the
Advancement of Teaching

Joseph P. McDonald
New York University

SERIES EDITORS

(Continued)

the series on school reform, *continued*

THE
TEACHING
CAREER

EDITED BY
John I. Goodlad and Timothy J. McMannon

Foreword by Patricia A. Wasley

Teachers College, Columbia University
New York and London

Published by Teachers College Press, 1234 Amsterdam Avenue, New York, NY
10027

Library of Congress Cataloging-in-Publication Data

The teaching career / edited by John I. Goodlad and Timothy J. McMannon ;
    foreword by Patricia A. Wasley
        p. cm. — (the series on school reform)
    Includes bibliographical references and index.
    ISBN 0-8077-4454-9 (cloth : alk. paper) — ISBN 0-8077-4453-0 (pbk. ; alk.
    paper)
        1. Teachers—Training of—United States. 2. Teachers—In-service
    training—United States. 3. Teacher effectiveness—United States.
    4. School improvement programs—United States.
    I. Goodlad, John I. II. McMannon, Timothy J. III. Series
    LB1715.T429   2004
    370'.71'1—dc22   2003067175

ISBN 0-8077-4453-0 (paper)
ISBN 0-8077-4454-9 (cloth)

Printed on acid-free paper
Manufactured in the United States of America

11   10   09   08   07   06   05   04   8   7   6   5   4   3   2   1

Contents

Foreword

When I started teaching high school English in 1975, I came out of a newly minted, postbaccalaureate teacher education program. I had a full year of student teaching. My student teaching supervisor was one of my methods professors in arts and science, and instead of visiting my classroom occasionally, he was there every week and spent whole days there. He taught lessons himself; he watched me teach and teamed with both my cooperating teacher and with me. This approach to supervision had many of the elements that we are still recommending for teacher education programs.

The truth, however, is that when I entered my own classroom—regardless of my excellent preparation—I was simply a novice. Unfamiliar with the curriculum offered. Unfamiliar with my colleagues in my new school. Unfamiliar with the 160 kids I taught daily and their families. My first couple of years were one-foot-in-front-of-the-other years. Unmediated. Unsupported. Barely reflective. Devoid of feedback.

After a few years, I understood that the only way to move up on the salary scale was to go back to school. After scanning the providers of professional development—the local university, the school district, and the union—I elected to attend a month-long session in drama. It was marvelous fun. We learned the fundamentals of putting on plays: auditions, set construction, blocking, rehearsal scheduling, and so forth. I did that for three consecutive years.

I am sure that this experience did not hurt my teaching. But I taught the least successful students in a small, rural high school, and the drama courses did not help my reticent and largely unsuccessful students to be any better readers. In fact, as a high school English teacher, I had never had a reading course, and I didn't know how to teach reading. No one at my school was guiding my professional development choices or asking that I analyze data from my classroom to determine what I might need to work on.

I wish I could say that current conditions were completely different, but that, unfortunately, is not true. Teachers are still emerging from supposedly newly minted teacher education programs while policymakers and local school administrators still wonder why preparation programs can't get it right. Teachers still find themselves in classrooms where they are novices without support or guidance or meaningful feedback. They are still selecting professional development opportunities that capture *their* interests rather than focusing on their students' needs.

Expectations for teachers' accomplishments with students have changed dramatically. "No Child Left Behind," "all children can learn," "high standards and high stakes"—teachers hear these mantras regularly repeated by policymakers, the business community, and their bosses. Yet conditions in teaching have not changed substantially. An accumulation of research suggests that 55% of teachers leave the profession in the first five years. They leave because they feel unsuccessful with students and because they are not getting the kind of support they need.[1] They leave because they are poorly paid. The fact that so many teachers abandon the profession suggests that we are wasting the investment that school districts make in recruitment and selection and that universities have made in preparation programs. It also suggests that we will always have a huge need for newly prepared teachers.

Another problem is that there is still little coherence between teacher preparation programs and later professional development. Where school districts do have mentoring programs for beginning teachers there is little capitalization on what teachers were taught in their preparation programs. If there were coherence among the various dimensions of a teacher's early career, the likelihood is that teachers would feel better supported and that they might find the profession more stimulating and manageable for the long term.

It is in response to these issues that I began gathering colleagues to work on an initiative, Strengthening and Sustaining Teachers (SST). Funded by the Ford Foundation, the Carnegie Corporation, the General Electric Fund, and the Gates Foundation, SST is a five-year project that aims to build sustainable systems of support for teachers in Portland, Maine, and Seattle, Washington, from their preservice education programs through their fifth year in teaching. The goals are to reduce the attrition rate of teachers and to create two examples of more coherent early-career pathways. The SST project is coordinated by several organizations committed to the development of quality teachers: The National Commission on Teaching and America's Future (NCTAF), the Teacher Union Reform Network (TURN), the Institute for Educational Inquiry (IEI), Bank Street College, and the University of Washington. These coordinating partners are each connected to networks of states, universities, unions, and school districts, which we hope will be interested in this project once the pilot districts have had enough time to build the requisite interconnected pathway for emerging teachers. Each site includes partners from the teachers union, colleges of education and arts and sciences, and the local school district. Evaluation of the project is being conducted by NCTAF and the Center for Teaching and Policy. The project should be ready for close scrutiny in 2006.

The chapters in this book describe the issues that surfaced as we began our discussions about building such an ambitious and complicated system of support for teachers. Some of the chapters relate to the project specifically, and some examine in greater detail the issues that plague a beginning teacher's life. Overall, they paint a picture of teaching as a challenging, complex endeavor for which initial preparation, however good, is not sufficient. Teaching is a life of continuous learning that requires support from an array of groups that, in the past, have rarely worked in concert to provide it. What follows describes what is both necessary and feasible. Strengthening and sustaining the teaching career for the teachers we have and those to come is perhaps the most significant thing we can readily do to ease the shortage of competent, caring, qualified educators in the nation's classrooms.

Patricia A. Wasley
University of Washington

NOTE

1. National Commission on Teaching and America's Future, *No Dream Denied: A Pledge to America's Children* (Washington, D.C.: National Commission on Teaching and America's Future, 2003).

Preface

TIMOTHY J. MCMANNON

Writing in the 1850s, Henry Barnard, the first principal of the Normal School at New Britain, Connecticut, observed that aspiring teachers need a "martyr spirit"[1]; that is, they must be willing, to some degree, to sacrifice themselves for the good of their students and the good of society. Anyone familiar with the educational scene today knows that little has changed since Barnard's time. Teaching remains a profession that demands much of its practitioners and, by many measures, gives little in return. Low salaries, long hours, and bureaucratic regulations burden many teachers in the United States today.

The intrinsic rewards of teaching can be tremendous, however, and perhaps that is why the profession continues to attract many of the best and brightest young people our country produces. But attracting young people to teaching is not enough to ensure that all classrooms in our nation's schools are staffed by caring, qualified, and capable teachers; intrinsic rewards simply are not always enough to keep them in the profession. Good teachers often seize opportunities to move into other occupations where the pay or benefits are better. According to *Learning the Ropes*, a 1999 publication of Recruiting New Teachers, Inc., nearly 10% of first-year teachers in public schools do not make it to the end of the school year, and more than 20% leave in the first three years.[2] As a result, too many children, especially those in inner-city schools, try to learn in classrooms headed by an unending parade of underqualified or substitute teachers. No wonder policymakers are so willing to embrace programs that enable military veterans to slide into teaching positions or allow teacher candidates to gain certification through routes other than traditional preparation programs.

Some educators insist that there is a better way. Rather than accepting high attrition rates as an unavoidable part of the teaching profession, they say, we should take steps to ensure that new teachers remain in the profession by giving them not only adequate preservice preparation but also sufficient personal and professional support in the first few years. Rather than filling classrooms with people who have few qualifications other than a willingness to teach, we should make teaching a much more agreeable occupation for those who are already in it. And rather than pretending that teacher quality and student success result solely from the quality of teacher education programs, we should recognize that there are multiple contributors to a teacher's preparation. Genuine teacher preparation improvement goes hand in hand with genuine school improvement, and both depend on collaboration among teacher educators, school administrators, teachers, arts and sciences faculty members, unions, and professional organizations.

Bringing all of these stakeholders together to renew teachers' preparation, induction, and professional development is the purpose of the Strengthening and Sustaining Teachers initiative (SST). In 1999, the SST's coordinating partners—Bank Street College of Education, the National Commission on Teaching and America's Future (NCTAF), the Institute for Educational Inquiry (IEI), and the Teacher Union Reform Network (TURN)—selected Portland, Maine, and Albuquerque, New Mexico, as initial sites on which to focus their efforts. The University of Washington's College of Education joined as a coordinating partner in 2000, and Seattle became a project site in the fall of that year.

The chapters in this book grew out of the work of the SST partners and ongoing conversations on the complexities of not only preparing teachers for the classroom but also helping them to succeed in their first years of teaching. Each chapter addresses a topic of vital importance to teacher educators, school leaders, teachers, parents, and students. Underlying the whole is the belief that better teachers mean better schools.

In Chapter 1, Roger Soder describes the constraints that are placed on teachers today. Teachers are far from free agents able to wield complete control over their classrooms, schools, or profession. They are continually beset by state mandates, district directives, parental pressures, and other influences. But that does not prevent new teachers from dedicating their lives to the profession. Soder respects that commitment and reminds teachers-to-be that they need a strong sense of self and a strong moral grounding to weather the inevitable storms they will face if they are to have satisfying teaching careers.

John Goodlad outlines in Chapter 2 the challenges facing teacher education and offers a moral mission for renewing teacher preparation and schooling. He argues that this moral mission—developing democratic character in the young—will bring both coherence to our nation's educational system and meaning to the experiences of students and teachers in our nation's schools.

In Chapter 3, Richard E. Barnes describes the first two years of the SST initiative in Portland, Maine. Working their way through turf struggles, personnel changes, and other challenges, the SST partners—the school district, the union, and the college of education—built a foundation for ongoing collaboration toward improving student learning through renewing teacher preparation and induction. Barnes's account is a useful model for other educational partnerships seeking to bring together key stakeholders in teacher education and schooling.

In Chapter 4, Paul Heckman and Corinne Mantle-Bromley challenge educators to bring about real change in schools and teacher preparation programs. They propose three principles that can help school–university partnerships renew the cultures of both P–12 schools and teacher education programs: participants in such partnerships must challenge long-held assumptions about their work, raise basic questions about theory and practice, and work together and, if necessary, differently. These simple-sounding principles are a truly powerful recipe for genuine educational renewal, and the authors' descriptions of professional development schools and the Educational and Community Change Project show how these principles can be put into practice.

Daniel Katz and Sharon Feiman-Nemser report in Chapter 5 some of their findings from an investigation of practices in three highly regarded programs for new teachers. They focus particularly on three common elements of these induction programs: orientations, seminars, and mentorship, both formal and informal. Their analysis points inevitably to the need to make schools "good places for teacher learning as well as student learning."

In Chapter 6, Sheldon Berman draws on his experience as the superintendent of the award-winning Hudson Public Schools to describe the school district's role in recruiting, inducting, and retaining effective teachers. Building a culture of schooling on a districtwide mission and vision enables teachers to collaborate for their own growth and for the renewal of their schools. The results are good schools that welcome and nurture both students and teachers.

In Chapter 7, Thomas Gillett and Adam Urbanski address the crucial role of the teacher unions in attracting and retaining high-quality teachers for our schools. Working with teacher-preparing institutions and local school districts, the unions are helping to make teaching a more attractive career and our schools more effective places for learning. In other words, rather than impeding school improvement, as some critics maintain the unions have done, the unions are increasingly becoming leaders in educational renewal.

Nancy Jean Sahling and Betty Lou Whitford take an admittedly "early look" at the SST initiative in Chapter 8. Their conclusions, reached after eighteen months of research and observation, offer much hope for the future. The SST strategy, they argue, effectively brings together key educators as a balanced, committed group of professionals who are willing to cross traditional boundaries and share historically well-protected turf. In short, SST builds communities of interest working toward better teachers and better schools.

In Chapter 9, Richard Wisniewski peers into the future to discern possible scenarios for teacher education, teaching, and schooling. Will our educational system be much the same as it is today? Or will it be markedly different? Wisniewski does not claim to know, but he remains optimistic about the future, despite his discouragement with some elements of the social and political environment that envelops American schools today.

Optimism, in fact, is the common thread running through this book. Although none of the authors would take the pollyannaish stance that all is right with the world of schooling and teacher education, they see much that is hopeful in our schools, colleges, and universities. By building new relationships among previously separated institutions, educators can create better schools and a more attractive teaching profession that does not require martyrdom of its members.

ACKNOWLEDGMENTS

In a collection such as this, thanks must go first to the authors. Their cooperation and communication made the job of compiling and editing their essays much easier than it otherwise might have been. Each of the authors, in turn, has no doubt benefited from the assistance of many unnamed colleagues. We give them, too, our collective thanks.

We are also grateful to the innumerable participants in the SST initiative, whose work, ideas, and commitment to education are an inspiration.

Sincere appreciation goes as well to the foundations that have supported the SST initiative and the preparation and publication of this book. The book was made possible by grants from the Carnegie Corporation of New York and the GE Fund. The initiative has been supported as well by the Bill & Melinda Gates Foundation and the Ford Foundation. The statements made and views expressed herein are solely the responsibility of the authors.

Finally, a heartfelt thanks goes to Paula McMannon, my wife and colleague at the Institute for Educational Inquiry. Only she really knows how much of her work made its way into this book.

NOTES

1. Quoted in Charles A. Harper, *A Century of Public Teacher Education* (Washington, D.C.: American Association of Teachers Colleges, 1939), p. 53.

2. Recruiting New Teachers, Inc., *Learning the Ropes: Urban Teacher Induction Programs and Practices in the United States* (Belmont, Mass.: Recruiting New Teachers, Inc., 1999).

CHAPTER 1

"When I Get My Own Classroom"

ROGER SODER

The conventional view of school teaching is of an adult standing in front of younger people seated in a classroom. This is the image many future teachers have in mind as well. In getting ready to teach, they worry about being able to manage a class and make it a place of learning.

This is a legitimate concern, to be sure. But at least classroom management is largely within one's control. There are, however, unpredictable circumstances arising out of the fact that schools and classrooms are microcosms of the larger community and society beyond. Not only does this social–political context come into the classroom with students, it significantly influences virtually everything that goes on there and in the school as a whole. With being smart in school ranking low on the popularity scale in high schools—far behind being an athlete or being regarded as good looking—teachers of English, for example, are sorely tried in seeking to have adolescents become avid readers of Jane Austen, Charles Dickens, Emily Dickinson, Sherman Alexie, or Alice Walker.

There are groups keeping an eye on what books teachers select, school boards worrying about whether enough time is spent on mathematics in the elementary schools, "education governors" with school mandates in mind, and federal commissions concluding that our schools are not doing enough to keep the nation at the forefront of the global economy. Are teachers to remain mute when the arts, recess, and physical education are cut out to provide more time to prepare pupils to take standardized tests?

How are teachers to respond to the familiar slogan, "It's all for the children," when a good many regularities of school clearly are not? Are they to keep silent when the new superintendent decrees that one specified method of teaching reading in the primary grades will be mandatory after a certain date?

We have all heard the avuncular advice, probably many times: "To thine own self be true." To have a long, satisfying career in teaching, one had better be clear about who thine own self is. Otherwise, the course of that career will be pushed this way and that by changing winds blowing in different directions. Some proposed school reforms are downright silly. Some are soon forgotten only to surface again in different dress. Some should simply be ignored. Teachers must have a guiding credo of educational belief that tells them when to give a little, when to embrace recommended changes wholeheartedly, and when to stand on moral principle.

Nothing in teaching is more important, personal, and individual than the development of such a credo. Few matters are more difficult than standing by it when circumstances are threatening. What Roger Soder writes in this chapter should help teachers at all stages of their careers strengthen both their educational beliefs and their resolve to be active decisionmakers in regard to what goes on in their classrooms and schools.
—The editors

"When I get my own classroom." This refrain—sometimes invoked as a mantra or a talisman to ward off the unpleasant or the unknown—is often heard when teacher education students are asked to identify that moment when they will shift from "would-be" teachers to "real" teachers.[1] We heard variations from hundreds of students during the course of interviews as part of our Study of the Education of Educators.[2] The refrain might be taken at face value, with students simply telling us of the moment in time when the change will be made. But we heard with great consistency sentiments behind it, sentiments suggesting that what the would-be teachers had in mind was the day when they would be free and independent professionals in charge of their own classrooms, and free, for the most part, of constraints getting in the way of their doing the best for their students. This refrain and the sentiments behind it were echoed by many university supervisors of student teachers. When would-be teachers return from their internship settings complaining that they were unable to teach as they wanted, university supervisors are heard to advise these students to hang on, just do as they are told for the nonce, and wait until they get their own classrooms (when, presumably, they will be able to proceed as they see appropriate).

In the course of hundreds of wide-ranging hour-long interviews, we heard much more about another related and strongly held belief. We tried to get from students their sense of the political and social context of teaching, the perceived pressures from the various parts of the community, the tensions between what one might want to teach and what one was directed to teach. We asked them to consider what they would do if asked to work in districts and schools where the prevailing schooling philosophies were counter to their own. If, for example, interviewees indicated strong opposition to tracking of youngsters, we would ask what they would do if their employing school district mandated tracking. The common response was, in effect, "I'd move to a district that was in keeping with my beliefs." Well and good, we would say. And if a new administration and a new school board in that district turned to tracking and it looked like you wouldn't be able to move districts for one reason or another, what then? The common response brought us right back to the classroom: "I'd close the classroom door and do what I felt was in the best interests of the children."

In the course of visiting other institutions as well as talking to teacher education students in classes in my home institution, I have persisted with these root questions: When do you feel you will be a "real" teacher, and what will you do if district and school policies go counter to your fundamental beliefs? The responses vary little across time, across institutional type, and across the usual demographics. Despite all the talk about the school as the unit of change, about the isolation of the classroom teacher, about the ecology of schooling, about one's stewardship of the entire school, about the teacher as moral and political agent, and about the teacher as change agent, the responses are robust, healthy, and unchanging. For these would-be teachers, the classroom is the focal point; there they will act to the best of their ability as independent, autonomous professionals to deliver the best possible service to children.

These notions of independence and autonomy, of being answerable to oneself and one's clients, are not to be found solely among teachers. The struggling, independent artist comes to mind, the artist who will not "sell out" to pressures from patrons or the roiling mob. We can think here of Tosca with her famous pleading to the police chief, "Vissi d'arte"—I live for art, I don't want to have to get involved in anything else. And we can think of Mark Rothko arguing that the artist must be truly liberated: "Freed from a false sense of security and community, the artist can abandon his plastic bank-book," and only then "transcendental experiences become possible."[3]

The responses of those about to become teachers are consonant with widely held beliefs about what it means to be a member of a profession. A traditional key to being regarded as a professional is in effect a "license from society for autonomous professional status."[4] If the image of the independent practitioner marks the true professional, and if teachers want to be regarded as professionals rather than "semiprofessionals" or workers simply doing the bidding of administrators and school boards, then the "when I get my own classroom" view can be seen as rational and right on the mark.[5]

As for the notions of a teacher leaving an offending district and finding another district more in harmony with his or her beliefs, we are once more in familiar territory. Pulling up stakes is in the grand American tradition. Robert Wiebe tells us of the allure of open land during the early days of the Republic: "From the earliest days of settlement it invited those people who had differences to solve their problems by separation instead of accommodation. Rather than adjust, they parted." Thus, for example, "where hostile Catholics and Protestants found themselves neighbors, as in Maryland, they fought only as long as it took their camps to disperse."[6] And lighting out for the territory, going anywhere but where society is going to do you in to your great discomfort—that, too, is in the grand tradition, with would-be teachers resonating well with Huckleberry Finn. He has been there before, and they have some idea, they think, of what Huck is talking about.

The difficulty with this good, earnest, brave talk about independence and autonomy and one's own classroom is that it is based on a fiction. Teachers are not independent agents. Teachers, at least public school teachers, are employees of school districts, and districts are state corporations. Teachers are state agents. Beyond that, teachers are enmeshed, inevitably and necessarily, in a web of complex and contradictory relationships that impinge directly and indirectly on their work as teachers. Given these relationships, it is not possible in any meaningful sense to "have your own classroom."[7] Moreover, the brave talk about lighting out for the territory with Huck simply will not get us anywhere because that territory does not exist: the relationships that impinge on the teachers' work are everywhere, in every school district.

This is not to say that teachers and would-be teachers are off to their own version of Newgate Prison, abandoning all hope. In what follows, I try to offer some hope, through a consideration of six relationships that everywhere appear to have teachers cribbed and cabined. I believe that an understanding of these relationships will help would-be teachers (and the rest of us) to see clearly the political and social circumstances of teachers. Seeing clearly is the first step toward the development of grounded strategies for teachers to engage the world that holds them in thrall and to use these strategies in supporting, opposing, engaging, and transcending that world as they see fit.

SIX RELATIONSHIPS

Teachers in Relation to the State

The states—and here I mean the fifty political units of the American republic—exercise control over the schooling establishment and those who teach within it. As we have noted, public school teachers are state agents, given their employment within state-mandated corporations we call school districts, and their relationship with the state is complex. The following is a brief discussion of seven aspects of the teacher–state relationship.

The State as Source of Economic Support of Schools and Teachers

Public schools receive most of their operating funds from state governments. Resources are always scarce: there is never enough, in any society, for everything. In one movie version of *A Christmas Carol*, Scrooge celebrates his epiphany with a party at the Cratchit home. "Everything for everybody," Scrooge shouts with delight as he showers the children with presents. But only in Hollywood are resources so plentiful. In our world, there is always competition, and in the world of schooling, there is always competition with other state-funded programs. Roughly 80% of a given state's budget goes to K–12 schooling, higher education, and health and welfare. K–12 schools are in a highly competitive struggle merely to maintain current levels of expenditure. Given a general unwillingness to pay more taxes (indeed, given the popularity of state ballot initiatives to shrink tax revenues), and given economic doldrums, additional resources for K–12 schools, if they are to be made available at all, will most likely come about through holding the line or cutting programs for higher education and the poor. The teacher may have her own classroom, but the level of available resources directly affects the pupil–teacher ratio, availability of instructional materials, and kinds of classes that can be offered.

Curriculum and Pedagogy Dictates of the State

A teacher might have her own classroom in the sense that her name is on the door. But as to what she is going to teach, and how she is going to teach it, the state has a great deal to say. There are learning objectives dictated by the state, and there are textbooks and curriculum guides to be followed. Some states have rules indicating how much time is to be spent on specified subjects; some dictate what special "teacher-proof" canned curriculum units are to be used. After the state has dictated the precise learning objectives, the precise curriculum, and the precise amount of time to be allotted, teachers find it small comfort (and more than a bit hypocritical) to be told that the state is merely providing standards, and it is up to the professional teacher in her supposed independence to determine how to have all of her children attain those standards. All told, as John Goodlad notes, "the volume and variety of state legislative activity has contributed to obfuscating the central education charge," and the most Goodlad can conclude is that the entire area of state mandates is a "conceptual swamp."[8]

Testing Dictates of the State

Statewide testing has long been a part of the business of schooling. In recent years, such testing has become increasingly pervasive.[9] These tests take time, of course. They take time to administer, and they take even more time to prepare for. If statewide tests are administered in May, many teachers find that they are encouraged or directed to start preparing students for the tests no later than February. The teacher is in her own classroom. But what does owning the classroom mean when a significant portion of the year has to be devoted to test taking and cramming for tests?

Moreover, if the teacher wants to deal with matters that are not part of the statewide tests, there may well be problems. It is difficult to make a case for the importance of subjects or notions to be taught if those subjects and notions are not part of the tests. Recently, a former Washington State Superintendent of Public Instruction called for statewide assessment of civic education, arguing that as long as the state tests emphasized only reading, writing, mathematics, and science, civic education will be "haphazardly taught."[10] However, given that statewide tests tend to be the fill-in-the-bubble variety, that which can be mass-tested is limited to the easily measured and, as it often happens, the trivial. Teachers are thus in a double bind. Only those subjects that are included on statewide tests will be given resources and time, but to include something in statewide tests is to invite trivialization.[11]

The State's Role Superceded by the Federal Government

Although a major relationship is between the state and the teacher, the federal government has also established a relationship with the teacher, mediated through the state. Although the U.S. Constitution speaks not at all about schooling, the federal government has gradually increased its involvement (although not its share of resource provision) over the last forty years. Federal involvement began to increase significantly with the Supreme Court's ruling on school desegregation in *Brown* v. *Board of Education of Topeka* in 1954. Four years later, the National Defense Education Act was passed in response to *Sputnik* and what appeared to be the successful challenge of the Soviet Union in the space race. Even with the pervasive Russians-are-coming mentality, there was considerable concern expressed about federal involvement in schooling. Political opposition was couched in the name of states' rights, although lurking not very far behind this resistance was in fact opposition to school desegregation. Both the court decision and the federal legislation had direct impacts on teachers and the classroom, as did the mammoth Elementary and Secondary Education Act (ESEA) of 1965.

The most recent federal involvement is the 2002 reauthorization of the ESEA, the No Child Left Behind Act (NCLB), passed with little opposition and with few of the thundering outcries against federal intrusion that would have been heard just several decades ago. The NCLB's extensive intrusion into state and local schooling matters appears to be taken as a matter of course, even though cost studies show that the many demands of the federal legislation will not be met with federal monies; rather, the states themselves will have to reallocate monies already scarce in order to meet the new regulations.[12] Reallocation of state monies will have a direct impact on what the teacher does in the classroom and school.

The State and Compulsory Attendance Laws

Given state-mandated, compulsory attendance, teachers (public school teachers, at any rate) mediate a relationship between state and parent and child. If for no other reason than mediating this relationship, the teacher's behavior is under constraints. Children are required by the state to be surrendered to the state for the good of the state. Teachers are directly involved in the surrender, for it is they who will receive and take temporary custody of the children. Compulsory schooling thus means that "My own classroom" is the parent's classroom and the state's classroom as well.

Teacher Preparation and the State

States license those who would be teachers, and states approve programs that prepare teachers. Every state has the authority to dictate appropriate curriculum, and that authority has often been exercised with federal enthusiasm, posing many challenges to those who are charged with the actual operation of programs.[13] An indication of the relative powerlessness of teacher preparation programs to deal with state intrusion is offered by legislation passed by the Texas legislature in the late 1980s mandating a maximum of eighteen semester hours for the so-called professional component of teacher preparation programs. Were the legislature in its wisdom to attempt to cap the number of hours in a medical school program or attempt to tell university medical schools what should be tested in, say, a gross anatomy course, the medical establishment would oppose with success any such attempts. Teaching and the preparation of teachers, by contrast, are relatively easy targets for regulation. Not only does every legislator who has ever attended school consider himself or herself an education expert, but education as a field lacks the social status and political power necessary to ward off intrusions. Those would-be teachers waiting until they get their own classrooms might well observe their own preparation programs and the astonishing extent of state regulation and intrusion; such observation would provide clues to what future teachers can expect in the way of independence.

The Teacher, the State, and the Law

As can be seen from the discussion above, the law is interwoven throughout all aspects of the teacher-state relationship. There is little in the teacher's professional life (and in some respects private life) that is not regulated by law. Laws have been enacted to tell teachers what to teach, what not to teach, when to use lesson plans, how to touch children, how to behave outside of school, how not to criticize superiors, what clothes to wear, and what language to use.[14] The detail of the regulation is considerable. For example, the portions of the published versions of the Revised Code of Washington and the Washington Administrative Code pertaining to the common schools run to some twelve hundred pages.

These many laws and rules and regulations may be all to the good in protecting children from bad teachers. But curtailment of the freedom to act limits teaching, in much the same way that de Tocqueville warned of the consequences of a "regulated, mild, and peaceful servitude" with "a network of small, complicated, painstaking, uniform rules through which the most original minds and the most vigorous souls cannot clear a way to surpass the crowd."[15]

Teachers in Relation to the School District

The number of school districts in the United States has been drastically reduced from a high of just over 127,000 in the early 1930s to fewer than 15,000 today. With state salary schedules for teachers and with limits on what local districts can raise through levies, districts have lost much of their power for discretionary action with, as we have seen, the states and the federal government gaining control. However, the teacher–district relationship still exists, and teachers are still constrained in their actions by districts. There is the constraint of testing, with many districts going beyond state requirements in their sometimes self-imposed fixation on test scores. There are constraints on behavior, and although some of the more flagrant invasions of privacy have been eliminated (e.g., no marriages allowed for female teachers, no consumption of alcohol and tobacco, and the like), districts have more than a little influence over what teachers can and cannot do in and out of the classroom.[16] There is, as with the state, competition for resources. Classroom teachers are involved in constant competition in what is close to a zero-sum game. There are only so many minutes of instructional time in the day and in the school year. To require some classes is to put other classes in the shade. Thus, for example, the Bellevue, Washington, district decided to make passage of Advanced Placement classes a requirement for all students; as a result, art is no longer a graduation requirement, and speech communication, once required in high school, is now to be relegated to a middle school course.[17]

School boards, either of their own accord or in response to parental and community pressure, approve, disapprove, or alter curricula and curricular materials. Boards can choose to ban books or allow banned books to be addressed in limited ways to limited student audiences. There may be fewer districts than formerly, but those that remain exercise considerable influence.

Who the teacher actually sees in the classroom is a matter of district policy. A district that engages in tracking and in developing programs for the "gifted" will have a significant impact on classroom composition. How districts respond to and augment state and federal policy regarding special education students will also have an impact on who the teacher sees in her or his classes. "When I get my own classroom" becomes, from the district's point of view, "when you step into our classroom."

Teachers in Relation to Parents and Guardians

As John Goodlad put it in *A Place Called School*, "We want it all." Parents want schools to focus on academics as well as vocational preparation as well as social goals as well as personal goals.[18] Many parents are concerned about social mobility for their children. Many parents believe in the connection claimed in the old saying, "To get a good job, get a good education." Many parents want their children in "gifted" programs, not only for the supposed economic payoff down the line, but because some "gifted" programs seem to involve better teachers, lower pupil-teacher ratios, and more resources.

These different views of what schools are for emerge not only in our own time, but for all time. As Aristotle noted, people are

> by no means agreed about the things to be taught, whether we look to virtue or the best life. Neither is it clear whether education is more concerned with intellectual or with moral virtue. The existing practice is perplexing; no one knows on what principle we should proceed—should the useful in life, or should virtue, or should the higher knowledge, be the aim

of our training; all three opinions have been entertained. Again, about the means there is no agreement; for different persons, starting with different ideas about the nature of virtue, naturally disagree about the practice of it.[19]

There are disagreements with regard to purposes and practices. Moreover, there is no particular agreement as to how these various purposes and practices are to be adjudicated. In dealing with what to teach and how to teach, the teacher must consider contradictory claims and views of her clients (and she must consider, too, just who is to be considered a "client"). The teacher will no doubt have her own views to consider, too, and if those views are contrary to those of her clients or the district, then further choices must be made. One changes one's views, one bends to authority or demand, or one holds to an internal set of standards. Or one holds the internal standards in temporary suspension and out of prudence exhibits superficial acceptance of the outside demands, with the hope that once the bad part is over, one can return to behaving in accordance with internal standards. No matter what the response or strategy, there are costs. For the teacher to accede to parental pressure while personally holding to contradictory views is to sell part of one's personal and professional soul. To hold true to one's beliefs can be admirable, as was the case when Socrates faced the crowd criticizing his teachings— admirable, but costly.

Teachers in Relation to the Community

A school exists in a community. The community includes school boards, parents, and representatives of the state. As such, the teacher–community relationship overlaps with the other relationships discussed thus far. However, there are other parts of the community that bear on how teachers conduct themselves. In every community one can expect to find political groups attempting to persuade schools and school districts to teach and behave in certain ways. These groups may also act in concert on given issues. For example, in the late 1970s, a combination of the Seattle Urban League, the National Association for the Advancement of Colored People, the Church Council of Greater Seattle, and the Seattle Mayor's Office (and, ultimately, a host of some eighty other political and community groups) persuaded the Seattle School District Board to proceed with a districtwide plan to desegregate the schools. The plan involved significant changes in the structure of the school day, student enrollment patterns, and curriculum.[20] Focus was placed on human relations, group interaction, and multicultural education, with teachers expected to deal with a wide variety of issues related to the new plan. Under such circumstances, there was considerable community and district intrusion into "my own classroom."

In many communities, political interest groups routinely put pressure on school districts to alter a curriculum. The issues may change from year to year (evolution, creationism, sex education, peace education, patriotism, and so forth), but the principle of intrusion remains active. Political interest groups routinely demand removal of what are seen as dangerous or immoral books from required reading lists or from the school library. Again, the titles may change (the Harry Potter books are currently stirring some people to action against satanic influences, and thus Harry joins Huck Finn and Holden Caulfield and a whole host of other inspired characters condemned for depravity or worse), but intrusion—threatened or actual—is commonplace.

Many of these challenges are, thankfully, turned aside by wise school boards. But the point is that the challenges are made, the intrusion is there, and teachers once on the job learn very quickly that the selection of class texts is a community and political affair, not just a decision to be made in one's own classroom.

Teachers in Relation to Others in the Workplace

Teachers do not work alone, even though talk about isolation in the classroom is a commonplace. Teachers negotiate goals with principals, department heads, and colleagues. The question of who is actually going to teach what to whom and when is open to negotiation. The desires and assignments of some teachers will affect what happens to other teachers. If a teacher with many years of seniority and some influence in the school wants to teach Advanced Placement and "gifted" programs, that teacher will most likely get what he or she wants, including smaller class sizes, leaving the newcomer with the larger enrollments in the basic or remedial courses.

Teachers in Relation to Their Occupation or "Profession"

Even in their own separate classrooms, teachers act in relation to their collective image of their occupation. As with any occupation, the field of teaching has over time established sets of norms, standards for how one is to behave under given conditions. Moreover, teachers have long sought recognition and legitimation as a profession, and part of being considered professional is the establishment of a code of conduct.[21] Some of the norms of behavior are learned in a teacher preparation program; these norms, along with others, are reinforced in the school setting. Teacher behavior is constrained not only by internal norms common to us all, but also by the external norms of the would-be teaching profession and the norms of professional associations and labor unions.[22] These constraints militate against the notion of the independence of being "in my own classroom."

THE RELATIONSHIPS CONSIDERED

Thus far we have outlined relationships between teachers and the state, the school district, parents/guardians, the community, the workplace, and the profession of teaching. Considered alone or in combination, these relationships ensure that today's teachers are far from being independent commanders of their own classrooms. Rather, teachers are constrained in numerous legal, moral, social, and political ways. Will these relationships and their resultant constraints necessarily continue in their current form? Or is it possible for teachers to alter them?

A brief consideration of the past gives us ways to respond to these questions. In one form or another, the basic elements of the relationships have been with us since the emergence of human society in its current form some several thousand years ago. By definition, in that human society there have always been elements of some sort of governing structure or state; there has always been a community; there have always been parents; there have always been tensions between state and community and parents over enculturation of youths, and at least for the last several thousand years, there has been some form of instruction of the young by those assigned the formal role of teacher.

From the beginning, teachers have had to deal with constraints emerging from these relationships. Consider one of the first teachers in history whose story is known to us. We all know what happened when Socrates continued to teach in the face of political opposition. In the *Gorgias,* Callicles warns Socrates that he will be dragged into court, perhaps by "some scoundrel of the vilest character." Socrates replies bluntly, "I should be a fool, Callicles, if I didn't realize that in this state anything may happen to anybody."[23]

In modern times in the United States, we find that the schools have always been controlled by one unit of the state or another, and teachers have always acted under constraints. One of the early battles over control of schools was between local communities, mostly in rural areas, and urbanized school bureaucracies.[24] But whether the local community retained control of schools or lost that control to a larger bureaucracy, teachers in the schools were employees of a system, a system over which the teachers themselves had little or no control. Over the years since the founding of the National Education Association in 1857, teachers have gained some control over their work. But the fundamental relationships have not altered: the state in one manifestation or another—federal government, state government, local government—dictates who is to come to school, what is to be taught, how it is to be taught, and how to assess and evaluate the entire business.

Barring an entirely new way of construing human society, it appears that the fundamental relationships between state and community and parents and teachers cannot be renounced. The state will exist, and the state will insist that schooling be regulated and supervised and held accountable, all in the interest of the state. Communities and parents will exist. But if relationships cannot be renounced, cannot they be altered in ways to at least reduce the constraints they impose?

The experiences of some occupational groups suggest that the constraints caused by these relationships are indeed mutable. For example, in the United States we can observe major changes in the power of the medical profession over the last two hundred years. Physicians, like all others, must work within a state and community context. Until the second decade of the 20th century, physicians had relatively little control over their work. But with the advent of "scientific" medicine coupled with cultural authority—what Paul Starr termed "legitimate complexity"—physicians and others in the medical business developed and institutionalized considerable control.[25] That control has diminished over the last two decades, with physicians ceding power to both the state and insurance companies. The relationship between physician and state and individual has not—and cannot—be renounced, but the constraints of that relationship on the conduct of the physician's work have been altered. In the struggle for control over their work, physicians were able to develop and wield a great deal of power because of their enhanced professional status and the high prestige they developed in the community.

If political power coupled with the cultural power of high status and legitimacy are critical factors in reducing constraints over one's work, then it is clear that teachers have never been in a good position in the struggle for control. Speaking two thousand years ago, Juvenal commented as follows on the earnings of teachers: "When the school year's ended, you'll get as much as a jockey makes from a single race."[26] Nothing much has changed. The literature since the time of the Romans suggests that teachers have had little political power and have suffered comparatively low status.

And what of the future? Might teachers be able to lessen the constraints in the decades to come? The example of American physicians does not provide much hope for teachers. If physicians, despite comparatively high prestige and considerable political power, are finding that their work is increasingly under the control of the state, we can hardly expect teachers to fare any better. There is nothing to suggest that teachers will be able to find other ways to increase their power and prestige.

Julien Benda suggests that any society has to decide whether it wants its teachers to be servants or guides.[27] It seems a reasonable bet that our society will continue to see our teachers as servants.

If the foregoing analysis is anywhere near the mark, are teachers left with anything besides pious or resentful acceptance? Is there nothing to be done? My response is that the first order of political business is to understand clearly what the situation is and where one stands in relation to that situation. By looking at the relationships and consequent constraints head-on, teachers can develop a realistic sense of who they are and what they can and cannot do. Moreover, they will shake free of the fiction of professional independence and the dream of inviolate classrooms. Teachers can proceed to construct a professional existence based on a grounded sense of who they are in relation to themselves and others.[28] With that grounded sense, teachers might be able to engage politicians and policymakers in struggles to lessen some of the constraints of the relationships, to make their work a bit more creative and less robotic. Perhaps, in the end, prudent acceptance of a limited public role while nonetheless maintaining a satisfying private role is the best that teachers can do. In the wise words of Loren Eiseley, "In the days of the frost, seek a minor sun."[29]

And yet, for all that, skeptical and perhaps wiser voices yearn to be heard. My analysis and advice might be cool, rational, shrewd. Even if not all that much can be done, I seem to be saying, at least we can agree that forewarned is forearmed. Some would-be teachers might imagine that they are hearing not a call to arms but a call to disperse, and they might well want to thank me for leading them away from the precipice.

But for most would-be teachers, my conclusions and advice might be deemed accurate but not acceptable. Most would-be teachers sense that teaching and deciding to teach involves something more than listening to a rational and shrewd Polonius holding forth on the dangers and pitfalls of the teaching world. They have some informed sense of the constraints and difficulties outlined in this chapter, to be sure. They are not innocents, going ahead where angels fear to tread. They know the odds are not particularly in their favor in the same way that mountain climbers know the odds of conquering Annapurna. But odds against is rarely a compelling argument.

I know that even for myself, my own analysis and advice will not dissuade me from a teaching career. My home institution, the University of Washington, always has budget shortfalls, there is always pressure from the outside, the state education bureaucratic apparatus has its own views of what should be done here, but none of these pressures and constraints dissuade me. I will teach no matter what. (This willingness to teach no matter what is part of the problem, perhaps. The persistence of the many teachers who will teach despite the problems leads to a tendency to put those problems aside, and they continue by default. To paraphrase Tiresias talking to Oedipus, we ourselves are the enemy we seek—because of our willingness to accept the tradeoffs between teaching and the threats to teaching.)

Would-be teachers know the negative aspects of teaching. They know that teaching will not make them rich. They know that teaching will not give them high status in the community. But that is not why they turn to or are called by teaching. In talking with teachers and would-be teachers over the years, I remain convinced that most people go into teaching for solid, morally defensible reasons. They sense that to be a teacher is, well, to be a teacher, and teaching has its own moral grounding, its own demands, its own rewards. They sense, in effect, what we discussed in the first volume that emerged as part of our Study of the Education of Educators, *The Moral Dimensions of Teaching*. The book was given positive reviews, with sales over a decade maintaining unusually high levels for a work of this kind. I suspect that the strong response stemmed from the resonance many teachers felt with the arguments in the book, and with the notion that teaching was surely more than implanting knowledge or securing high test scores or intoning the tenets of values clarification. Teachers and would-be teachers had a strong sense that they were indeed moral and political agents, morally responsible to and for those they chose to teach.

During the course of a recent road trip to Kansas and back to our home state of Washington, my wife and I were stopped by a construction worker on an isolated two-lane road near Devils Tower.

"It's a one-way road up ahead. You'll have to wait here maybe fifteen to twenty minutes for the pilot car to take you through," she told us.

No problem. We noticed her car by the side of the road, with the usual college sticker in the back window.

"You're at the University of Nebraska," my wife said.

"That's right," replied our traffic worker.

"And what are you studying there?" I asked.

"Elementary education." Without missing a beat and without any cues from us, she continued: "I know there are a lot of hassles, and I don't like all the tests we keep running kids through, because they waste a lot of time, and I already know where the kids are anyway, and I don't like the way the curriculum is dictated by the state education people, but—"

"But what?" I interrupted.

"I want to be a teacher. I'm going to be a good one. I can't wait."

We talked until the pilot car came along with the eastbound traffic. Our turn now. We waved. "Thanks, and good luck to you," we said. We were on our way. So was she.

NOTES

1. A note here on how I am using the word "teacher." In a general sense, we are all teachers. All of us teach ourselves. And we teach others. I learn a lot in watching my young grandson, Matthew, teach his younger brother how to play trains. But there is another sense of "teacher," the formal sense that we need to be concerned with here, the formal role of teacher in a formal schooling system. It is the formal sense of teacher that I deal with in this chapter.

2. For a summary of Study findings regarding student perceptions of teaching and preparing to teach, see John I. Goodlad, *Teachers for Our Nation's Schools* (San Francisco: Jossey-Bass, 1990), Chapter 5.

3. Quoted in Herschell B. Chipp, ed., *Theories of Modern Art: A Source Book by Artists and Critics* (Berkeley: University of California Press, 1968), p. 548.

4. Stephen J. Kunitz, "Professionalism and Social Control in the Progressive Era: The Case of the Flexner Report," *Social Problems* 22 (October 1974): 25. For additional discussions of professions and independence and autonomy, see Terence J. Johnson, *Professions and Power* (London: Macmillan, 1972); Eliot Freidson, *Professionalism: The Third Logic* (Chicago: University of Chicago Press, 2001); as well as Freidson, *Professional Powers: A Study of the Institutionalization of Formal Knowledge* (Chicago: University of Chicago Press, 1986).

5. For a consideration of teachers' desires for professional status and strategies for obtaining that status, see Roger Soder, "The Rhetoric of Teacher Professionalization," in John I. Goodlad, Roger Soder, and Kenneth A. Sirotnik (eds.), *The Moral Dimensions of Teaching* (San Francisco: Jossey-Bass, 1990).

6. Robert H. Wiebe, *The Segmented Society: An Introduction to the Meaning of America* (Oxford, England: Oxford University Press, 1975), p. 29.

7. It should be noted that teachers are not alone in having to deal with a web of relationships. Physicians—at one time the leading occupational group claiming professional status—have always had to deal with intrusive relationships, particularly in recent years with widespread changes in the economics of healthcare delivery systems. What with many physicians working on salary for HMOs, the demands of insurance companies, and the pressures of malpractice suits, the supposedly autonomous professional physician is rarely to be found.

8. John I. Goodlad, *A Place Called School: Prospects for the Future* (New York: McGraw-Hill, 1984), p. 48.

9. See, for example, Kenneth A. Sirotnik, "Promoting Responsible Accountability in Schools and Education," *Phi Delta Kappan* 83 (May 2002): 662–673.

10. Judith Billings, "WASL Minus Civics = Sinking Schooling," *Seattle Times*, 28 February 2003, p. B7.

11. For a discussion of the double bind of not testing and losing resources versus testing and becoming trivialized within the context of civic education, see Roger Soder, *Learning to Be Good Citizens in a Democracy: Reflections on Assessment and Evaluation Practices in Civic Education*, Occasional Paper No. 2 (Seattle: Institute for the Study of Educational Policy, University of Washington, 2002).

12. For an outline of ten state-cost studies pertaining to NCLB requirements, see William J. Mathis, "No Child Left Behind: Costs and Benefits," *Phi Delta Kappan* 84 (May 2003): 679–686.

13. For a useful discussion of the regulatory context of teacher preparation programs, see Goodlad, *Teachers for Our Nation's Schools,* Chapter 4.

14. For useful summaries of laws and regulations, see David Ruben with Steven Greenhouse, *The Rights of Teachers: The Basic ACLU Guide to a Teacher's Constitutional Rights* (New York: Bantam, 1984); as well as Louis Fischer, David Schimmel, and Cynthia Kelly, *Teachers and the Law* (New York: Longman, 1999); and Howard K. Beale, *A History of Freedom of Teaching in American Schools* (New York: Charles Scribner's Sons, 1941).

15. Alexis de Tocqueville, *Democracy in America,* Vol. II, Part 4, Chapter 6, trans. Harvey C. Mansfield and Delba Winthrop (Chicago: University of Chicago Press, 2000), p. 663. For an insightful discussion of the tensions among creativity, freedom, and autonomy and thick bureaucracies, see Robert Nisbet, *The Present Age: Progress and Anarchy in Modern America* (New York: Harper & Row, 1988), Chapter 2, "The New Absolutism."

16. See Beale, *A History of Freedom of Teaching in American Schools.*

17. See, for example, Cara Solomon, "Schools' 'High Standards' Resisted: Bellevue Residents Object to District's Emphasis on Advanced-Level Courses," *Seattle Times,* 3 June 2003, p. B1, available at http://seattletimes.nwsource.com/html/education/134881989_riley03m.html.

18. Goodlad, *A Place Called School,* pp. 33–60.

19. Aristotle, *Politics* 1337a, b, *The Basic Works of Aristotle,* Richard McKeon, (ed.) (New York: Random House, 1941).

20. For details, see Ann LaGrelius Siqueland, *Without a Court Order: The Desegregation of Seattle's Schools* (Seattle: Madrona, 1981).

21. For a discussion of the professionalization of the teaching occupation, see Soder, "Rhetoric of Teacher Professionalization"; see also Alan R. Tom, *Teaching as a Moral Craft* (New York: Longman, 1984).

22. It is ironic that teachers and those who claim to support them place so much emphasis on the image of "profession" at a time when the external dictates of what teachers are to teach, how they are to teach it, and how everyone will know whether they are teaching it have never been greater. We are in a time not of professionalization but, rather, of deprofessionalization.

23. Plato, *Gorgias,* trans. Walter Hamilton (New York: Penguin, 1971), p. 139.

24. For a useful discussion of this battle, see David B. Tyack, *The One Best System: A History of American Urban Education* (Cambridge, Mass.: Harvard University Press, 1974), pp. 13–77.

25. Paul Starr, *The Social Transformation of American Medicine* (New York: Basic Books, 1982), p. 71. For an overview of the changing power of the medical profession, see Soder, "Rhetoric of Teacher Professionalization," pp. 56–63.

26. Juvenal, "Satire No. 7," in *The Sixteen Satires,* trans. Peter Green (Harmondsworth, England: Penguin, 1970), pp. 335–336.

27. Julien Benda, *The Treason of the Intellectuals*, trans. Richard Aldington (New York: Norton, 1969).

28. Parker J. Palmer, *The Courage to Teach: Exploring the Inner Landscape of a Teacher's Life* (San Francisco: Jossey-Bass, 1998). See also James March, "Yo sé quien soy," in Kenneth A. Sirotnik and Roger Soder (eds.), *The Beat of a Different Drummer: Essays on Educational Renewal in Honor of John I. Goodlad* (New York: Peter Lang, 1999), pp. 275–283.

29. Loren Eiseley, *The Immense Journey* (New York: Random House, 1957), p. 178.

CHAPTER 2

A Guiding Mission

JOHN I. GOODLAD

Education is commonly regarded as a good thing. But it can serve bad ends just as readily as good ones. Actually, it is a neutral concept. The good must be built into both the purposes and processes of educating. Teaching the young in schools is a moral endeavor that must be guided by a clear moral mission.

We closed our introduction to Chapter 1 with a comment on the personal, individual nature and importance of developing a credo of educational belief to guide one's teaching. This does not mean, however, that this credo can be whatever a schoolteacher chooses. In a democracy, one's teaching credo must align with the public good—in other words, with democratic principles.

The central message of Chapter 2 is that the entire schooling apparatus must align with democratic principles—of mission, operating conditions, and strategies of improvement. A reviewer commenting on this manuscript prior to publication said that this message is too obvious to warrant elaboration. That is about as silly a statement as we have heard in a long time. Yes, a lot has been written about the relationship between education and democracy. There is nothing of greater educational good for our schools to do than develop democratic character in the young: an understanding of justice, equity, and freedom and the exercise of civility, civicness, fairness, honesty, compassion, and the like that a robust democracy requires.

Recent studies reveal, however, little attention to these in the preservice or in-service education of educators. Nor did this centrality of school mission enter into presidential debates in elections of the 1990s or the early years of the 21st century. Is this an obvious message for all the groups and institutions that must join in supporting and sustaining teachers? Unfortunately, it is not.

We are reminded of the relationship between education and democracy in commencement addresses at both the high school and college levels and, quite often, in patriotic ceremonies on national holidays. But then we seem to assume that democracy will take care of itself. We seem to believe that higher test scores in academic subjects indicate higher productivity in the development of democratic character. But they do not. The correlation is weak.

We must come to understand that dispositions such as civility, honesty, civicness, dependability, and cooperation are products of the everyday teaching of our cultural surround. But only our schools are in a position to attend to them deliberately. Few

things are more critically important to the future of democracy than a system of pub-
lic education committed to ensuring in its citizens deep understanding and appreciation
of their freedoms and responsibilities. Fulfilling this commitment depends on recruiting,
educating, and supporting competent, caring, qualified teachers

—The editors

Everybody teaches. Some of this teaching is deliberate; most of it is not. We teach and learn simply by being in the company of others: our children, friends, neighbors, associates at work, and the people we encounter in the market. Teaching does not necessarily involve talking, nor does it necessarily involve learning. Muted language is a great teacher: for example, frowns, body movements, and eye contact. Many of the facial expressions that accompany oral language accompany sign language, too. What we model over time teaches powerfully. Only the air we breathe is more ubiquitous than the teaching that surrounds and educates us daily, for better or for worse.

Schools, then, are not the whole of teaching—nor are school and home together. Indeed, with respect to time available to them for their teaching today, the two are becoming minor players. Time in bed takes up about a third of the years between the ages of six and eighteen, school about 12%. A large part of the remaining 55%, once dominated by the teaching of the home, is now consumed by electronic media. Their teaching penetrates even the time allocated to sleeping and schooling. The media generally claim only to entertain and give information, but their teaching is powerful nonetheless.

The career of teaching the young in our schools is a special case of teaching, more buffeted by the twin contingencies of politics and supply and demand than is any other profession. These two sets of contingencies are closely entwined. The inability of even a few school districts in a state to fill vacancies in classrooms brings almost immediate pressure on the legislature to ease licensing requirements. Teacher shortages are exacerbated during cycles of robust economies, and the loosely latched gates into teaching swing open. The demand for quantity then overwhelms issues of quality. Given little differentiation in material rewards between the well-prepared and the under- or ill-prepared teacher, such circumstances are a deterrent to the rigors of striving for excellence in teacher education.

The problem of ensuring an adequate supply of well-prepared, career-line teachers is further exacerbated by the heavy dependence of schooling—and, therefore, of teaching, teachers, and teacher education—on the vagaries of a multi-tiered political infrastructure. Local, state, and federal political interests penetrate every aspect of public schooling, from educational purpose to classroom practice. With respect to teacher education, the authority of those held accountable for preparation programs is overshadowed by that of external policymakers. No other domain of professional education has its programmatic requirements so mandated in length and breadth by external forces.

Aware of these circumstances, we should not be surprised by the number of young people considering teaching careers who report being discouraged by both their parents and their teachers or who prepare to teach but then do not. Nor should we be surprised that a third of those who enter the teaching profession leave within the first three years. We pay a severe price for our neglect of the teaching career.

The above is part of the bad news. The gratifying good news is that, in spite of these and other disheartening conditions, this nation is blessed with a core of competent, well-qualified, dedicated, caring teachers whose presence goes far toward sustaining what arguably is the most stable institution in our changing, dynamic society. Some of those individuals I worked with decades ago I meet in other situations today. Many of them are now principals or teacher educators and are almost invariably closely connected to the ecosystems of elementary and secondary schools.

The rest of the good news provides a challenge to this chapter and those to follow. That is, we also possess considerable insight into attainable alternative circumstances that would make teaching much more career friendly. These alternatives include greater attention to incentives; more focused recruitment, preparation, and induction; and professional and personal renewal. Each of the chapters that follow will address a major component or accompaniment of this array from the perspective of enhancing the teaching career.

Implicit or explicit in each chapter is the necessity of coherence among these components. Research reveals considerable incoherence. I argue the need for an organizing element to tie together the now poorly fused segments of the teaching career. This, I maintain, is a shared mission of common purpose and a common understanding of the conditions that the component parts of the whole must put in place in order to sustain this mission.

TEACHER EDUCATION: A TROUBLED ENTERPRISE

An observer from abroad wryly commented that higher education is America's substitute for a royal family. But in the march of our system of higher education to world-class status and admiration, teacher education was left behind. It began in the new normal schools of the 1840s as primarily a female enterprise at a time when women were granted little intellectual recognition.[1] Whereas medical research first looked for lessons to be learned from ongoing practice of its male practitioners, early educational research looked scarcely at all at practice and its predominantly female practitioners.[2]

With each transition of a normal school to teachers college and then to state college or university, the status of teacher education within the institution declined. Several of our top-ranked universities prepare no teachers and have no departments or schools of education. Several of the top-ranked schools of education prepare no teachers or maintain small, boutique programs.[3] Ironically, the movement of schools of education in flagship universities to exclusively graduate status has given neither higher status to teacher education nor the greater security and approval anticipated. No universities lacking schools of education have added them to their rosters of professional schools. And proposals to abandon all schools of education, whether graduate level or not, abound as never before.

Nonetheless, the good news is that there have been in recent years stirrings within universities, among college and university presidents, and in higher education organizations regarding the need to place teacher education higher in their priorities—and, indeed, the dangers of not doing so.[4] In a piece entitled "Teacher Education Must Become Colleges' Central Preoccupation," Vartan Gregorian, former president of Brown University and current president of the Carnegie Corporation of New York, argues the theme eloquently.[5] Again ironically, those for whom the message should have the most significance do not seem to get it: The future of schools, colleges, and departments of education lies not in the profundity and abundance of their research (most policymakers could not care less about educational research) but in the demonstrable quality and abundance of the teachers they produce. Otherwise, those who condemn such educational entities to oblivion, notwithstanding often-dubious intentions, will prevail. What we then invent to fill the void might not be schools of education but, of necessity, agencies for the teaching career.

Fortunately, the pieces that are necessary for a robust teacher education enterprise exist. These pieces include, in particular, the need for college- or university-based faculties in both the schools of education and the arts and sciences to work in close collaboration with educators in the elementary and secondary schools for the renewal of both teacher preparation and the K–12 schools. Since these faculties and institutions need to be closely coupled, they must be renewed together and simultaneously if the linkages are to be positively symbiotic—that is, each piece must add to what the others need and be acutely aware of and sensitive to this mutuality.

I turn now to dissonance and incoherence within the teacher education enterprise, knowing full well that causes of troubling internal circumstances also come from without. But those are a subject for some other time. Let us concentrate on matters for which those who are in and around schools and universities will be held accountable. The reader should understand that there are exemplary exceptions in current practice to each of the troubling observations that follow. But one would need to look very carefully—and perhaps unsuccessfully—to find a teacher-preparing setting entirely free of the shortcomings described.[6]

The Teacher Resource Pool

The bulk of our current teachers prepared themselves for teaching careers during their undergraduate years in crowded curricula extending on the average at least 15 credit hours beyond their anticipated 120. To graduate in four years, they added courses in some semesters or attended summer school or both. Some simply added a semester or two to the normal eight, making theirs in effect five-year programs. Many wished they had anticipated the added load early on, and some said that they would have preferred a less-rushed educational experience. Known in advance, they said, an expectation of five years to completion would not have deterred them.

Many of these students came to college or university with the possibility of a teaching career in mind; some had harbored this prospect for years. But few chose an institution because of the reputation of its teacher education program. Rather, they commonly chose an institution for reasons of propinquity—from within the state and from nearby. Others did not have teaching as a clear goal or even have it in mind at all. They also came from close by.

Perhaps because of this "built-in" supply, there is little university recruitment of potential undergraduate teacher education candidates. But this is not a full explanation. Many universities offering programs in engineering recruit vigorously in nearby secondary schools from which many of the institutions' students come. The apparent assumption that future teachers will just come, without any particular encouragement from colleges and universities, may contribute to the low percentage of minority students in the supply pool, even as diversity increases in the elementary and secondary school student population. Unfortunately, the percentage of minority students preparing to teach in urban universities is frequently lower than the percentage of minority enrollment in the institution overall. The reasons for a low percentage of these students in the teacher education supply line are complex.[7] It is past time for states and their institutions of higher learning to give this matter more attention.

During the past decade, a significant number of future teachers have been prepared in postbaccalaureate programs ranging in length from nine months to two years, with the shortest offering certification and perhaps some credits toward master's degrees and the longer ones usually offering both certification and the degree. These programs appeal particularly to people with years of experience in other work, sometimes offer financial inducements, and are sufficiently varied to attract a diverse array of candidates. They also fit the ethos of graduate schools of education unaccompanied by undergraduate teacher education. However, the two routes to teaching, graduate and undergraduate, often coexist. This coexistence, both within and among institutions, results in a bipolar stream of people entering the teaching career, aged in their early 20s for one group and often 30s and older for the other.

The two paths briefly described above certainly do not exhaust the entry channels. The postgraduate program, much more than the undergraduate, fosters choice, and the candidates come from many places and backgrounds. There are other choices for the college graduate, some requiring only a few weeks of summer orientation followed by entry into teaching under the mentoring eye of an experienced teacher (who is commonly teaching elsewhere in the same school).

The charge that the entry gates and routes to teaching are carefully guarded is nonsense. Actually, almost the opposite is true. There are numerous alternative paths to a teaching career, a situation that pertains in no other profession. The curricular requirements of law and medical schools are very much the same nationwide and are not pushed this way and that by state mandate. Likewise, the licensing requirements for lawyers and doctors are also very much the same from state to state, the professors in the law and medical schools are aware of and contribute to the construction of the state examinations, and their graduates proudly display the certificates of graduation of their respective universities. Is what we commonly accept as good for our major professions too good for those who teach our children? Currently, anyone with determination and a modicum of effort can find an unlatched gate or a stile over the fence so as to enter teaching.

Programmatic Myths and Realities

In a newspaper piece, the dean of a major medical school observed that untrue reports of new cures, once into the public domain, take on a credibility that is virtually impossible to extinguish. Such is the case with a litany of incorrect or outdated claims regarding the conduct of teacher education. One that did have some credibility decades ago is that at least 80% of candidates for elementary school teaching majored in that field, in a curriculum combining both content and pedagogy. However, as long ago as 1988, in our sample of six types of teacher-preparing institutions across the United States, colleagues and I found only one in which a few students took as much as 50% of their courses in the school or department of education. On the campus of a flagship university, the dean of arts and sciences complained about the excess of education courses in the preparation program of his own institution and praised that of journalism majors: about one-third journalism and the rest general education and electives outside of journalism. He was astounded to learn that our ongoing examination of teacher education there revealed almost precisely the same balance. He said that he would look into it. What those making this outdated claim either do not know or, more likely, omit to note is that differentiating students according to majors or specializations is a classification device that says little about curricular distributions.

It is interesting to note that recitation of the above enduring myth is often accompanied by the recommendation that schools of education be closed down. Were the alleged situation to exist, it would make more sense first to look into state-mandated requirements and then to set a deadline for the *institution* to correct the situation or have its authority to prepare teachers withdrawn.

Unfortunately, the repeated exhortation of this and other myths appears to rest more on prejudice (and frequently ignorance) than on evidence accompanied by an interest in remediation. The mythical ethos surrounding the conduct of teacher education tends to obscure the problems and shortcomings that do exist and confound the necessary processes of renewal and change. It is important to remember that the critical relationship between good teachers and good schools has been recognized only quite recently. Major reports on school reform from 1892 to 1986 made few references to teacher education; those on teacher education reform during the same period paid scant attention to schools.[8] Even though the influential Conant reports on schooling (1959) and teacher education (1963) in the United States appeared only a few years apart, little on the other is found in either.[9]

Over the past decade, it has been almost impossible for teacher-preparing settings to escape the stirrings toward necessary change. Consequently, given the number and variety of these, it is almost equally impossible to know precisely where each setting is in the change process and where exemplary responses to shortcomings exist. Here is a partial list of what inquiry has brought to the agenda of remediation:

- *The welcoming call and admission of students to undergraduate teacher education programs has been, in general, casual.* As described earlier, institutional recruitment has been limited or nonexistent. Given that most programs begin in the junior year, and given the common lack of effort to identify interested students early on, these and others who might become interested drift away—often enticed by the inducements of recruiters into other fields. Many of the students we interviewed late in their teacher preparation programs spoke of the various pressures to enter other fields they had encountered during their earlier college years.

Institutions of higher education offering postgraduate programs rightfully claim the attention of potential teachers to this alternative route. But without programs at the undergraduate level, a larger number of first-rate candidates may have been lost to teaching, particularly among those students who came undecided about careers in the field. With no teacher education faculty or student candidates to talk with and overtures from other fields enticing them, they pursued other paths. The mandated exclusion by some state legislatures of education courses from the undergraduate curriculum also has undoubtedly reduced the supply of teachers. Ironically, many of those courses got there in the first place because of the states' teacher licensing requirements. Fortunately, a number of public colleges and universities have been creative in circumventing such mandates in seeking to satisfy students' interests.

- *The casual identification and admission of students has contributed to their casual entry into preparatory courses and to incoherent programs.* Few of the hundreds of teacher education students that colleagues and I interviewed could recall ever having been formally admitted. Admission to the institution and passing the course grade requirements—nearly all of which had been raised during the two or three years prior to our visits—brought them to student teaching (commonly in their senior year) where, again, receiving satisfactory grades was usually the prime or only criterion.

Courses could be taken in any order, suggesting the absence of a carefully planned sequence. It was common to find directors of teacher education checking off courses covering mandated state requirements but uncommon to find teams of professors engaged in determining the mission, purposes, and components in content and pedagogy of curricular sequences. Asked if there were now students engaged in student teaching who ought not teach, the members of campuswide teacher education committees invariably answered in the affirmative.

It should be noted that most students interviewed simply assumed that, once admitted to the institution, the maintenance of satisfactory grades across the board guaranteed admission into any undergraduate department or field. A criticism of teacher education is that many candidates have mediocre academic records. In many settings, we found resistance to or rules against deviation from institution-wide adherence to a common grade-point standard.

- As earlier stated, an oft-repeated myth is that teachers are prepared only in teacher education programs in schools, colleges, or departments of education (SCDEs). When some teacher candidates do poorly on tests, such as in mathematics and science, SCDEs are blamed. The requirements for college graduation, however, are set by the institutions. Although most students enjoy the luxury of electives in the freshman and sophomore years, choice is often guided by and restricted to courses introduced into these years by the professional schools. *The SCDEs have been conspicuously absent in the determination of general education requirements, yet teachers are the college graduates who draw the most on the disciplines of general education as the very tools of their occupation.* This would not worry us if general education in the liberal studies were educating citizens and especially teachers in the civil and civic attributes that responsible citizenship in a social and political democracy requires. Unfortunately, the idea that professors in the SCDEs and the departments of the arts and sciences should join in determining the general education of teachers is both new and little implemented.[10]
- *There is plenty of research to show that field experiences, student teaching, and internships are rated highest for relevance to teaching among all the preparatory components by both future (and experienced) teachers and teacher educators. Yet the involvement of professors in both the SCDEs and the arts and sciences declines precipitously as their students get increasingly involved in practice.* Adjunct, temporary, and part-time instructors and then cooperating teachers in the schools get increasingly involved as this journey from the college campus to the schools progresses.

It is also apparent that this mixed group of college and school personnel plays a marginal role in the determination of the policies, programs, and practices of the teacher preparation enterprise. Further, the several clusters of the total faculty conduct their respective components of the enterprise separate from one another and with little intergroup communication. The fact that most colleges and universities have campuswide committees, usually with a representative or two from the schools, suggests otherwise. But most of their agendas address matters of administration and compliance with state and accreditation requirements. It is ironic to note that in SCDEs of flagship research universities only a small fraction of the faculty on whom institutional reputations depend engage more in teacher education than in teaching courses in their education disciplines.

- Critics frequently make the claim that the so-called professional curriculum of future elementary school teachers is "stuffed" with how-to courses of little intellectual demand. The courses picked out are usually in the teaching of something or other: reading, mathematics, sciences, and the other subjects of school curricula. This charge opens up one of the most challenging and controversial issues of the entire enterprise. The campus battle over who should teach these subject-matter methods courses is still alive and explosive. The many future elementary school teachers we interviewed commonly looked to these and classes on classroom management as their future salvation and wanted more—as squirrels might want to collect acorns for the long winter. Some future secondary school teachers expressed envy and wondered why such courses were largely missing from their curricula.

  What appeared to be missing for future teachers in both elementary and secondary programs was deep penetration into cognition and its implications for teaching, whatever the field. Absent are practice-connected principles of pedagogy upon which to build the teaching career as John Dewey proposed,[11] some of them subject or content specific, as Lee Shulman has more recently argued so effectively.[12] Correcting these omissions clearly calls for close collaboration among practitioners, cognitive psychologists, and specialists who understand deeply both the structure of their disciplines and the connection of the disciplines to the knowledge domains of the human conversation. Without the solid grounding in fundamental concepts and principles that the above implies, legions of teachers go on looking for the acorns throughout their teaching careers. But, of course, the implications for teacher education carry us far beyond the limited scope of conventional practice and the shackling imposed by policies driven by conventional wisdom rather than careful inquiry.

- Schooling is characterized by an ethos and a deep structure that together face a widely shared set of expectations for it—from the custodial to the academic—on the part of both the public and teachers. Teacher education is geared largely to the institution of schooling and, consequently, to these expectations. *Therefore, what is commonly viewed as the most impactful part of a teacher's preservice preparation—student teaching—is also commonly viewed as an apprenticeship in what exists.* The loose coupling of the university side and the school side of the student teacher's placement in an experienced teacher's classroom virtually ensures that practices in that classroom will dominate in the learning repertoire of the neophyte.

This makes the choice of school and classroom critical to the resulting introduction into teaching. Yet research reveals the process to be repetitively casual. The sheer numbers of students to be placed limit the range of choice. This is particularly the case with large producers in small towns with few schools. Just finding enough teachers willing to take on student teachers is often a problem. Sometimes students are turned loose to find their own placements. The "teaching hospital" of medical education provides an attractive model, but even medium-sized teacher preparation programs would require dozens of schools in which to place cohorts of interns. And these "teaching schools" need to be renewing places, open to new ideas and change, unless we prefer to continue cloning the schools we have. But until we move beyond test scores as the criterion of school quality, teacher education will continue to be driven by this low level of conventional wisdom regarding the purposes of our schools rather than by our steadily growing and largely neglected body of knowledge regarding cognition and pedagogy and the educational needs of a democratic society.

TOWARD RENEWAL

What I have described here is not a placid lake of little-known and little-explored environmental circumstances. The water has been studied by researchers and churned by commissions. Typically, that call to arms regarding the condition of our schools, *A Nation at Risk* (1983), said little about teacher education.[13] But it did prick the consciences of some leaders in higher education and bring them and their institutions together in the realization that better teachers mean better schools and that they could contribute to this end.[14] Nonetheless, this link had always been ignored or seen as tenuous; therefore, direct intervention in school "reform" dominated the radar screen into the 21st century.[15]

Meanwhile, all the old myths about teacher education and the SCDEs' iron grip on it began increasingly to resurface. But there were also legitimate criticisms stemming from studies, discussions among higher education organizations, commission reports, and more. Issues of national accreditation of teacher education programs and national certification of teachers moved onto the screen.[16] There was a kind of convergence of elements of the work of all of these in the report of the National Commission on Teaching and America's Future (1996).[17] As I surmised earlier in this chapter, it is hard to believe that any teacher-preparing setting in the United States failed to be stirred into the realization that changes in expectations for it were in the offing. What many probably did not anticipate was that mandates to change would come swiftly, arbitrarily, and sometimes mindlessly.

What many policymakers, still almost entirely preoccupied with direct school reform, failed to realize was the degree to which the public had come to embrace—and perhaps had believed all along—the idea that good schools in the absence of good teachers is an oxymoron. For about two years, I have enjoyed using a single-item multiple-choice test in discussions with and talks to diverse groups. I present four dominant proposals for current school improvement and ask those assembled to choose the one—just one—offering most promise for investing our resources productively:

1. Standards and tests mandated by the states
2. A competent, caring, qualified teacher in every classroom
3. Retention of children who fail to meet the standards set for their grade
4. Schools of choice for all parents

Selection of the second is almost unanimous. From an audience of about one thousand people attending an annual meeting of the National School Boards Association, for example, all but one person chose it. The intrepid dissenter then went to the microphone and explained that, while supporting the second proposal, she wanted to be sure that teachers had standards for which they are held accountable. The goal put forward by the National Commission on Teaching and America's Future was that of our having a competent, caring, qualified teacher in every classroom by 2006. This goal was overly optimistic, as history will attest, but continuous progress toward it should be the object of our attention each day.

Mission

Colleagues and I have been engaged for several decades in research and development pertaining to educational change, schooling, and the conduct of teacher education. We are impressed with the good ideas that abound and with the efforts of many educators to renew their settings, but we remain awed by the challenges involved. What troubles us most is the general absence of *an ethos of commonly shared mission* beyond that of academic preparation. I deliberately chose this italicized phrase instead of the common one, *shared purpose*. "Purpose" suggests ends for which means are yet to be found. But "mission" implies both ends and means together in an ethos that simultaneously embraces not only where we are going and what we will do to get there but also where we are now.

Effective renewal is characterized by this ethos. There is a substantial literature documenting moral lineage in human dignity, civility, and civic well-being. Lisbeth Schorr draws upon this operational concept of mission to describe productive work in strengthening families and neighborhoods: "Successful programs create an organizational culture that is . . . 'tight' about their mission and simultaneously 'loose' about how the mission is carried out."[18] Eliot Levine, whose book *One Kid at a Time* brought Schorr's work to my attention, describes how a school's mission pervades the work ethic, staff deliberations, conviviality, and caring commitment of the entire enterprise.[19] His description comes close to depicting the islands of school renewal and—even less common—of teacher education renewal that colleagues and I have encountered over the years.

We have rarely found what might be termed a "macromission" for the intended education of the young in a social and political democracy—an ethos encompassing the conditions most likely to foster the sensitivities and sensibilities of both responsible citizenship and a productive, satisfying life. In crisscrossing the country to conduct two comprehensive studies, we were unable to find either in schools or in colleges and universities engaged in teacher education any evidence of or discourse about this larger institutional or programmatic mission. To assume that a macromission, as I have described it, is ubiquitous in the surround and, therefore, guides the daily functioning of our educational system places a considerable strain on the imagination. Likewise, to assume that the close coupling of the several major components of the teaching career will in itself provide a common mission for all involved with them is an irrational leap of faith.

Yet it is clear that both educators and a large percentage of the American people share and readily articulate a rather comprehensive set of purposes for their schools.[20] I have been asking diverse groups of people whether they value personal and social goals at least as highly as the vocational and academic. They almost universally respond in the affirmative. And most polls and surveys reveal a high percentage of agreement on the view that our public schools must be tied to the democratic principle of equal educational opportunity for all.

Nonetheless, in our discussions with future teachers and teacher educators in institutions across the country, we encountered considerable discomfort with the idea of school commitment to a common set of values. Words such as "values" and, especially, "moral" were challenged: What values are to be taught? Whose are to be downplayed? Are teachers to be the moral stewards of children's learning and of the school's public purpose as well? Interestingly, we received a good deal of feedback regarding the importance of the discussions elicited and how much they had stimulated subsequent conversation.

Back home, we discussed our experiences in the field and began to exchange position papers on what our schools are for and, therefore, what the preparation of teachers is for. We came up with a four-part mission statement that, we realized in retrospect, began with a two-part macromission for both enterprises and moved on to a two-part, more contextual mission for teacher education. It is less of the former and much more of the latter that we have found commonly in the ethos of so many of the schools described, to use Theodore Sizer's words, as "places of learning, places of joy." The mission that emerged from our work is the following:

- Enculturating the young in a social and political democracy
- Providing to the young disciplined encounters with all the subject matters of the human conversation
- Ensuring responsible stewardship of schools
- Practicing pedagogical nurturing

Caught up as colleagues and I are in the idea of education as a moral endeavor, we struggled over whether to include it in the mission as a fifth component. We came to realize that the concept is a necessary dimension of the four—the part of the ethos that most imbues the otherwise neutral word "education" with both intentionality and context. Here is how Kenneth Sirotnik embedded the moral in his take on the first of the above mission statements in his concluding chapter of the book in which several colleagues and I addressed the moral dimensions of teaching:

> Some contributors to this book show a bit of discomfort with non-relativist positions, even though . . . establishing a set of first principles is exactly what this book is all about. I would suggest that none of the authors . . . would endorse or even negotiate a new conception of "justice" based on racial determinism, hedonism, nihilism, or no ethical stance whatsoever. . . .
>
> But if universalism is still a troublesome concept, then I would urge readers to at least ponder the rationale that unites the states of America. To be sure, America is a collection of multiple communities defined by different interests, races, ethnicities, regions, economic stratifications, religions, and so forth. Celebrating these differences is part of what makes this nation great. But there is a community—a moral community—that transcends the special interests of individuals, families, groups, that stands for what this nation is all about: liberty *and justice* for all. This "community," of course, is an abstraction. It is a "moral ecology" held together by a political democracy and the fundamental values embedded in the system.[21]

It is from this moral ecology, I would argue, that the whole of our education—formal, informal, and nonformal—must derive its ethos. And it is this moral ecology that both drives and sustains the most worthy and satisfying teaching career. It is the ethos that must bind together the disparate components of and actors in the teacher education enterprise.

The Renewing Self in a Renewing Culture

What disciplined inquirers describe as characteristic of effective social programs and institutions is an ongoing process of simultaneous individual and cultural renewal.[22] The linear model of inputs and outputs that characterizes the "reforming" of schooling and teacher education ignores such renewal and, indeed, stifles and eventually extinguishes it. The narrow, punitive agenda of the current standards/testing/accountability reform era has, probably unwittingly, polluted the moral ecology of potential individual and institutional renewal that began to stir among educators in the 1980s in spite of the failure of our political leaders to provide the resources necessary to the warlike educational "crusade" called for in *A Nation at Risk*.[23]

Reform is a negative, nasty concept. It is one frequently used in referring to the rehabilitation of criminals, drug addicts, and juvenile delinquents, and ironically, the improvement of schools. It implies things gone wrong to be righted by some outside intervention. The word rarely appears in the rhetoric of improving health, social, or business practices. In regard to these, by contrast, there is an extraordinary appeal to the insatiable public appetite for self-improvement books, videos, speeches, conferences, and the like.

Teachers are extraordinary in their readiness for and willingness to spend their own resources of time and money for self-improvement opportunities. If the resources spent on "reforming" them and their schools were spent on supporting teachers' motivation to do better, the high level of satisfaction parents now express toward their schools would be even higher.[24] The time is long past for all of us—educators, too—to abandon the concept of reform and its accompanying impositions on teachers and schools and give serious attention to individual and cultural renewal. Renewal can never be imposed, but the human propensity for it can be nourished and supported. It occurs because individuals want it and will it.

A major problem with the feast of self-improvement inducements that surround us is their hedonistic appeal. Corporations are well aware of this. Their appeal to the worker is not just to be all that you can be but to be all that you can be for the company. The "power breakfast" is not to motivate one just to run faster, but rather to run faster for the company's bottom line. This does not necessarily mean to be creatively deviant, even though corporate rhetoric may extol creativity. What counts in the cultural value system is how creativity and other traits that are said to be valued are actually used.

What counts in teaching is much less clear, considerably less stable, and not necessarily conducive to personal satisfaction or tangible reward. At the time of this writing, what counts in teaching in most places in the United States is clear and narrowly directed—to test scores. And just as critics view what counts in the business world as narrow and even immoral in its inattention to the common good, the same is said by critics of what now counts so dominantly in schooling. Teachers challenged by the educational mission of developing democratic character in the young wonder if they have chosen a career other than the one they had envisioned. The implication that they and their work need to be reformed contributes nothing to their sense of worth and motivation for self-renewal. Power breakfasts would do more harm than good. Yet teachers, like other workers, crave attention to and support for what they do.

There is a considerable industry devoted to so-called staff or professional development, driven by both internal and external interests. It adheres very closely to the self-improvement paradigm that prevails in the marketplace in general. A major difference is that little of it is in response to teachers' felt needs. Rather, it stems largely from others' felt wants: for a different method of teaching reading, for teachers to understand quality circles, for tougher approaches to grade promotions, for greater use of technology, and so on. Analyses reveal little attention to educational purpose, what education is, pedagogical issues, what should be removed to make room for the new, or teachers' views. Teachers leave their classrooms and schools for the supposed tune-up when their needs would be better served by joining together to improve conditions in their own workplace.

As stated above, a major fallout from the past several decades of inquiry into educational change is the lesson that the most productive symbiosis is that of a renewing self in a renewing culture. Over the past decade, colleagues and I have brought together in a leadership development program dozens of cohorts composed of teams representing the arts and sciences, colleges of education, and school faculties from teacher education settings all across the United States. They have addressed the four-part mission presented earlier, at least sixty major conditions necessary to the robust conduct of this mission, and an implementation strategy focused on the simultaneous renewal of their respective programs and those people (such as themselves) responsible for them.[25] While most speak eloquently of their own renewal, they almost invariably link this to the generation of culturally renewing processes in their own settings and the intensely intellectual discourse involved. Although many of the old regularities of their settings remain, the changes effected in some and the coming together of long-separated, sometimes discordant, cultures have had a powerfully renewing influence on these leaders and their colleagues. Their testimonials reveal the powerful symbioses of simultaneous cultural and individual renewal.

In the literature of teacher and teacher education improvement, there is far more attention to the individual than to either cultural settings or their relationships. Indeed, as I stated earlier, reports on school or teacher education reform rarely mention one another. It is as though teachers and teacher education have little to do with the quality of schools. Consequently, to speak not only of renewing the several different cultures involved with the teaching career but also of renewing them collaboratively, guided by a common mission, is to propose a challenging innovation.

CONDITIONS

Although what currently counts in determining the quality of our schools is exceedingly narrow, public expectations for them have steadily expanded. Perhaps we should consider this expansion as giving credit to schools. With so much of our infrastructure in flux, we look to them as among the most stable of our institutions. Although there is considerable disagreement over giving top priority to personal, social, vocational, or academic goals, parents grow uneasy when any one of these appears to be neglected. There is a close parallel here with the uneasiness that arises when any one of the traits we identify with democracy (such as civility, civicness, opportunity, freedom, or individual responsibility) appears to be eroding in the fabric of our society.

In part because of this parallelism, colleagues and I began to use the layered concept of developing democratic character in the young as the all-encompassing public expectation for our schools. Unpacking the implications of this for schools and their educators has been central to the readings and discussions that have brought together in common cause in our leadership development program representatives of the several cultures of schooling and teacher education.[26] The school–university partnerships of the National Network for Educational Renewal are committed to forwarding the Agenda for Education in a Democracy that emerged out of our inquiries into educational change, schooling, and the education of educators described previously.

The curriculum we developed for this leadership program has guided varied others in local settings. I do not recall any reactions over the years that suggest the irrelevance of this mission to the ongoing work of any of the cultures represented. The view often expressed by participants early on, however, was that their various cultures generally lacked serious discussion of the purpose of the work in which they are engaged. Many admitted the absence of sustained conversation about either the component parts of this mission or the conditions of the workplace required to sustain them. Most of the settings involved in the leadership program have in varying ways sought to fill this vacuum. And most regard the building of critical inquiry into the regularities of the workplace to be a necessary condition of their cultural infrastructure, whether it be that of a school, a teacher education program, or some other institution. Such inquiry is particularly crucial where the boundaries of the cultures relevant to the teaching career come together.

The remainder of this chapter reviews some of the critical stages in ensuring a competent, caring corps of teachers nationwide, several of the critical issues in each stage that cry out for attention, and some of the intercultural innovations that have emerged in recent years to improve coherence among the parts that impinge on the teaching career. The intent is to nourish the discourse that characterizes cultures of individual and institutional renewal, not to prescribe one-size-fits-all solutions to the problems of teacher preparation and schooling. Further, it should be understood that renewal is always work in progress and never the implementation of some imagined perfect model program or human being.

Recruitment

If a plethora of public and institutional inducements is the way to attract a steady supply of promising candidates for teaching, this nation should be ashamed. If enormous diversity in the pupil population of our schools is a wake-up call for increased diversity in the teaching corps and for preparing all teachers in the understandings and skills that educating the young requires, this nation is asleep. If the distribution of college scholarships correlates with the college hierarchy of students most welcomed, then, obviously athletes outrank teacher candidates by far. Without adding several other obvious "ifs" to this list, it becomes startlingly clear that the present high level of satisfaction of most parents with their schools and teachers is a miracle.

There is little more to be said about the problem of teachers' income, particularly the slow advance during the critical years of raising families. Action has fallen far short. Some states—notably Georgia[27]—have taken steps to provide financial support during the preservice stage of preparation. But little of the needed collaboration for a campaign exists. The key players in such a campaign would be policymakers, school district administrators, university officials, and the media, with this last group needing to focus on a much more uplifting role of school teaching than has been presented in the past.

Admissions

Just as the recruitment of promising candidates, especially of minorities, ranks low in the institutional repertoire of commitment to teacher education, the admissions process suffers from inattention. In too many colleges and universities, there is no clear entry point. The major identifying milestone is reached when students apply for student teaching placement. The major, and sometimes only, criterion for admission is grade point average. Most of the many students that colleagues and I interviewed—all close to graduation and program completion—were unable to recall any overt action regarding their demonstration of admissions criteria. Campus committees with jurisdiction over all internal matters pertaining to teacher education universally answered "yes" to my query, "Are there students who have now completed or are well along in student teaching who never should have been assigned to a classroom?"

School–University Partnerships

Partnering is another of those vanilla-flavored ideas to which we commonly nod our heads in unthinking approval. But good partnering—as in a good marriage—is hard work. Ideally, each partner has something the other lacks or needs and a willingness to contribute to the other's needs. In other words, there is a potentially powerful positive symbiosis. Most universities take pride in providing a variety of community services, including to schools. A spirit of *noblesse oblige* guides and enhances. But much more is required of a school–university partnership for teacher education, teaching, and the improvement of schooling.

Exemplary "teaching schools"—in concept similar to teaching hospitals in medical education—are essential to exemplary teacher education programs. Although there are now comprehensive standards for partner or professional development schools in the accreditation of teacher education programs, the functioning of the necessary school–university partnerships is still in a developmental stage. Much more is essential than the mere assignment of ten student teachers to ten classrooms in a designated professional development school. These ten need to be a cohort immersed in the functioning of the whole school and engaged as both a cohort and as members of the faculty in individual and institutional renewal. University faculty members from both the college of education and the arts and sciences should be on the scene quite regularly and be involved, just as school personnel must be partners in the college or university component of the teacher education program. The partner school concept offers a unique opportunity for simultaneous renewal.[28]

Centers of Pedagogy

Accounts of turf battles among the cultures contributing to the teacher education enterprise are legendary. Research into these and the functioning of the loosely linked school and university contributors is relatively new and scattered. Work such as that of the Center for the Study of Teaching and Policy (headquartered at the University of Washington in collaboration with Indiana University, Michigan State University, Pennsylvania State University, the University of California at Santa Barbara, the University of North Carolina, and Education Matters, Inc.) in pulling this together and providing thoughtful answers to critical questions about teacher education is long overdue.[29] Also needed is that complex genre of inquiry that documents and monitors those innovative solutions to problems that are either too much or too little heralded.

One of the latter variety is the department of pedagogy proposed a century ago by John Dewey while he was at the University of Chicago. He did not get the approval he sought from the trustees and President William Rainey Harper. Few details are available, but it appears that what he had in mind would have embraced in a continuum the early childhood, elementary, and secondary laboratory schools and run up through the undergraduate college and graduate divisions. He viewed concepts and principles of pedagogy to be the organizing elements of a curriculum in the same way scholars in the arts and sciences view those of their disciplines. He decried generic methods of teaching and the teachers of such in his effort to place pedagogy at the very center of scholarly inquiry.

It is reasonable to deduce from his letters of proposal that he saw teaching at all levels being a common endeavor and hence as providing the glue that binds them together in the several institutional cultures I have described. All would engage in essentially the same conversation while differentiating the specifics of application. Since the time of his proposal, rather than melting away, the boundaries of these cultures have hardened. A contemporary version of his proposal—for centers of pedagogy—is intended to break down these barriers for teacher education and assumes that a common conversation on pedagogy would emerge. There has not been a rush to implementation.

Influenced by the idea of a center of pedagogy,[30] settings in the National Network for Educational Renewal with strong school-university partnerships began to move toward new organizational structures to better connect all of the major constituencies engaged in the preservice teacher education endeavor. Brigham Young University (BYU), for example, with a decade-old partnership with five neighboring school districts in place, created in 1996 the Center for the Improvement of Teacher Education and Schooling to coordinate more effectively the collaborative processes involving partner schools, the college of education, and the arts and sciences departments, many of which were operating near-autonomous programs for the preparation of secondary school teachers. Beginning with a year-long Institute for Educational Renewal during the 1997–1998 academic year, the University of Texas at El Paso (UTEP) has moved toward a center of pedagogy to strengthen teacher education and public school practice simultaneously. In November 1995, Montclair State University opened its Center of Pedagogy, apparently the first in the nation.[31] Building on a school–university partnership already in place, members of three groups of partners—from schools, the arts and sciences, and the College of Education and Human Services—have equal status in the center's policymaking and conduct. Later, the partners created a doctoral degree program emphasizing pedagogy for teachers wishing to stay in teaching.

It is interesting to note in the early histories of the initiatives at BYU, UTEP, and Montclair State the extent to which the implementation of the center of pedagogy concept forced attention to the dysfunctional, chronic disconnections among the several cultures engaged in teacher education. Also noteworthy is the importance of serious discussion of mission and necessary conditions in seeking common purpose; such discussions are crucial to understanding and making real that moral ecology to which Sirotnik refers.

Induction

The point of most serious disjuncture in the teaching career is that of suddenly becoming "teacher" and no longer "teacher-to-be." For some it is the realization of a dream, for some others a nightmare become real. Interestingly, the transition is akin to that of children being "pre-school" on a Sunday evening in late summer and "in school" on Monday morning. Neither transition is given the caring, understanding, supportive attention it deserves.

College-based teacher educators are themselves dealing with a crop of new aspirants. They have no time for and give little thought to the entry experiences of last year's student teachers. The close ties of professors in the arts and sciences are to those students who majored in their fields and are now their graduate students, not to those who majored in their disciplines and are now beginning their teaching careers.

The decibel level is high as teachers greet one another just before the superintendent's address at the districtwide welcoming ceremony on the day before schools open and students arrive. But their minds are on tomorrow—some with keen anticipation, some with dread. The culture of each individual school and its relationship to the larger district and community cultures beyond will have much to do with the playing out of anticipation. The concepts of the teaching role and the nature of the preparation already received will also be powerful factors. Combined, they will contribute enormously to the career decisions of the one-third of these neophytes who will not be in classrooms three years later and the two-thirds who will be. To deal with the alarming level of attrition solely on the basis of demographic statistics such as salaries and benefits, important though these are, is to ignore the profound effects of individual school culture, the social and political intrusions that shape this culture, and the place of schools and their teachers in the ethos of public support and the nation's priorities.

Mentoring

Teachers mentoring teachers, especially their least-experienced colleagues, is an idea whose time has come. It is also an idea of deceptive simplicity—simple in the sense that people helping one another is an age-old and unarguably moral concept, deceptive because much more than the obvious one-to-one relationship is involved. As I stated earlier, there is extraordinary worldwide agreement on principles and concepts necessary to peace and harmony among the whole of humankind. But there is also incredible contradiction among these at all levels and in all domains of human interaction.

It is exceedingly difficult to deal with the effects of controversy out of their context. Beginning teachers, for example, may be able to effect technically the hundreds of decisions they make each day only to have the process overwhelmed by the dynamics of the classroom ecology. They might have been ranked high on human relationships among their peers in college but may now be overly sensitive to and perhaps irritated by the demands of some parents. These and other complexities, many unpredictable, make the mentoring relationship much more varied and complicated than often is assumed.

Early in the higher education phase of my teaching career, I returned from summer vacation to find myself in charge of the division of teacher education, an organizational unit lodged somewhere between departmental and professional school status in the university of my employment. I was told that my departing predecessor, going to a deanship an hour's drive away, would be available as my mentor. He proved to be very diligent in his visits and sincere in his offers to help. But I needed and wanted him only when he was unavailable. We grew mutually frustrated over my inability to frame critical questions during our sessions together and over his absence during crises. We agreed to discontinue.

Since then, I have observed a broad array of mentoring relationships that have led me to a couple of conclusions. First, the technical kinds of help to which mentoring so readily lends itself can in many instances be economically and productively provided in a mentor-and-group setting anywhere. But all of those work-in-progress dilemmas, circumstances, and happenings that call out for sage counsel require a mentor who is part of the same school culture. Any mentoring arrangement derived from a standard school district formula is doomed to failure. The mentoring domain is currently dynamic and high on the list of promising practices for the support of teachers, especially early in their careers.

The School District

There has long been internal tension regarding the balance of centralization and decentralization in the district's relationship to its schools. The production and marketing of commercial products such as Pepsi-Cola require carefully monitored standardization. But schools are human intensive and, consequently, even more than gardens, have varying nutritional needs. Strangely, the foolishness of a state's mandating the seeds, fertilization, and watering schedules in common for all the varying locations and soils of gardens and farms seems to be more obvious than that of marketing the same instructional materials and method of teaching reading for all the school children of the state. There is plenty of evidence from the past couple of decades of inquiry into school change to support the proposition that both teacher satisfaction and student learning improve when well-prepared teachers enjoy decision-making latitude in the diverse ecosystems of their classrooms.[32] Teachers, like other workers, tend to gravitate, when possible, to higher-paying districts, but they also are known to make parallel and even lower-paying moves to districts known for their cultivation of site-based renewal.

Forward-looking districts are to be commended for their efforts to ensure that teachers have an array of support services that include psychological counseling. But the need for such is likely to be considerably reduced when districts and both principals and teachers unions are closely joined in supporting cultures of individual school renewal. Good work is closely linked to the well-being of human beings.[33] Few things are more satisfying than promoting and doing good work.

Unions and Associations

When I began my teaching career, the union-oriented federations and associations of teachers were in their infancies. Some were focused primarily on salaries and working conditions, some on instructional and curricular support, and others somewhat ambiguously divided between the two. From the 1950s into the 1960s, the comprehensive National Education Association (NEA), which in its public relations rhetoric and in considerable substance had appeared to be more committed to matters of professional improvement, moved vigorously toward matching the public perception of the union role—that of teachers' salaries, benefits, and working conditions. One major result was the moving out from under the NEA umbrella of such organizations as the Association for Supervision and Curriculum Development and the American Educational Research Association. Another was increased tension between and separation of employers and employees and administrators and teachers. Implementing the concept of individual school renewal became compounded by principals, charged with leadership, being identified in bargaining as tied to the central administration. Teacher strikes exacerbated this separation of principals and teachers in school settings.

During the concluding decades of the 20th century, the American Federation of Teachers (AFT) and the National Education Association grew closer together in their increased interest in enhancing teachers' salaries and benefits and promoting professional services. There have been serious talks of an amalgam of the two along with increased attention to the public purpose of improving our schools nationwide. It is significant that one of the partners in the Strengthening and Sustaining Teachers initiative, the Teacher Union Reform Network (TURN), is an improvement enterprise representative of both the AFT and the NEA. These recent developments bode well for a supportive, coherent infrastructure for the teaching career.

Beyond the Beginning Years

Critical and in need of strong support though the first three years of teaching most certainly are, there is for many teachers a flattening and burning out of enthusiasm after a decade or so, accompanied and undoubtedly influenced by a common disconnection from the intellectual and social wellsprings of renewal. Opportunities to get out of teaching beckon. Estimates show that single career lines of forty years are sometimes occupied by as many as five different teachers.

To assume that career lines are refreshed by these infusions is wrongheaded. We do not hold similar assumptions with respect to lawyers and physicians. And this situation is expensive. We do preservice teacher education cheaply, but to have to fill a career line four or five times over is anything but cheap.

The revolving-door syndrome is not one with relatively obvious innovative solutions. It represents a complex interweaving of legacies from a long-neglected occupation, the loose and uncertain effect of a high level of universal schooling on the nation's economy, the absence of commitment to a common mission on the part of the diverse cultures that impact the teaching career, the inertia that comes from myriad unclear responsibilities, and more. The surest road to the satisfying, productive teaching career that attracts and retains a high level of able, committed professional practitioners is a society that recognizes and nourishes the critical relationship between education and democracy. The surest road to such a society is a people dedicated to the development of democratic character in the young. Among such a people will be many who proudly seek and steadfastly pursue teaching careers characterized by reflective learning in nurturing environments.[34]

September 11, 2001, will go down in our memories as a day of anguish and infamy. It is a day that should drive home the implications of Tocqueville's prescient observation that democracy is an arduous apprenticeship of liberty: There can be no higher mission for our schools and their teachers than ensuring for all the education that individual and cultural democratic character requires.

NOTES

1. For intimate knowledge of 19th-century schools and pedagogy, one is advised to read the letters, diaries, and memoirs of some of the women involved. (For a classic of the genre, see Bruce A. Ronda [ed.], *Letters of Elizabeth Palmer Peabody* [Middletown, Conn.: Wesleyan University Press, 1984].) Few other artifacts remain. On slowly moving recently through an outstanding museum of U.S. history, I noted the conspicuous absence of items pertaining to schooling.

2. See the essays in Donald Warren (ed.), *American Teachers: Histories of a Profession at Work* (New York: Macmillan, 1989).

3. For a provocative, illuminating account of a clutch of schools of education that achieved high ranking during the concluding decades of the 20th century, see

Geraldine J. Clifford and James W. Guthrie, *Ed School* (Chicago: University of Chicago Press, 1988).

4. See, for example, "The Letter: 37 Presidents Write . . . ," *American Association for Higher Education Bulletin* (November 1987): 10–14; and The Renaissance Group, *Educating the New American Student* (Cedar Falls: University of Northern Iowa, 1993).

5. Vartan Gregorian, "Teacher Education Must Become Colleges' Central Preoccupation," *Chronicle of Higher Education*, 17 August 2001, pp. B7–B8.

6. Colleagues and I found none in our comprehensive sample of settings studied. The few that had quite coherent college- or university-based components did not connect closely with the school-based components. See John I. Goodlad, *Teachers for Our Nation's Schools* (San Francisco: Jossey-Bass, 1990).

7. See the analysis in June A. Gordon, *The Color of Teaching* (New York: RoutledgeFalmer, 2000).

8. Zhixin Su, "Teacher Education Reform in the United States (1890–1986)," Occasional Paper no. 3 (Seattle: Center for Educational Renewal, College of Education, University of Washington, 1986).

9. James B. Conant, *The American High School Today* (New York: McGraw-Hill, 1959); and *The Education of American Teachers* (New York: McGraw-Hill, 1963).

10. There has been, in recent years, considerable support for these two groups of faculty members to work closely together in the conduct of teacher preparation. But there has been little attention to the need for them to plan and ensure comprehensive general education for all future teachers.

11. Comprehensive analyses of Dewey's educational ideas abound. For a balanced treatment, see Alan Ryan, *John Dewey and the High Tide of American Liberalism* (New York: W. W. Norton, 1995).

12. Shulman has advanced his concepts in varied publication outlets. See, for example, Lee S. Shulman, "Those Who Understand Knowledge Growth in Teaching," *Educational Researcher* 15 (February 1986): 4–14. Earlier, Bruner caused an educational stir with his persuasive conception of teaching that employed understanding of the structure of the discipline to stimulate children's learning of it at an early age. See Jerome S. Bruner, *The Process of Education* (New York: Vintage, 1960).

13. National Commission on Excellence in Education, *A Nation at Risk* (Washington, D.C.: Government Printing Office, 1983).

14. Particularly significant was the joining of university provosts and education deans to create the initial Holmes Group. See its first report, Holmes Group, *Tomorrow's Teachers: A Report of the Holmes Group* (East Lansing, Mich.: Holmes Group, 1986).

15. Each successive president, beginning with Ronald Reagan, and most governors quickly learned of the political mileage to be gained by putting school reform at the top of their agendas. The need to pay attention to the education of teachers lagged far behind.

16. At the time of this writing, there is a clear divide between two groups of protagonists in the "teacher quality wars." One group rejects the idea that quality is associated with an education degree and sees the need for teachers to have only

an academic major and "subject-matter" courses. The other group aligns itself with a balance of general education, subject-matter specialization, and pedagogy in the preparation program, as well as program certification and teacher licensing much as with the other professions. See David G. Imig, "Battling the Essentialists," *AACTE Briefs* (November 19, 2001): 2.

17. National Commission on Teaching and America's Future, *What Matters Most: Teaching for America's Future* (New York: The Commission, 1996). This report pulled together many of the recommendations that have emerged in common from various studies and other reports on what is necessary for solid improvement in the conduct of teacher education. The agreements are such that there should be no need for further studies and reports until these recommendations are widely implemented.

18. Lisbeth B. Schorr, *Common Purpose: Strengthening Families and Neighborhoods to Rebuild America* (New York: Doubleday, 1997), p. 8.

19. Eliot Levine, *One Kid at a Time* (New York: Teachers College Press, 2002).

20. Two major studies, one of secondary schools and the other of both elementary and secondary schools, published close to the time of release of *A Nation at Risk*, sampled large numbers of adults regarding their choices of school purposes. Unlike the commission's report, which emphasized economic goals, both studies described much broader expectations for balance among the personal, social, vocational, and academic. See Ernest L. Boyer, *High School* (New York: Harper & Row, 1983), and John I. Goodlad, *A Place Called School* (New York: McGraw-Hill, 1984).

21. Kenneth A. Sirotnik, "Society, Schooling, Teaching, and Preparing to Teach," in John I. Goodlad, Roger Soder, and Kenneth A. Sirotnik (eds.), *The Moral Dimensions of Teaching* (San Francisco: Jossey-Bass, 1990), p. 307.

22. See, for example, John W. Gardner, *Self-Renewal: The Individual and the Innovative Society* (New York: Harper & Row, 1964); and Robert N. Bellah and Associates, *Habits of the Heart: Individualism and Commitment in American Life* (Berkeley: University of California Press, 1985) and *The Good Society* (New York: Knopf, 1991).

23. Ted Sizer put forward a biting criticism of the failure of the National Commission on Excellence in Education to pay attention to the large body of data available to it regarding both the extant conditions of schooling and what these implied for its comprehensive improvement. See Theodore R. Sizer, "Back to *A Place Called School*," in Kenneth A. Sirotnik and Roger Soder (eds.), *The Beat of a Different Drummer* (New York: Peter Lang, 1999), pp. 103–115.

24. The 33rd Annual Phi Delta Kappa/Gallup Poll (2001) reported support for public schools to be the highest since this poll began. See Lowell C. Rose and Alec M. Gallup, "The 33rd Annual Phi Delta Kappa/Gallup Poll for the Public's Attitudes Toward the Public Schools," *Phi Delta Kappan* 83 (September 2001): 42–43.

25. For the core curriculum and its use in settings of the National Network for Educational Renewal, see Wilma F. Smith and Gary D Fenstermacher (eds.), *Leadership for Educational Renewal: Building a Cadre of Leaders* (San Francisco: Jossey-Bass, 1999).

26. The common readings have been many. Five that colleagues and I have edited bring together the views of a wide range of individuals who have given serious thought to the powerful relationship between education and democracy and the apprenticeship of liberty that our educational institutions should provide: John I. Goodlad, Roger Soder, and Kenneth A. Sirotnik (eds.), *The Moral Dimensions of Teaching* (San Francisco: Jossey-Bass, 1990); Roger Soder (ed.), *Democracy, Education, and the Schools* (San Francisco: Jossey-Bass, 1996); John I. Goodlad and Timothy J. McMannon (eds.), *The Public Purpose of Education and Schooling* (San Francisco: Jossey-Bass, 1997); John I. Goodlad, Roger Soder, and Timothy J. McMannon (eds.), *Developing Democratic Character in the Young* (San Francisco: Jossey-Bass, 2001); and Stephen J. Goodlad (ed.), *The Last Best Hope: A Democracy Reader* (San Francisco: Jossey-Bass, 2001).

27. See the Georgia Student Finance Commission's web page on the PROMISE Teacher Scholarship Program at http://www.gsfc.org/GSFA/SCL/dsp_teacher_prom_scholarship.cfm.

28. For a comprehensive analysis, see Richard W. Clark, *Effective Professional Development Schools* (San Francisco: Jossey-Bass, 1999); and Russell T. Osguthorpe et al. (eds.), *Partner Schools: Centers for Educational Renewal* (San Francisco: Jossey-Bass, 1995).

29. See the results of the center's analysis of research reported in peer-reviewed journals: Suzanne M. Wilson, Robert E. Floden, and Joan Ferrini-Mundy, *Teacher Preparation Research: Current Knowledge, Gaps, and Recommendations* (Seattle: Center for the Study of Teaching and Policy, University of Washington, 2001).

30. See John I. Goodlad, *Educational Renewal: Better Teachers, Better Schools* (San Francisco: Jossey-Bass, 1994), pp. 235–273.

31. See Robert S. Patterson, Nicholas M. Michelli, and Arturo Pacheco, *Centers of Pedagogy: New Structures for Educational Renewal* (San Francisco: Jossey-Bass, 1999).

32. See, for example, the sustained lines of investigation carried out over the years by Michael Fullan and Seymour B. Sarason. "Must" reads are Fullan's *Change Forces* (New York: Falmer Press, 1993) and Sarason's *Revisiting "The Culture of the School and the Problem of Change,"* 3d ed. (New York: Teachers College Press, 1996).

33. For a concept of good work that combines excellence with ethics, see Howard Gardner, Mihaly Csikszentmihalyi, and William Damon, *Good Work: When Excellence and Ethics Meet* (New York: Basic Books, 2001).

34. For a compelling account of teaching as a moral journey, see Kay A. Norlander-Case, Timothy G. Reagan, and Charles W. Case, *The Professional Teacher: The Preparation and Nurturance of the Reflective Practitioner* (San Francisco: Jossey-Bass, 1999).

CHAPTER 3

Learning to Walk and Talk Together: Strengthening and Sustaining Teachers in Portland, Maine

RICHARD E. BARNES

For two decades, the Southern Maine Partnership has been committed to the simultaneous renewal of schools and teacher education. It has been for much of this time a member of the National Network for Educational Renewal that, in turn, is guided in this renewal effort by a common agenda—the Agenda for Education in a Democracy. On becoming a pilot site (with Seattle schools and the University of Washington) in the Strengthening and Sustaining Teachers (SST) initiative, the Portland, Maine, partnership set out to bring into close collaboration several of the major groups constituting the cultural context of teaching in the schools of that city.

When Richard Barnes gave up the deanship in the College of Education and Human Development at the University of Southern Maine, he became immersed in this partnership in a way that few deans of like settings have ventured to take on. What emerges is a candid account of the inner workings of relationships that surely removes from our minds any benign images we might have of institutional partnering. The positive symbiotic joining of the organized interests of quite different groups is absolutely essential to the well-being of our educational enterprise, particularly its teachers and their students. But, as Barnes's narrative reveals, it is time we lost our innocence regarding the levels of resolve and ability required to bring about success in such collaboration.

—The editors

Why would the three of us choose to take on the challenge of this project yoked together as if we are in a four-legged race at a Fourth of July picnic? It would seem to be impossible enough for each one of us running—or walking—separately.[1]

The above question is one that the three members of the steering committee for the Portland, Maine, Strengthening and Sustaining Teachers (SST) project might have been forgiven for asking frequently during the first twenty-four months of the project's life as one of the urban sites for the SST project. Stumbles by the steering committee members—leaders of a school district, a teachers union, and a university college of education—seemingly threatened to pull down a precarious collaboration at nearly every step. Despite the existence of a long local history of collaboration on school–university partnership activities, SST has created a new dimension for partnership. Three powerful institutions with distinct yet overlapping missions and interests were creating simultaneously new opportunities for and threats to collaboration in the name of promoting teacher development within a framework of partnership for school and university renewal.

This chapter discusses the first two years in the evolution of new relationships among the University of Southern Maine (USM), especially its College of Education and Human Development (CEHD); the Portland Public Schools (PPS); and the Portland Education Association (PEA), the local NEA-affiliated teachers union, as they implemented the vision of SST. By the end of these two years, the Portland SST project was still in the early stages of influencing the daily practice of teacher educators, school district leaders, teachers union leaders, and classroom teachers. The path toward a new culture of professional practice in the school had become clearer but still seemed long. Principals, teachers, and university faculty members working in partner school sites were engaging in SST activities, but many kept an eye on the exits, unsure of what lay ahead and not yet convinced that working together would yield the promised results. The SST leaders, however, became increasingly optimistic over time. The president of the Portland Education Association, the director of educational planning for the Portland School District, and the dean of the USM's College of Education and Human Development—the three veteran leaders of the SST steering committee—had yoked themselves together. After each early setback, the partners stood up, rubbed their bruised shins, and gave each other high fives as they regrouped, faced the next way point, and forged ahead.

The focus here is on the elements of the Portland site's journey that caused the steering committee's optimism. The account begins with a description of the school–university partnership that paved the way for Portland's inclusion in SST and a brief history of the previous working relationships among the three partners. Initial efforts to implement the vision and goals of the Portland SST project led to several critical decisions. These decisions frequently placed each of the three partners in conflict with the other two and ultimately helped forge the collaboration that exists today. The chapter concludes with a discussion of the lessons learned and a plan for continuing work that may ultimately realize the vision for SST.

PORTLAND'S SELECTION AS AN SST SITE

Portland was chosen as one of the initial SST sites because of the strength and history of the school–university partnership in the Portland area. Through its membership in the National Network for Educational Renewal (NNER), the Southern Maine Partnership (SMP) has been committed to the simultaneous renewal of schools and of teacher education through the Agenda for Education in a Democracy.[2] Headquartered in USM's College of Education and Human Development on the university's suburban campus nine miles west of Portland, the SMP was founded in 1985 by six rural and suburban school districts and USM. Present membership includes thirty-four districts throughout the southern tier of the state; the Portland district has been a member since 1991.

Within four years of the SMP's founding, teachers and administrators in partnership schools were working alongside university teacher educators in a total redesign of USM's teacher education program, with all the students, courses, and faculty based in a series of partner schools nominated by SMP districts.[3] As USM sought to expand its new postbaccalaureate teacher education model, the Extended Teacher Education Program (ETEP), the university looked to Portland, which had served as a host site for student teaching placements. The university's partner schools for teacher education have expanded beyond the original two high schools and one middle school to include four elementary schools, some with high enrollments of language-minority students. When the university began a new undergraduate program for certification in elementary and middle school teaching—a program designed on a strong liberal arts/general education model[4]—the Portland school district was chosen as one of three initial sites. As the number of partner schools for teacher education was increasing, Portland principals and teachers in several schools were becoming involved in other professional development activities sponsored by the SMP.

THE PARTNERSHIP
CONTEXT AT THE BEGINNING OF SST

Portland has the largest school district in Maine. With a K–12 enrollment of just under eight thousand students and a professional staff of about eight hundred employees, it can barely be called an urban district by national standards. Yet the schools mirror many of the traits of their more urban cousins, even as they manage to avoid others. The schools host a growing number of language-minority students, currently 12% of the citywide total and over 50% in some schools. In a city of many middle-class neighborhoods, several schools serve areas where 80% or more of the school enrollment falls below federal poverty guidelines. In a state where the average school district has just one or two elementary schools and may or may not run its own high school, Portland is relatively complex. With a large central office staff, two comprehensive high schools, an arts-and-technology high school, three middle schools, an alternative school, and thirteen elementary schools, the district, more than any other in Maine, projects a feeling of bureaucratic organization. The Portland Education Association (PEA), the largest local union affiliate in the Maine Education Association, has a reputation for being aggressive at the bargaining table and is the only local unit in Maine to have purchased released time from classroom responsibilities for its president to attend to union matters.

Unlike urban districts in other states, however, until very recently the Portland Public Schools did not have difficulty attracting a strong pool of qualified applicants for its teaching vacancies. Salaries have remained competitive with surrounding suburban districts, class sizes have been reasonable, and support services, even in the most challenging school environments, have been considered strong. The system has had stable leadership from the superintendent's office and school board, and the curriculum support and professional development systems have been well funded.

Over the years, partnership relations between USM and the PPS waxed and waned. Portland teachers' and administrators' participation in SMP activities was spotty at best. SMP staffers focused more on the partnership's work in those districts committed to long-term change projects than on short-term training or consulting jobs. After the SMP's startup, college leaders turned their focus away from teacher education in Portland. The ETEP program, often seen as only loosely connected to the core activities of the partnership, even in districts with strong SMP participation, became even more isolated from its sponsoring partners in Portland because of a lack of strong site leadership from both the university and the district. In 1998, the relationship among the PPS, USM, and the SMP began to turn around. As dean of the College of Education and Human Development, I worked with our director of teacher education, PPS's director of elementary education, and PPS's superintendent of schools to appoint new university and school coordinators for the USM's ETEP program. The four of us also established Portland as a start-up site for a new undergraduate teacher certification program. Turnover in the leadership of PPS's Office of Instructional Planning led to a reconnection with SMP projects and activities. The stage seemed set for the SST project to make an entrance.

In this brief history of the partnership between the PPS and USM, the teachers union is conspicuously absent. In their work with Portland schools, USM faculty members either approached or were approached directly by administrators and individual teachers. The Portland Education Association remained on the outside, even though the teacher education programs received supplemental program development funding from the NEA and accepted Maine Education Association support in organizing meetings with teachers. It never occurred to those involved with the partnership that the PEA could or should have any formal role in establishing or implementing policies for recruiting teachers in developing projects and activities in partner schools. University-based partnership members assumed that the PEA was uninterested in the teacher professional development in which the university was engaged. The PEA was seen as the voice of the teachers on contractual matters; its activities were largely regulatory and part of the bureaucratic culture that characterized much of the university's work in Portland. As SST started, USM participants soon learned how mistaken they were in this belief. PEA leaders had many questions and concerns about how USM implemented its programs and defined partnership in teacher education matters, and they welcomed SST as an opportunity to enter the stage.

THE SST PROJECT: ITS VISION, MISSION, AND GOALS

Discussion of the Portland SST project must be understood within the context that the three partners established for themselves. In August 2000, after several months of data collection from nearly a hundred different people—including teachers, school administrators, and arts and sciences and teacher education faculty—a design team chosen by the three partners created a plan for the SST work. The preface to the plan contained the following to guide the project over the planned five years of its life:

> *The Vision:* [By the year 2005] The Portland Public Schools and USM's teacher development program [will] combine preparation, induction, and continued professional development into a series of sequential and seamless experiences that operate as a whole, ensuring that all students are learning for their future.
> *The Mission:* The SST project is a collaborative effort of the Portland Education Association, the Portland Public Schools, and the University of Southern Maine to promote high levels of student learning through sustained, high-quality teacher development.

The SST initiative involves a set of four inextricably connected components:

- A shared vision of teaching and learning;
- Teacher preparation;
- Teacher induction; and
- Professional development

These components blend the skills, conditions, and dispositions needed to support long-term teacher development with the goal of creating a measurable, successful impact on learning for all students.

Through the SST initiative:

- Our schools will be organized to promote teamwork and collaboration— as the way we do business—not just for new teachers, but for all staff. . . .
- Our schools will value the deprivatization of practice where teachers share, observe, and discuss each other's teaching methods and philosophies. They will become communities of practice.
- Our teachers union will become a progressive agent of change—marshalling energies to promote best practices, ongoing and meaningful staff development, and differentiated staffing options to support teachers as learners and leaders in their field.
- University personnel will have a heightened sense of visibility and input to our work—functioning as our partners in learning and support for all our teachers.
- Our work will be successful if we establish and maintain a focus on teaching and student learning—as opposed to a focus on external structures and processes (e.g., shared decision making, scheduling, etc.).[5]

The loftiness of this vision and goals masks the tensions that arose at the start six months earlier, when the three partners first met to discuss the feasibility of participation. It is that gathering, and other critical events along the way, to which we now turn in order to understand and appreciate how this four-legged race is being run.

THE FIRST CONFLICT: WILL THE UNION REPRESENT ALL TEACHERS?

Shortly after receiving our individual letters inviting us to join together in the SST initiative, the three potential partners gathered for our initial discussion of the proposal. The meeting was held at the PPS central office and was attended by the superintendent of schools, the director for educational planning (who would later be asked to represent the district on SST matters), the president of the PEA, and the dean of USM's College of Education and Human Development.

At that initial meeting, the PEA president made it clear that, as a condition for its agreement to participate in SST, the union wanted the right to name all teacher members chosen to serve in any SST-sponsored activity. The superintendent vigorously objected. "This is a professional development opportunity for all teachers, not just PEA members. Our collective bargaining agreement, school board policy, simple fairness, and common sense all require that the benefits of participation should be available to everyone. The district can never agree to this."[6]

The union president countered that the PEA had been invited to represent the teachers' voice in the project and could not very well do so if the district was free to name additional teachers as key participants in planning the project.[7] It became clear that the PEA president had already discussed the implications of the union's participation in SST with her executive committee, and they supported her position. The dean probed both sides with questions about the district's recent experience working with policy development committees of mixed union and administration members and about the percentage of PEA membership in the schools. He learned that the teacher evaluation system had recently been totally revamped by such a committee and that both sides were satisfied with the result. On other policy committees, where union membership was not required by the contract, the PEA leadership was not usually consulted on the makeup of the teacher contingent. As to the extent of union membership, approximately 85% of eligible teachers belonged to the union, and membership in individual schools ranged from 45% to 98%. The school with the lowest membership level was led by an outspoken principal who had battled with some teachers over the direction of school renewal initiatives and who had developed a reputation for being hostile to the union. It was also a school with which the university maintained strong partner school relations. With this background information in hand, the dean agreed to prepare a draft memorandum of understanding that might form the basis for an agreement permitting both sides to move forward.

On February 17, with some additional negotiating, a memorandum of understanding was signed, still labeled "draft," and the three partners sent a letter agreeing to participate in SST. Some of the key provisions of the memorandum that proved to be important in several later activities are:

1. All teachers on the project design team or teams, or major subcommittees of such teams, will be members of the Portland Education Association in recognition of the PEA's role as one of the three collaborating partners.
2. The project design team(s) will work with the three sponsoring organizations to define what projects for teacher preparation, induction, and professional development occurring within the Portland Public Schools will be formal parts of this project.

3. Teachers chosen to play formal roles in the project (serving as mentor teachers, lead teachers, etc.) will be expected to meet all qualifications set forth . . . and these qualifications will be in clear alignment with project purposes. When all other formal qualifications are met, the design team or selection committee will make every effort to appoint PEA members to these roles. The spirit of the Collective Bargaining Agreement . . . will not be violated in this process.

4. This project will be considered an affirmative experiment in collaboration by the three parties, one purpose of which will be to seek new ways of defining working relationships. Any changes to administrative practice and policy for the Portland Public Schools that may result from this project will not be considered to have any legal or contractual impact on the collective bargaining agreement itself or on any grievance that may be filed. Such project-related activities will not be used by any of the three parties to make a unilateral claim of prior or past practice, or be cited as precedent setting with regard to any formal contractual agreements between two or more of the parties.

5. Disputes about interpretation of these broad principles will be brought from the design team(s) to a designated committee of three leaders, one from each partner organization, for resolution. If any dispute persists over time and cannot be resolved after good faith efforts, including requested intervention and/or facilitation from our national partners in the project, any one of the three partners has the right to formally withdraw from participation in the project. Any such withdrawal will be duly reported to all outside funding agencies, project directors, and evaluators, both national and local.[8]

EARLY SUCCESSES IN TEACHER INVOLVEMENT

At the same time that the memorandum of understanding was being negotiated, the three partners reviewed the status of their collective activities related to the goals of SST. This environmental scan—and a subsequent gap-analysis activity that was completed by the director of educational planning, the president of the PEA, and the dean at the initial national SST meeting in Albuquerque on March 23–25, 2000—formed the basis of the Portland site's first major activity. The three, calling themselves the steering committee, agreed that they needed to survey teachers, teacher preparation candidates, administrators, and university faculty members on the current effectiveness of Portland's teacher support programs. The steering committee agreed to start with getting widespread input from teachers with more than three years' experience.

The committee's first public activities were to place a notice about the project in the PEA newsletter and issue an invitation to all union-member teachers in the city who were interested in becoming involved in SST to notify their building representatives. Because of the frequent consultations with her executive committee and building representatives, the PEA president felt that building leaders were prepared to explain the potential benefits to teachers who inquired. The notice explained that, as a first activity, a group of forty-five teachers would be chosen to attend a "dine and discuss" evening work session along with four or five administrators and three USM faculty members as observers. The purpose was to learn more about what was working well and what was not in the current teacher induction system. The partners agreed that all teachers chosen would be paid for their time at the dinner.

Over one hundred teachers asked to participate, and the decision of whom to invite was made by the PEA president who, interestingly, consulted her steering committee partners as well as her executive committee as part of her decision-making process. Attendance at the actual dinner meeting was high, and a core group of PEA members quickly wrote up summaries of the teachers' comments and disseminated them to everyone on the original attendee list. Accompanying the written summary was a notice about the establishment of a design team that would meet from May through the summer and be responsible for establishing the first-year project plan. Response to this was strong, and again the PEA leadership consulted committee partners before making final decisions on the design team's teacher representation.

The early activities reflected the steering committee's decision to make participation by classroom teachers its top priority during the planning and initial implementation phases. Building experienced teachers' trust in the value and power of the project, particularly among active PEA members, was at the forefront of early activity. Administrators, university professors, preservice teacher candidates, recent graduates undergoing induction, and teachers completing their second or third years of teaching were interviewed during the first two months, but in separate gatherings and in a lower-profile setting. The composition of the thirteen-member design team was set at seven teacher members (all classroom teachers except for the PEA president), one principal, three PPS central office administrators (including the director for educational planning, who became the new interim superintendent midway through the team's work), and two university representatives: the dean and the director of teacher education. The plan for the first year called for strong teacher majorities on all of the work groups: induction support programs in three volunteer pilot schools, a redesign of the ETEP program in the Portland partner schools, and a group to develop a mentor training program. Nine members of the design team traveled to Seattle at the end of July to share the draft plan with the national coordinating partners and our then-sister site representatives from Albuquerque. Four of the nine were classroom teachers, and the PEA president was a fifth teacher representative.

THE FIRST PHASE OF IMPLEMENTATION

As we headed into the first implementation year, spirits and expectations were high. Given the initial emphasis on designing an induction program, efforts at the beginning of the 2000–2001 school year were concentrated on recruiting three pilot schools—one each at the elementary, middle, and high school levels—and creating a mentor training and support system. Each school would be given $5,000 in regrant funds to design an implementation plan. The USM partner on the steering committee deferred to the other two members in selecting the pilot schools and concentrated on lining up USM faculty representation on the mentor system. A request for proposals was sent out to schools, inviting them to submit applications to be pilot schools. Criteria for being accepted were distributed to teachers and administrators in the schools. The following excerpts from the criteria serve to illustrate the emphasis given by the plan:

The partner school must

- have enough new teachers in the building to support the SST project;
- have demonstrated or be able to ensure positive teachers' support for the project;
- have been a cooperating site for the ETEP or TEAMS [teacher education] program;
- have demonstrated one example of successful implementation of some aspect of the SST initiative;
- see its participation as part of a larger district/union/university initiative;
- commit to renewing and improving the culture of support for teaching and learning in a "community of practice."

Partner school teachers and administrators must

- be willing to share in the design and revision of the program;
- commit to work cooperatively with the three partners (PEA, PPS, and USM), a point person in the building, new teachers, mentors, cooperating teachers, and administrators;
- support and share the SST ideal professional development program, including but not limited to differentiated work loads, mentor training, professional development, and work with preservice programs.[9]

Principals or teachers were to contact either the director of educational planning or the PEA president if they were interested in or had questions about the process. The next step for the interested school was to schedule a faculty meeting with the three steering committee partners, who would participate in a question-and-answer dialogue about the expectations for participating schools. Following the presentation, the faculty would vote on its participation, and the partners agreed that principals and the PEA building representative could work together in putting together a school-based design team. Nothing was said at steering committee meetings about union membership on the school-based design team, other than an implicit assumption that the PEA would have a voice with the principal in choosing the teachers to lead the project at the school level. When no schools at the middle and high school levels initially surfaced, steering committee members solicited interest from two schools where they knew internal support and resources were present.

ANOTHER STUMBLE OVER
THE ROLE OF UNION LEADERSHIP

When the first three schools returned their votes with a list of teachers selected for their school design committee, called an "SST building-based governance board," a problem quickly surfaced at the steering committee level. The PEA president stated that the middle school had proposed a governance board with at least one nonunion teacher member and could not be approved for funding. The other two partners initially took the position that this was not a problem. The PPS and USM representatives argued that the PEA members of the school in question had voted overwhelmingly to support SST. They also noted that all teachers in the school—union and nonunion alike—as well as the principal supported the teachers selected for the governance board. Citing the memorandum of understanding of February 2000, the USM dean and the PPS superintendent stated that only during the project design phase was union membership mandatory for teachers, and that at this early implementation phase, nonunion members could become involved as long as the PEA retained the leadership voice for teachers. The PEA head also cited the memorandum, arguing that the project was still in a "design" phase, because the first-year plan called for pilot school teachers and administrators to design induction programs for their schools.

The dispute caused reverberations in all three of the pilot schools. Although the composition of two schools' boards was not in dispute, the principals expressed concerns. The issue of union membership had not been raised in the first place, and so it was only by chance that all selected governance board members belonged to the PEA. Furthermore, these principals were uneasy about entering into an agreement that would bar qualified nonunion members from a project that paid a stipend with district-sponsored grant monies. At the middle school, both the principal and teachers expressed dissatisfaction with what several saw as a creation of a post facto rule that was not aligned with "standard" district policy on professional development projects. The middle school principal summarily announced that he was withdrawing from participation. The USM dean expressed great concern, as this school was a strong partner school in the teacher education program. Could there be, he wondered, a middle ground that could win the school's return? At this point, the PEA representative again cited the memorandum of understanding and asked for our national coordinating partners to meet with the steering committee to seek resolution.

Mediation occurred at a midyear meeting of the national partners of SST in Santa Fe. Two members of the national partners, a representative from the Teacher Union Reform Network (TURN) and one from the Institute for Educational Inquiry (IEI), met for several hours with the Portland steering committee and the teacher representatives from the two participating pilot schools in attendance. The interim director of educational planning, who had taken over the PPS leadership role on the steering committee, quickly agreed with the PEA president on her interpretation of the February 2000 memorandum of understanding. After discussion, the USM dean conceded the point and accepted that the SST project was still in a design phase in Portland, this time at the school level.

The mediation session helped deepen the three steering committee members' understanding of the SST agreement's importance as a formal statement about institutional responsibility for creating cultural renewal in the schools and university. The two mediators helped uncover a new layer of honest dialogue among the members of the Portland SST initiative in attendance. PPS central office leaders and the university representatives admitted that until they were truly ready to grant the PEA formal authority to appoint teacher leaders, they could not expect the union to assume responsibility for transforming teachers' attitudes about peer responsibility for induction and professional development. The PEA president spoke eloquently about how difficult it was for her to stand up to the PPS central office and to the university on matters of professional development.

Cultural norms in Maine schools and state statute assign decision making on professional development to the school administration. In spite of the rhetoric of teacher-led professional development, school administrators and university representatives almost invariably chose the teachers who got to lead. With the exception of the traditional areas of union negotiations over wages, hours, working conditions, and procedural issues in personnel matters, the teachers' collective voice was not represented in any formal way. If significant numbers of teachers disagreed with professional policy decisions, they could turn to their union for ways to resist, passively or actively. But law and tradition barred the union from having a direct voice in setting the course for professional development or any other aspect of educational policy.[10] By the end of the Santa Fe meeting, the other two partners were talking about how they could support the PEA president in their work with administrators and with the many pockets of resistance she would find within her own membership.

TENSIONS BETWEEN THE
UNIVERSITY AND THE OTHER PARTNERS

Problems also arose between the university and the schools, usually on an operational or basic communications level but, on at least one occasion, on a policy level as well. There were several nagging operations-level difficulties, most of them arising because the USM partners lacked day-to-day institutional contact with the district partners, and in most work groups, only one person represented USM, while PEA and PPS each had multiple representatives. The most long-running difficulty was in gathering research data. The university researcher had repeatedly sought baseline data on several measures of teacher employment in the district to be included as part of the national evaluation study but had met with passive resistance from the district. Although the PPS and PEA partners involved with SST agreed that it was important to know how many teachers were fully certified upon hiring, how many had previous teaching experience, and how many left teaching with three years' experience or less, obtaining these data proved difficult. Although district spokespersons were certain that the data were readily available in the district's personnel database, this proved not to be the case. In fact, because the PPS had not been as hard hit by the beginnings of the teacher shortage through the first year of the SST project as had some of its neighboring districts, there had been no perceived need to track the district's teacher induction or retention records closely. Not until the second year of the project, when Portland found itself in late August scrambling to fill vacancies in several subject areas, did the extent of the need for a widespread induction program hit home at an operational level. Forty-one new teachers were hired at the beginning of the 2001–2002 year, ten more than a year earlier (or a 32% increase).[11]

During the second year of the project, cooperation on data gathering improved all around. The steering committee allocated more time for the teacher coordinators to work with the central office human resources staff to gather data, improve their own data collection systems, and to assist with surveying and interviewing participants in various SST activities.

A second area of university–school tension involved the two projectwide design teams. Unlike the pilot school teams, teacher education faculty were represented on the design teams charged with reexamining the preservice teacher education partnership and the development of a mentor training and support system. The teacher education design team had been in existence for many years as a site advisory council for the ETEP program. Through the SST initiative, the advisory council was charged with planning a significant redesign of the academic program and its delivery, as well as a restructured schedule for classroom placements and selection of mentor teachers. As work proceeded, some PPS teachers and administrators expressed frustration at the apparently slow response by the university. When Portland educators presented strong evaluation data showing that mentor teachers and intern students judged some university teacher education courses to be ineffective, they were upset that the university representative could not promise change, even if she agreed that change was necessary. The university representative, a faculty member in the department of teacher education, reminded the group that some courses were in the control of faculty in other departments and could be changed only with those departments' agreement and involvement, and linkages with those departments were sometimes problematic. PPS personnel were understandably frustrated and wondered about the breadth and depth of the USM commitment to the SST reform agenda. Other changes recommended by the team would require either scheduling or policy changes that needed teacher education department approval. These changes encompassed both minor and major reforms ranging from rescheduling the time of day that courses were taught to recommending admission of part-time students. The changes were strongly supported by the university representative, but the pace for obtaining such approval seemed unnecessarily slow to the school partners.

The mentoring system design team had a similar tension that led to a policy disagreement at the steering committee level. Most of the team's work proceeded without controversy and consisted of identifying priority areas for mentor recruitment and training. Everyone agreed on such areas as selection criteria for mentors and the need for a common training system for mentors of teacher education interns and for mentors in the induction support program. When the USM dean and the faculty member took it upon themselves to decide the model for mentor training, however, the PEA president objected, saying that this decision was not in the spirit of collaboration. The dean took the position that collaboration did not mean a consensus decision on every question and that the nature of the partnership is to recognize the individual strengths and expertise of each partner and, when appropriate, defer to that expertise.

In the end, the disagreement was resolved and helped to forge further trust in the steering committee partnership. The dean conceded that ideally he should have discussed his recommendation with the full steering committee rather than acting on his own in order to take advantage of an opportunity to save money on training costs. The partners agreed to grant each other their respective realms of expertise while also creating zones of mutual autonomy in decision making. Trust that each partner would not abuse that autonomy was developing and would grow even more as they continued to work together and engage in evaluation of their work collectively and individually.

ADMINISTRATOR WARINESS;
OR, "ISN'T THIS JUST ANOTHER GRANT PROJECT?"

As the project entered its second full year in August 2001, the SST initiative's ability both to bring about change at the surface level and to penetrate the cultural norms of the schools became the overriding issue for the steering committee. The SST goals articulated the year before—to create, in the words of the new superintendent, "'communities of practice' integral to the conduct of our daily business"—dominated the project's summer retreat. The steering committee recognized that SST had not only to help teachers change their view of their role in and responsibility for collective professional development, but also to help principals change their view of teachers' roles and responsibilities. The steering committee resolved to shift its primary attention from educating PEA members about SST to winning administrator support.

The year 2 plan widened the number of schools involved in induction support at the same time it began to make linkages to the teacher education program and to the preexisting certification support system for teachers. To widen the scope of the work and expand into new schools at the same time, the partners needed more support from key district office staff. Together with the superintendent, the district directors for elementary and secondary education were invited to the Portland site's summer retreat to learn the rationale behind the three-part partnership, particularly the PEA's role. With the national project director and three members of the national coordinating partners present, nearly everyone connected with Portland SST's first year gathered to refine plans for the second-year program. Although the retreat was helpful in focusing action plans for the core groups of project participants, the impact on the extended central office staff was less positive. Rather than becoming more comfortable with the role of the PEA as the official representative of teacher representation, the central administrators became more focused on the problems and inconsistencies that developed in the first-year pilot sites, reinforcing doubts they may have had about both the union's role and the project itself.

The problem areas were real. The pilot school teams proposed an elaborate induction support model, with mentors receiving a $3,000 stipend for their time supporting each new teacher over a two-year period. The amount was determined by looking at similar stipends offered to mentor teachers in Rochester, New York, and an estimate of the cost of induction support contained in a Maine Department of Education report on teacher recruitment and retention.[12] Although the $3,000 figure had been freely used in meetings with both the steering committee and the national partners in the first year, there had been no discussion among the three steering committee partners as to its appropriateness to the scope of work in Portland. Indeed, in one of the pilot schools, the emphasis of planning had been on integrating the mentoring work into the regular workday and reducing other teacher responsibilities, thereby reducing the need for added stipends. As the central office administrators noted, the $3,000 stipend created prima facie inequities with other stipends for mentoring preservice or new teachers either negotiated through collective bargaining or paid by the university.

In addition, the PPS administrators were wary of the union's leadership role in the building governance committees. As the new school year started, they relayed feedback from several principals alleging that the present certification mentoring program, administered by a committee appointed by the PEA in accordance with the collective bargaining agreement, was ineffective in providing support to new teachers and too removed from the principal's ability to influence the process. They were reluctant to create a new program that might remove administrators even further from the induction process. In the words of one, "We can achieve the same goal more efficiently by having the principal in each building create a building-level structure and process with her/his own teachers. Involving the union creates a lot of contract issues and unnecessary bureaucracy that will become a burden long after the grant money goes away."

As the fall progressed, the steering committee held two meetings with the superintendent and the central office team on the expansion of the induction program and the building governance committees into another elementary school, all three middle schools, and the other high school. The steering committee wanted to have a plan in place by the start of a late October meeting of all three SST sites and the national coordinating partners to be held in Portland. At these two meetings it became obvious that the resistance of Portland's central office administrators to the PEA's role was increasing, and the superintendent's support appeared to be weakening. The October start-up goal would not be met. Tensions between the union and the central office staff had been mounting on other fronts, intermingling with administrators' suspicions of the SST project. First, the emergency closing of an elementary school invaded by toxic mold led to a clash with the PEA leadership over the ways that the school relocation planning had been implemented. Second, a looming budget cut and continually declining elementary enrollments created concerns about staff layoffs for the 2003–2004 year. The possibility of permanently closing the school to save money surfaced, creating opposition among the parents and anxiety in faculty ranks.

Following the October meeting, the steering committee acted to meet the mounting resistance head-on. The director of educational planning met privately with the superintendent and asked for her unequivocal support of the SST model to emphasize the importance of involving the union in decision making if the district were to realize the goal of "communities of practice" in each school. The USM dean met separately with the directors to understand their areas of greatest concern. The PEA president met with the pilot schools' governing board members to discuss ways to make the governing boards' work more efficient and effective.

At the November meeting of the steering committee, the superintendent, and the PPS's two directors for elementary and secondary schools, the superintendent made clear her desire to support the SST project. She asked the directors to convene principals, to develop a list of their questions and concerns about participation in the project, and to bring those to the steering committee. In December and again in January, the principals shared their concerns with the steering committee and pilot school teacher leaders. The SST project leaders then met separately to consider the issues and redraft the guidelines under which building governance committees would operate. Interestingly, about 90% of the principals' or central office team's issues matched those already identified by the steering committee or teachers from the pilot schools.

At the end of January, five principals from the invited schools met with SST leaders, central office staff, and two representatives from the national coordinating partners for a two-hour discussion of the proposed changes. The two teachers serving as coordinators for SST presented handouts on the latest plan for implementing building-based mentoring programs. They reviewed the redrafted building governance committee document and also distributed a document written in question-and-answer format that addressed other implementation concerns raised previously by the principals and central office staff. There were few questions and many clear, positive signals that the administrators felt satisfied that pilot site teachers and the steering committee had listened to their concerns.

The series of meetings in January 2002, almost two years into the project, proved to be a major turning point in the partnership's development. Administrators and teachers demonstrated that they could listen to and respond to each other's legitimate concerns. It was also a period in which the university's role in developing the mentor support system became more legitimized. University faculty members' roles in redesigning the Portland SST handbook and the implementation plan for teacher support helped allay administrators' and teachers' concerns about the potential for superficiality in the support system.

LESSONS LEARNED: GETTING STRONGER BY TAKING RISKS AND SHARING OUR FEARS

As the above examples from the first two years' work show, partners in the Portland, Maine, SST project built trust and collaboration by paying careful attention to group dynamics and ensuring that dialogue was open and inclusive. The "forming, storming, norming, and performing" stages of organizational development were present in the key events described above, and each stage needed participants willing to undertake significant risk.[13] Each of the three partners provoked a "storm" at one or more points in the journey merely by standing up for its own perceived self-interest. Because the key participants valued the partnership, including the partner causing the storm, all were willing to spend time working through the problem to seek another level of consensus permitting forward progress. The fears that each partner faced and the risks each took are probably typical for other settings considering this move.

For the district, letting the PEA be the exclusive representative of teachers' voices constituted the biggest risk. History was replete with union leaders' efforts to block or limit changes in school practice often championed by nonunion teachers. Although the university's presence may not have been perceived to present the same level of danger, its outsider status created potential problems in managing the district's personnel development program. For the university, the union's lack of participation in previous university-based professional development programs and its unfamiliarity with the goals and principles of the university and district's partner school work caused concern and reservations about the quality of the teacher representation on work teams. The university was also wary of district administrators' past tendencies to undo or unilaterally change district–university agreements on teacher education when such agreements seemed inconvenient or unworkable.

The PEA leaders, however, took the biggest risks in the first two years. Unaccustomed to negotiating with the university on professional development issues, the president and teacher leaders were unsure when and how to disagree with university professors. Knowing that state labor law and tradition were not on their side, leaders were sometimes tentative in advocating for union positions on professional development policy with the district. Developing expertise in the field of professional development comparable to their expertise in labor law was a tall order. But union leaders' biggest area of risk proved to be with their own membership. Many members questioned the wisdom of venturing out of the traditional negotiating sectors. For teachers who resisted more involvement in professional development, the PEA's advocacy could be seen as undermining their desire to resist "management's add-on work," as professional development was often seen to be. Even worse, some worried that the union's new involvement might eventually lead toward PEA involvement in teacher evaluation and employment decisions.

The role of the national partners, sometimes acting as mediators, sometimes as facilitators, and sometimes as expert consultants, was key to the process. Although throughout the first year it was the PEA president who was first to insist on intervention by the national partners, all came to value their role equally. Without external support, especially from the TURN consultant, participants would have been unable to safely explore their underlying hopes and fears about the risks they took in giving some of their respective power bases over to the project. With support from the national partners and increasingly from members of the steering committee and the teacher leadership staff, they could admit their mistakes to each other and to their key constituents without fear that partners would use those admissions to partisan advantage. The process of developing changes in the building governance committees and mentoring procedures provides the best example.

FACING THE FUTURE:
IMPLICATIONS FOR FURTHER WORK

We in Portland have made progress, but we have a long way to go to achieve our vision for SST. Although we are now in a comfortable collaborative relationship within our SST group and even with others more peripherally involved in "SST business," we still have a tendency to fall into our traditional patterns when dealing with each other on matters outside the current scope of the initiative. Given the expansive mission we have for SST, we must continue to build on the trust achieved within the initiative and trade on it in our general relations with each other. But we recognize also that continuous joint renewal calls for changing some of the well-established regularities of each partner.

There are several ingrained patterns in our traditional working relationships that will continue to cause the three partners to stumble as we walk together along our new path. For the PEA and the district, there remains a tendency to air complaints with one another in language that emphasizes contract compliance and blaming, rather than mutual problem-solving responsibility. For the university, there is still a reluctance to bring in resources from outside of the College of Education and Human Development to address partnership needs. More specifically, the partners have identified the need to attend to the following issues that, although outside the immediate scope of SST work plans, will have profound effects on the ultimate success of SST in building a seamless continuum for professional development and communities of practice. We need to:

- Become more mindful of the basic tenets of the Agenda for Education in a Democracy that has guided the school–university partnership for many years. We are committed to educating teachers for more than the current priorities of the state. The principles that we believe in are not abstract but have enormous implications for the conduct of the collaboration called for in the SST initiative.
- Promote the value of National Board for Professional Teaching Standards certification for teachers in the district and provide support for teachers aspiring to certification. Not only might this appeal to the veteran staff, but it also could help those teachers currently in the third through fifth years of teaching to see themselves as being at the beginning of their careers, not already nearing a glass ceiling.
- Develop partner schools that are constantly moving toward the best educational practices and not simply immersing teachers and students in traditional ways. Partnering in this process means much more than simply getting along with each other.
- Broaden teacher involvement in the program evaluation of our work to go beyond collecting data and participating in focus

groups. Such involvement would not only lead to better evaluation and refocusing for the future but also could lead to greater understanding of and commitment to the values behind SST.

- Significantly involve the arts and sciences departments that provide both general and specialized preparation in what schools are expected to teach. They must be key players in ensuring that students are prepared to assume responsible roles in sustaining a democratic form of individual and community life.
- Continue efforts to involve districts beyond Portland in promoting the goals and strategies of SST. The PPS, as a member of the Southern Maine Partnership and other regional school district collaboratives, does not exist in a vacuum. Other districts are experiencing the same problems as those facing the PPS, with some having even more severe needs.
- Make a greater effort to work with teacher union leaders, at both the local and state levels, to have them become more active change agents for their districts and their own members.
- Develop or seek out dependable means of assessing students' progress in the social and personal domains of school purpose as well as the academic. Left unassessed, these are not considered by either the students or their teachers to be of importance.

We believe that the relationships necessary to supporting and sustaining productive, satisfying teacher education and teaching careers are in place. We face two key challenges, however, the first of which is to find out whether we are truly joined in an educational mission that transcends our daily activities and guides collaboration toward consciously shared ends. It would seem that we are. The early dominance of logistics and the protection of turf not previously shared has been increasingly replaced by a sense of common purpose. Our second challenge is to ensure a permanent process of dialogue, decisions, individual and collective action, and evaluation that characterizes sustained renewal. Renewal is not a project; it is a condition of good health. For the good health of our educational institutions, we need to ensure the good health of our educators as well as those they teach.

NOTES

1. Comment made by Sally Loughlin, director of educational planning for the Portland Public Schools and an SST steering committee member, during a presentation on the SST project at a Maine Education Association teachers' conference, Augusta, January 12, 2002.

2. The development of the concept of an "Agenda for Education in a Democracy" in the Southern Maine Partnership roughly parallels its development as a construct for the work of the National Network for Educational Renewal. For an overview, see Kenneth A. Sirotnik and Associates, *Renewing Schools and Teacher Education: An Odyssey in Educational Change* (Washington, D.C.: AACTE Publications, 2001). For more detailed explorations of specific elements of the work, see the Agenda for Education in a Democracy book series (San Francisco: Jossey-Bass, 1999): Wilma F. Smith and Gary D Fenstermacher, *Leadership for Educational Renewal: Developing a Cadre of Leaders*; Robert S. Patterson, Nicholas M. Michelli, and Arturo Pacheco, *Centers of Pedagogy: New Structures for Educational Renewal*; Richard W. Clark, *Effective Professional Development Schools*; and Kay A. Norlander-Case, Timothy G. Reagan, and Charles W. Case, *The Professional Teacher: The Preparation and Nurturance of the Reflective Practitioner.*

3. The initial models for the redesign were drawn from several sources. See, especially, the Holmes Group, *Tomorrow's Teachers* (East Lansing, Mich.: Holmes Group, 1986); the Holmes Group, *Tomorrow's Schools: Principles for the Design of Professional Development Schools* (East Lansing, Mich.: Holmes Group, 1990); and John I. Goodlad, *Teachers for Our Nation's Schools* (San Francisco: Jossey-Bass, 1990).

4. The program was modeled on that described in John I. Goodlad, *Educational Renewal: Better Teachers, Better Schools* (San Francisco: Jossey-Bass, 1994).

5. "Sustaining and Strengthening Teachers for Student Learning," Portland, Maine, Site Year-One Plan (August 31, 2000), pp. 10–11.

6. Reconstructed from the author's notes from a meeting on February 9, 2000.

7. Author's notes.

8. "Memorandum of Understanding between the PEA, the PPS, and USM on Their Collaboration on the 'Strengthening and Sustaining Teachers' Project," February 17, 2000.

9. "Sustaining and Strengthening Teachers for Student Learning," pp. 23–24.

10. Harry Pringle (ed.), *Maine School Law* (Standish, Maine: Tower Publishing, 1996), pp. 77–81.

11. Portland Public Schools records made available to the SST research project.

12. National Commission on Teaching and America's Future, *Urban Initiatives Partners Newsletter* 2, no. 2 (Summer 2000); Maine Department of Education, Commission on Educator Recruitment and Retention, *Final Report* (February 2001).

13. These terms are a staple of the organizational development and group process consultation fields. See, for example, Gordon A. Donaldson Jr. and David R. Sanderson, *Working Together in Schools: A Guide for Educators* (Thousand Oaks, Calif.: Corwin Press, 1996), pp. 55–60.

CHAPTER 4

Toward Renewal in School–University Partnerships

PAUL E. HECKMAN AND CORINNE MANTLE-BROMLEY

The culture of a school is powerfully educative. It can readily run counter to what individual teachers say they are trying to do. We all know of schools that are joyful centers of learning. Looking behind the scenes, we discover that an enormous amount of planning and collective work is required to make and keep them such. And we know of schools where there appears to be a kind of bargain between students and teachers: do not push us too hard and we will not make life difficult for you. Schools like this are not hospitable places for idealistic teachers who seek to create interest and excitement in learning.

Ironically, the dominant socialization into teaching is focused on one's solo performance in the classroom, not on collegial effort. Indeed, both novels and research into preparation and later practice depict isolation in individual classrooms and little serious discourse about schoolwide matters or issues of possible common concern. Neither the design of school buildings nor the daily and weekly schedule invites serious discourse. Satisfying schools—for students, teachers, and parents—are those in which all of these stakeholders are brought together regularly in continuing processes of renewal, confirming what is being done well, what is amenable to relatively quick change, and what requires long-term study and effort. There is an ample body of literature on how best to proceed.

The authors of this chapter have engaged in such work. They are very aware that preparation for renewal is not commonly part of the education of future teachers, and they are equally aware that the deep structure of schooling resists renewal. Indeed, both teacher preparation and the structure of schooling are geared to expectations for preserving what exists, not changing it. Paul Heckman and Corinne Mantle-Bromley call for cultures of teacher education programs and schools that encourage countervailing ideas, challenge conventional practices, and foster cultures of inquiry.

They argue against the convention of developing models that others are to transport into the circumstances of their settings. Rather, they contend, processes must begin with careful assessment and discussion of local circumstances. Participants in renewal efforts then make decisions, take actions, and appraise the degree to which these actions addressed the initial problems or issues. Decisions made and actions taken are always subjected to later scrutiny; participants may even revisit the validity of the entire cycle.

Strong leadership is necessary but not sufficient to bring about change. The entire culture must be shaped and renewed, a process that requires broad participation. We have pointed out that a close partnering of schools and universities is necessary to renewing the culture of teacher education. Getting over the idea of the university as the lead partner and taking on the necessary concept of equal partners is not easy. Not only are schools and universities equal partners in both the preservice education and continuing practice of teachers, but they are equally responsible for their own institutional renewal and for assisting each other in this endeavor.

Positional leaders such as school principals can and must contribute significantly to the whole by creating the necessary conditions for effecting what Heckman and Mantle-Bromley refer to as second-level changes. These are usually changes in regularities and systemics now commonly seen as norms—the ways things should be. This is a hazardous role for these leaders to play, largely because they are frequently charged with and rewarded for strengthening the familiar. This is why the involvement of a critical friend—a drummer with a different beat—is so important. We are not talking about the occasional consultant. More than expertise is essential. There must be trust. Trust is built over time, and building institutional cultures of renewal takes a great deal of time. The "quick fix" is appealing but is almost always the best assurance of postponing, not effecting, change.

—The editors

Robert Linn recently stated, "It is far easier to mandate testing and assessment requirements at the state or district level than it is to take actions that involve actual change in what happens inside the classroom."[1] Our experiences support Linn's conclusion: Although it may look like a great deal is changing, classroom practices and structures remain much the same as they were fifty years ago. Our vision for what could be and our optimism regarding the potential of collaboration, however, have kept us searching for ways to alter significantly how young people learn and how new teachers are taught. Our search has led us to a set of principles that we believe could transform classrooms, schools, and teacher education programs into vital centers of child, youth, and adult learning. The principles, however, are difficult to enact. They assume changes in the organizational cultures of schools and institutions of higher education—changes that have been resisted for decades.

ORGANIZATIONAL CULTURE

Understanding the nature and power of school culture and its influence on the conditions that we will be discussing in this chapter is our first priority. We believe that the nature of a school's culture determines whether or not educational renewal is likely to flourish in precollegiate schooling and in professional preparation programs in partner schools. To take school culture seriously requires understanding the limits of an individual in any organization's culture. An organization's existing culture will usually influence an individual's thoughts and actions in the organization more strongly than will the individual's prior training and experience. This means that ignoring the nature of a school's culture will reduce the influence of efforts to make teaching and teachers more effective through various professional credentials, certificates, or programs.

What is this culture thing? It is socially learned beliefs, values, and related actions. It is always there, influencing what happens, but never apparently so. Our minds have absorbed what is sensible or nonsensical in our daily experiences in the various cultures where we spend our time. Culture increases the complexity of understanding what one knows, shaping and placing boundaries around how one gains new insights and how one learns from new experiences, especially in a society of so many co-cultures.

For example, when an individual brings outside views to an organization, those inside of the organization commonly see the outside ideas or practices as either similar to what is already going on or as irrelevant. This judging is a consequence of the organization's existing culture. The culture encourages individuals to make sense of the new through the lenses of the old, the guides for thought and action that exist in the organization as its culture. Those who are outside of an organization do not understand ideas in the same way as those who are inside it. This is one of the problems of human learning that confronts all who are interested in change in individuals and in educational organizations. Richard Schweder puts the matter this way: "We could not possibly know that others are rationally justified in their conception of things . . . if we could not make rational sense of their conception of things 'by our lights' or, as Gellner puts it, 'against the backcloth of our world.'"[2] In other words, if we can make rational sense of others' conception of things, then their conception of things is not *that* different from ours, for it must make sense in terms that are understandable to us. It is *our* rationality that we explore when we confront *their* conception of things, for how else could we understand others, unless their meanings, beliefs, and modes of justification were in some sense available to us?

Schweder is pointing out a paradox. Individuals know and understand their world through the lens of their cultures. They do this with a mind that is constantly "world making." That is, minds make sense of the world. Within a culture, minds make *shared* sense of the world; that sense both allows for understanding the world one way and poses problems for understanding it differently. One knows only what one knows, and this knowledge is the foundation for new learning. New insights come out of these old guides for action. Furthermore, the culture encourages certain ways of knowing and often limits others.

Paul Berman and Milbrey McLaughlin confronted this paradox in 1974, analyzing data about what happened to features of schooling innovations supported by federal funds in the late 1960s and early 1970s. These innovations were brought from outside of the school to be implemented inside it. If they were accepted at all in the school, the practices eventually looked more like the prevailing school program than they did like the innovations in their ideal form. Berman and McLaughlin explained this regression of innovations to the mean as mutual adaptation. Faculty and staff members inside of the school adapted the characteristics of the innovations to fit those features that were most familiar to them and to fit the school culture. In other words, the culture of school required innovations to correspond to the existing cultural mold of the school, irrespective of what those innovations were intended to do.[3] By extension, partner schools seeking renewal—ongoing examination of current practice with the possibility of enacting fundamental change—face this same dilemma in efforts to improve simultaneously teacher education programs and P–12 schools.

The culture of an organization is also at work when individual educators, either novice or expert in what they know and do but unfamiliar with a particular school culture, come to work in a new school setting. New arrivals to existing organizations receive powerful messages regarding how work gets done and how people interrelate. The pressure to assimilate—to adopt the existing beliefs, attitudes, and behaviors—is strong, so strong that it is almost always successful. With little overt intention to do it, the new individual comes to embrace the guides for action that others in the school share. The influence of the existing school culture is and always will be greater than the influence of any one individual on that culture. Bradd Shore explains why this is so:

> Both personal and conventional cognitive models are kinds of "mental models," what cognitive scientists like to call mental representations. In many ways, the cognitive processes that underlie the creation and use of such conventional models are basically the same processes that are involved in the formation of any "mental models." Mental models, such as my mental maps for driving to work or picking up the kids from school, are creative and adaptive simplifications of reality. Thus they do not contain many colors or sounds. And they delete the vast amount of visual detail that is actually available along these routes, retaining only abstract-

ed, schematic information relevant to my purposes. Details are reduced in complexity and at times eliminated altogether, while salient features of an environment are selected and sometimes exaggerated or otherwise transformed by a process of formalization and simplification—a process I call "schematization." In this sense, every mental model is part memory, part invention. But there is an important difference between personal models and cultural models. Cultural models are constructed as mental representations in the same way as any mental models with the important exception that the internalization of cultural models is based on more socially constrained experiences than is the case for idiosyncratic models. Cultural practices that constrain attention and guide what is perceived as salient are not left open to much personal choice but are closely guided by social norms.[4]

These personal and cultural models have much to say about why the culture of the school must be understood, how that culture can be altered in ways that create new personal and organizational models of learning and new organizational structures, and how these new guides, images, and models can be sustained over time.

Regularities of Schooling

In 1984, John Goodlad's book *A Place Called School* provided for the first time a detailed account of what was going on in the nation's schools and classrooms. Despite federal and foundation support for innovative practices since the late 1950s, a dominant set of schooling practices and structures existed in the thirty-eight schools of the study's national sample. These same practices had characterized schooling for nearly a century. The more things had changed in schools, it seemed, the more they were staying the same.[5]

Here is a composite—a cultural snapshot—of Goodlad's findings about classroom life for students and teachers:

Walking into a school, an observer notes a long, dimly lit hallway. Entering any classroom along this hallway, the observer finds an adult who is called a teacher standing in front of a group of twenty to thirty seated children. Several features of the classroom life of this room stand out. First, these children are all of the same age, and the teacher calls them "graders": first graders, second graders, and so on. The grade is determined by the age of the children. Six-year-olds are called first graders; seven-year-olds are called second graders. The children work on material that also has grade-level distinctions.

Second, teachers overwhelmingly talk at students who are far more passive than their teachers. Students answer more questions than they ask. They fill in blank spaces with predetermined answers on sheets of paper, workbooks, and textbooks. Student engagement in these tasks is often less than high. Few belly laughs reverberate in these classrooms.

Third, much of the effort in classrooms and throughout the school is devoted to correcting deficiencies in or to sorting students. Those who are deficient are separated from those who are not and provided remediation. Little attention is paid to identifying and embracing the assets and knowledge of the children.

Finally, students have little direct influence over what and how they study. Few opportunities exist for them to find their interests and act on them. In turn, teachers have relatively little influence over many decisions that directly affect them. They follow directives provided by those in charge of them.[6]

These predictable regularities of schooling and classroom practice have great hold on the lives of teachers and students and have existed for a long time in schooling. John Goodlad, Seymour Sarason, and Paul Heckman are among those who have argued that the culture of schooling provides the holding power for these predictable patterns and explains why they remain.[7] The chances of altering these patterns of practice will increase only when considerable effort is intentionally directed by educators in these settings to develop a new culture of schooling, a culture powerful enough to guide the development of new practices and structures in classrooms and schools.

Regularities of Teacher Education

One can imagine that the complications of changing embedded school culture only increase when teacher educators from colleges and universities, who have their own sets of deeply held beliefs and assumptions about teaching and learning, are added to the mix. Several years after his study of schooling, Goodlad expanded his inquiry to include teacher education in colleges and universities. He and his colleagues studied the preparation of teachers in twenty-nine institutions that ranged from small liberal arts colleges to major research universities. The study revealed significant variations in some foci of their research, often but not always based on institutional type. The researchers found several programs that consistently stood out in their conception and enactment of what good teacher preparation could be. During the study, they regularly encountered teacher education students who were deeply committed to becoming teachers and serving children well, and they found teacher education faculty members who were perceived as caring and accessible to the preservice teachers. They also found the persistence of a parallel set of regularities of teacher education programs, which, like those of schooling that we have just discussed, were often weak and ineffective in educating their students. "The pervasive common themes," Goodlad noted, "cannot be ignored."[8] The following second composite paints a picture of what many program features in Goodlad's comprehensive study of teacher education programs were like.

> The university student who intends to become a teacher is rarely recruited into teaching. Instead, she commonly begins to take education classes because of an interest in teaching, and at some poorly marked juncture, is "in" the program. As vague as entry is, even more ambiguous is any process of monitoring once she is in the program. This preservice teacher is aware of the low status that P–12 teaching holds on her campus and in society and has likely been pressured by faculty members outside of education, by peers, or perhaps by a parent to use her talents somewhere other than teaching. Her grades are good, but the education classes she takes are perceived by others to be less rigorous than those in other departments.
>
> This soon-to-be teacher finds her education courses dominated by lecture and is mostly passive in class. She is largely on her own throughout the program, rarely relying on her peers or getting to know them or participating in any informal socialization into teaching. In general, this preservice teacher and her peers find little programmatic clarity or coherence in goals, beliefs, or general program purpose. They rarely see their arts and sciences classes as connecting to their education course work and often criticize their education classes for their lack of utility. They regularly criticize the lack of connections between their field experiences and campus courses and suggest that communication and coordination across the program are limited.
>
> The preservice teacher readily accepts the current-reality focus of her program and experiences no expectation to change extant practices or to engage in school renewal activity once she begins to teach. She values most highly her fieldwork, and if she experiences a clash between what she is taught in her education courses and what she is expected to do in her field experiences, she yields (and is encouraged to do so) to the practice of the school or the individual teacher.
>
> The preservice teacher's most influential experience is her student teaching. Her placement with a teacher is most often deter-

mined at the district or administrative level. Alignment between a teacher's practice and the preservice teacher's preparation is not likely to be a consideration. Her university supervisor for this experience is most often a low-status, non-tenure-track employee of the university who has no programmatic control or responsibility and little interaction with education faculty on the college or university campus.

The preservice teacher's education professors suggest that the control of program substance and quality are beyond their purview, as are the required arts and sciences courses their students must complete. They find frustrating the increasing restrictions placed upon them by state regulating agencies and keenly feel a sense of prestige deprivation regarding their work. The arts and sciences faculty members often agree with the low-status position of teacher education, viewing the academic ability of education students as low and the research of the education professors as substandard.[9]

To complete this dismal picture, the top-level administrators on campus are not likely to place the preparation of teachers among their highest priorities or list it among their proudest accomplishments. Furthermore, research and publication are becoming increasingly important in tenure decisions, and service to the local community is less and less recognized or rewarded, decreasing the motivation of education professors to work closely with schools.[10]

The researchers found numerous regularities within the education schools, colleges, and departments that clearly discouraged ongoing renewal of teacher education. Of grave concern was the lack of connection between preservice teachers' course work and their experiences in the field. Goodlad and his colleagues proposed that educators in schools and in teacher education institutions engage in the difficult, ongoing work of changing the norms of their respective institutions, in part by regularly interacting with and learning from each other's perspectives, knowledge, and experiences.[11] In order to prepare new teachers well, they argued, preservice teachers needed field experiences that manifested the skills and attributes that the teacher education programs were teaching and course work that took into account schools' realities and their efforts at renewal. In order to keep their schools' renewal efforts moving forward, teachers and administrators needed a ready supply of well-prepared new teachers who could assume full-time responsibilities that included not only teaching but also engagement in ongoing reflection and renewal. If these parallel efforts were to be done well, teacher educators needed to become a part of the schools' faculties just as the schools' teachers and administrators needed to see themselves and be seen by others as teacher educators. These changes needed to occur while maintaining perspectives sufficiently different to provide alternate views of each other's work. This rationale led to the creation of professional development schools (PDSs) or partner schools, places where teachers and teacher educators together worked toward simultaneous educational renewal.[12]

A complicating factor is that, historically, neither school nor teacher education culture has provided much "wiggle room" regarding valued perspectives, ways of knowing, or experience. Capitalizing on each other's differences—using each other to provide alternative ideas that could lead to significant learning and change—demands each party's willingness to think outside of boxes the walls of which seem higher and the windows of which seem smaller than ever before.

FIRST- AND SECOND-ORDER CHANGE

Paul Watzlawick and colleagues distinguish between first- and second-order change,[13] a distinction that is important to our vision of what could be. First-order change requires that educators accept the organization's existing culture—its assumptions, theories, and beliefs—and then seek improvements based on that culture. Educators have long engaged in seeking improvement, but most often as first-order change from within the existing culture's belief structures that maintain the status quo. The more some things change, the deeper the existing culture (which caused many of the problems to begin with) becomes embedded in the work. In other words, first-order change does not get us very far toward genuine organizational renewal.

Second-order change, on the other hand, results from a process of careful observation linked to ongoing questioning of current beliefs. That is, it happens only when the existing culture is challenged by countervailing ideas. Hundreds of years ago, for example, most people mistakenly believed that the earth stood at the center of the universe. Careful observations of the night skies revealed facts that could not be accounted for under that theory and eventually led to new understandings fundamental to our current conceptions of motion and gravity.

Educational renewal—the ongoing development of new thoughts and actions about teaching and learning—resides in these countervailing or "perpendicular" ideas. They have the potential for bringing about second-order change in teacher education and schooling by challenging existing cultural guides for educating children, youths, and prospective teachers. The regularly encountered belief that children from minority backgrounds often come to school with cultural deficits leads to activities that are based upon this belief. What if these children actually come with rich bodies of knowledge that could be used to connect to new knowledge development? How might this perpendicular idea change what we do in schools and classrooms?

Challenging and abandoning ineffective ideas and actions in schooling (like the cultural-deficit belief described above) require what Chris Argyris and Donald Schön have called organizational learning.[14] The kinds of learning that they have in mind mirror first- and second-order change. Argyris and Schön discuss one type of learning that simply refines understandings about the organization's guides for action. The resulting refinements—first-order changes—may improve but will not substantially alter those guides. The second type of learning provides the basis for altering understandings and actions. The potential for this second type of learning, parallel to what we are calling second-order change, is what must exist if schools are to serve all children well. It is this second kind of learning and change to which we urge attention.

Change That May Not Change Much: First-Order Change

Two vignettes highlight the difficulty of establishing new cultural norms that contribute to ongoing educational renewal that is second-order and symbiotic in nature. The vignettes describe conversations that one of us had with PDS participants in two settings recognized for their progress in intensive school–university collaboration. These and two additional settings participated in a study of the progress that PDSs were making toward their theoretical potential. Hundreds of teachers and preservice teachers and dozens of college or university staff and faculty members from nine PDSs in the four settings were surveyed, and many also participated in either individual or focus group interviews. Data from this study are referred to throughout the remainder of this chapter.[15]

The first vignette involves a teacher educator we will call Leslie, who worked closely with the local high school. Her students—preservice teachers from the nearby university—were interning in classrooms throughout the school and taking a semester of classes back at the university campus prior to their final semester of student teaching. When asked whether she provided feedback to the school's teachers or if her role was strictly working with the university students, Leslie eagerly talked about telling teachers what the preservice teachers were impressed with: a skill, a particular lesson, a student's progress. "What about feedback that isn't so positive? Do you talk to teachers about anything that troubles you or the university students?" she was asked. Leslie responded hesitantly: "My interns and I have just been talking about how many students are sleeping in the backs of classes. We see it all the time, and nobody seems to do anything about it." When asked if she talked to anyone at the school about their concern, she responded, "Oh, no, I couldn't do that."

The second vignette involves three preservice teacher interns who were completing an internship in a midsize elementary school that was partnering with a large university and an equally large teacher preparation program. The interns were asked about a gap between what they were taught in their education course work and what they saw and learned at the school. They looked at each other and giggled nervously. "Well," one young woman started, "it's pretty big." After more nervous laughter, they explained that most of their university professors did not know what the school's teachers were doing and that the school was not doing what the university professors taught. "We are always having to explain to the professors what is happening in the school. They have no clue."

We draw two conclusions from these remarks about schooling, teacher education, and the connections between the two. The first is that despite efforts to connect and then alter what goes on behind the doors of K–12 classrooms and teacher education courses, the cultures that have guided and manifested themselves in these educational settings do not simply disappear when efforts are undertaken to join together schooling and teacher education. The second is that guiding principles have to be established and their necessary conditions rigorously monitored if students, teachers, preservice teachers, and teacher educators are to develop new understandings of the purposes of education and if they are to gain knowledge about, for example, human cognition, learning, and development. These guiding principles must be powerful enough to alter substantially the cultures of both educational settings and create a collaborative culture between the two for encouraging and sustaining new conceptions of education for students and educators. Otherwise, the difficult work of collaborating across school and university boundaries may leave us with a basketful of first-order changes that ultimately serve to maintain current structures, beliefs, and assumptions that have long guided schools and teacher education.

The two vignettes occurred in school–university partnerships that were considered by many to be exemplary: Both partnerships engaged school and collegiate educators in the design of their collaboration, both required extended field experiences of their preservice teachers, both included collegiate course work taught on the school's campus, and both required extensive school- and collegiate-level supervision of the preservice teachers. Many changes, however, appeared to be first-order in nature, leading to innovation that left existing beliefs and assumptions solidly in place. Several examples follow.

Increased Field Experiences

Teachers have long believed that preservice teachers needed more than the traditional eight- or ten-week student teaching experience to prepare for their first year in the classroom. Not surprisingly, then, for teachers in the studied PDSs, the move to extended field experiences did not require changes in their beliefs or assumptions. The lengthened practica did require changes in teachers' notions of what one does with an intern, however, since the teachers were not willing to "give up" their classrooms for months at a time. Teachers and interns in the study were experimenting with more small-group instruction, with team teaching, and with creative turn-taking. The resulting changes, however, did not remain when the interns left the classrooms.

Before widespread implementation of PDSs, the teacher educators from colleges and universities had been far more nervous about the extended field experiences than were their school-based colleagues. They worried that preservice teachers would place even more value on the practical knowledge of teachers and less on the foundational knowledge gained from their study of theory. Overwhelmingly, the teacher educators in the study who regularly worked in the schools agreed that extended time in schools was improving the teaching skills of the preservice teachers. Many of them recognized that their colleagues back on the college or university campuses were not convinced that extended field experiences had led to improved teacher preparation. This split in beliefs resulted in conflicting messages for untenured professors and tense disagreements regarding who should supervise the field experiences and what can and should be expected in remaining university-based classes. These tensions provided evidence that second-order change was being resisted at the postsecondary level.

Increased University Interaction with Schools

Each of the four teacher preparation programs in the study was based on the belief that both school and university faculty members would benefit from increased interactions with each other. The study's participants overwhelmingly agreed that interaction had increased. Strong relationships with one or perhaps several university faculty members had become a regular part of the schools' fabric. The maintenance of these relationships over time, however, was proving to be problematic. One partnership had moved university faculty members out of direct PDS participation, replacing them with doctoral students who were then supervised by the university faculty members. In another setting, the university began hiring teachers from the district to work closely with the partner schools. Several faculty members remained connected to the schools, but they were required to oversee ten or more partner schools each, severely limiting their time with any one school. In the other two settings, where the university connections were the strongest, all or most of the school-based university instructors were full-time university employees but were not on tenure-line appointments, where status and authority reside. The university connections were, it appeared, sliding back to the previous model of tenure-line faculty working on campus and lower-status representatives of the university working in the schools.

Changes in Teaching and Learning Practices

Participants at each of the studied PDS settings could easily talk about improved student–teacher ratios, new materials, and the infusion of new energy that the partnerships had influenced or created. It was far more difficult for the experienced participants to think of how the partnerships had altered their beliefs about learning or teaching. It is not that these changes had not happened; it is that they did not happen easily or consistently. Important progress had been made, but not enough.

The very existence of these PDSs or partner schools is a huge first step. Now numbering in the hundreds, perhaps thousands, these intensive collaborative efforts have resulted in relationships between school and collegiate educators that have increased their understanding of each other. Claims abound that the best of these partnership efforts are preparing new teachers better for the realities of today's schools. Our grave concern, however, is just that. These partnerships, difficult to create and even more difficult to sustain, may actually be reinforcing existing beliefs and assumptions, further entrenching current regularities (both effective and ineffective ones) of schools and of teacher education programs instead of becoming powerful tools for the second-order changes that our schools and our teacher education programs need.

Students who historically have been poorly served by our nation's schools will not be better served by educators doing the same, but more so and better. Students will be better served when we uncover the beliefs and assumptions that are getting in our way of reaching them. There is little evidence that school–university partnerships in general are promoting second-order change regarding teaching and learning—challenging deeply held beliefs and assumptions so that powerful new approaches to schooling arise. School–university partnerships may be an important condition for such powerful change; they are not, however, sufficient. What principles need to be established in these partnerships if deep adult learning—learning that leads to second-order change in schools and teacher-preparing institutions—is to result from our work together?

Three Principles for Creating Second-Order Change in Schools and Teacher Education

We propose three principles delineating purpose, role, and action of school–university collaboration that we believe have the potential for significantly altering the cultures of schools and teacher education programs. Our hope is that we and others can explore these principles and create the necessary conditions in school–university partnerships that can lead to genuine educational renewal. Our principles are these:

1. *Participants must agree that a primary purpose of the partnership is to challenge long-held beliefs and assumptions about their own and each other's teaching and learning.*

Most participants in the previously mentioned study believed that the primary purpose of their PDS was to improve the preparation of new teachers—to get preservice teachers more experience with existing cultural guides and practices—before they had classes of their own. The partnerships were, in their eyes, entirely successful at doing this. The goal of expanding field experiences (with commonly described benefits of easier intern placement and lower student–teacher ratios) may be a valid reason for a partnership designed to maintain the status quo; the goal will do little to initiate or sustain educational renewal, however.

One elementary PDS, whose participants agreed that their own learning would be a primary purpose of their PDS (established after a unanimous vote of the school's faculty), required each of its twenty-plus teachers to work with a preservice teacher intern for the year, thus doubling the school's instructional staff. At any time, half of the staff (of in-service and preservice teachers) could then be released from classroom duties to discuss a reading or previously collected data or to plan for an anticipated change. The university instructor regularly taught the school's children, modeling new techniques that teachers and interns observed and later critiqued. This partnership created a vehicle for educators to examine their work, challenge their assumptions and beliefs, and institute changes in their cultural guides for action.

*2. There must be agreement that everyone's responsibility within the partner-
ship work is to raise the most basic questions about theory and practice.*

Why do we do what we do? What beliefs and assumptions undergird
the actions? What perpendicular ideas are strong enough to challenge
these beliefs? What might we do differently if we suspend a particular
belief? These and similar questions must be raised and answered if
school–university partnerships are to bring about renewal in schools and
teacher preparation programs.

Most of the hundreds of educators who were surveyed in the PDS
study agreed that, in general, the partnership had increased their reflection on teaching and learning. Working closely and regularly with preservice teachers required that they question what they did and why on a regular basis. Individuals, however, regularly made comments that demonstrated how deeply embedded their beliefs about knowledge and established roles actually were. One teacher, for example, said that teachers at
her school "were too professional to give feedback to each other." Another
teacher said of the university faculty members working at the school: "I
don't think they know what they're talking about. . . . We know what
works here." And a university faculty member agreed that constructive
criticism was dangerous and could easily be viewed as "meddling."
Although there were in each of the studied PDSs individual examples of
school and university participants learning from and with each other, the
widespread cultural assumptions that defined and confined roles had not
really changed.

In a partnership where beliefs about roles were beginning to shift, a
teacher and a teacher educator regularly co-taught class sessions for the
preservice teachers. Their intent was to raise awareness about the differences between theory and the school's practice. Sometimes, for example,
the teachers disagreed with a theory being taught to the preservice teachers. Meanwhile, the teacher educator sometimes felt that the school's
practice in a particular area was ineffective. This public recognition of
their differences respectfully raised difficult questions for the teachers, the
teacher educator, and the preservice teachers, opening a door for ideas
that were perpendicular to strongly held beliefs.

*3. Participants must agree to go about their work together and, where neces-
sary, differently.*

"Together" and "differently" will happen only when the second type
of organizational learning that we have previously discussed in this chapter happens. Principle 2 above highlights the importance of everyone

involved in partnership activities and institutions asking the fundamental questions. But more is required than only asking questions; principle 3 addresses this "more." The second-order learning and change previously discussed call for an ongoing search for perpendicular ideas that might challenge conceptions that are now held as guides for learning and human development in schools and teacher preparation programs. We advocate learning activity that not only challenges what currently exists but also explores the possibility of enacting the countervailing theories that emerge. Embracing that kind of learning does not, however, mean that all of the guides for actions that presently exist in schools and teacher preparation programs will change. Some of the guides may well prove themselves to be powerful enough for educating students for a long time to come, after careful examination and questioning. But that can be determined only as questions are asked and more powerful guides for thought and action are sought in the educational renewal of schooling and teacher preparation.

A specific example may help to clarify our meaning: Understanding the subject area of mathematics remains an important organizing concept of the curriculum of the schools for students and for their success as citizens in a democracy. Comprehending mathematics may be even more important for students' successes in present times than it has ever been. Probing questions about the nature of mathematics and mathematics achievement—the kind involved in second-order learning—may uncover more compelling ideas about mathematics and ways that it can be learned. Several ideas about mathematics and mathematics learning may be perpendicular enough to engender new cultural guides for mathematics learning in schools.

These ideas come from studying everyday use of mathematics by individuals whom Donald Norman calls "Just Plain Folks" (JPFs).[16] For example, a study of JPF men who install carpets in homes and office buildings quickly reveals that geometry and arithmetic play a central role in how these individuals do their work. However, their use of mathematics differs from that of conventional school mathematics. Their geometry is much more embedded in the activity, work, and tools of installing carpets. Joanna Masingila describes the difference between school and everyday mathematics in a way that suggests a different kind of mathematics learning for each:

> Whereas school learning emphasizes individual cognition, pure mentation, symbol manipulation, and general learning, everyday practice relies on shared cognition, tool manipulation, contextualized reasoning, and situation-specific competencies. Researchers who have investigated how per-

sons solve problems in school-like situations and solve mathematically similar problems in everyday contexts found that in the former situation people "tended to produce, without question, algorithmic, place-holding, school-learned techniques for solving problems, even when they could not remember them well enough to solve problems successfully." When the same people solved problems in situations that appeared different from school, they used a variety of techniques and invented units with which to compute.[17]

If educators in schools and teacher education programs embraced a mathematics that corresponded to what happens in everyday mathematical activity in the world of work, Masingila concludes, the nature of what is learned and how it would be learned in schools and teacher education programs might involve knowledge that "develops out of activities that: (a) occur in a familiar setting, (b) are dilemma driven, (c) are goal directed, (d) use the learner's own natural language, and (e) often occur in an apprenticeship situation allowing for observation of the skill and thinking involved in the expert performance."[18]

Consideration of the power of such a conception of mathematics and learning permits closer scrutiny of the present guides for school mathematics. If found wanting, as we believe they are, the old guides for school mathematics could be replaced by newly created ones based on these notions of the everyday mathematics of JPFs. Individuals involved in educational renewal could then consider the degree to which they will embrace and enact relevant new ways of engaging students, preservice teachers, and colleagues in teaching and learning based on these and alternative ideas about learning, mathematics, and other subject areas.

Returning to the study of school–university partnerships, we find that interactions in the four studied settings had been centered mostly on new teachers' preparation. Teacher educators in several of the settings had responded with minor program changes that resulted from partnership interactions. The school calendar was used instead of the university calendar, for example, or an assignment was adapted to the school's reading program. Most often, changes that were described were first-order changes (possible within the existing belief structure) or were merely seen as necessary compromises.

Second-order learning and change were seen only occasionally. Participants from one high school PDS began to question why an intern's content expertise had to match the mentor's for all field placements. The participants started experimenting with complementary placements, for example, pairing a history teacher with a literature intern. This change,

although seemingly minor, introduced interdisciplinary teaching and
began to break down historically hardened departmental boundaries,
leading participants to question why they had departments and how
department boundaries kept the teachers from connecting their content in
meaningful ways.

If the three above-stated principles (or perhaps these in combination
with other essential principles) are agreed to and we create conditions
that facilitate their enactment, we naturally begin asking questions such
as these: Why do we group children by age? Why do teachers work
alone? Why do field experiences *follow* the study of theory rather than
precede it?

In all likelihood, some questions will lead us back to current practice.
Much of our current work is worthy of retention. It is in the regularity of
questioning, however, that we will uncover beliefs and practices that cannot be defended given new knowledge and experience and must give
way to new beliefs and actions.

What follows is a description of a project undertaken in Tucson,
Arizona. The project enacted many of the ideals of the professional development school without calling itself such: It created a strong learning
community, embraced the development of new teachers, and used differences between school and university perspectives to strengthen teaching
and learning. It also broke numerous traditional boundaries, however,
and thus created multiple opportunities for second-order learning and,
when appropriate, change.

An Illustration of Second-Order Learning and Change

The Educational and Community Change (ECC) Project piloted preservice teacher education in three schools in Tucson, Arizona, aligning
teacher education with the purposes and design of the project under way
in the schools.[19] The ECC Project encouraged the creation of conditions for
the reinvention[20] and ongoing renewal of what was happening in classrooms not only *in* each of the three involved schools, but also *among* the
schools, the families of the students, and the neighborhoods. While not
part of a formal school–university partnership, the project was, nevertheless, a highly collaborative effort among the schools, neighborhoods, and
university participants. It sought the simultaneous renewal of the programs and work that partners in formally constituted school–university
partnerships usually attempt to achieve.[21]

When second-order educational renewal simultaneously happens in all
of the partner organizations, everyone benefits. The children and youths
experience increasingly engaging and dynamic educational opportunities,

making it more likely that they will continue to value learning. The schools' teachers engage in more effective, compelling, and caring work as they push their conceptions of effective teaching. Their growth as teachers and leaders has positive consequences for the children, the school, and prospective teachers who participate in the school culture. University faculty members do their major teaching, service, and research work in the renewing schools, ensuring strong connections between the realities of schools and their theoretical connections to teaching and in research. In the process, everyone involved creates new ideas and practices that encourage children's and youths' development and learning.

The ECC Project and its pilot teacher education program provide examples of anticipated benefits of the symbiotic relationship suggested above. The conditions that had been established for simultaneous educational renewal in each school and neighborhood involved in the project made it possible for these benefits to accrue. For example, every week for three hours during one school day, teachers and their principal met together to describe, discuss, and examine aspects of what they did with students. Teachers regularly sought ideas that would be counter to what they predictably used as guides for action in their classrooms. When they left these meetings, everyone made commitments to try out something new in his or her classroom: gathering more descriptive information about some aspect of their classrooms, for example, or exploring a new idea that had been discussed that day. They would then bring back to the group the following week some aspect of their new efforts and understandings for further discussion and examination.

This kind of inquiry into teaching and learning at the ECC Project sites led to a number of substantive changes in thoughts, actions, and structures of classrooms and of the schools. These changes include:

- Students' voices, ideas, and thoughts became prominent in classroom work.
- Teachers worked together in teams of two or three with multi-age groups of students, reducing the usual isolation of one teacher from another and of age groupings of students from each other.
- Teams of students and teachers remained intact for two to three years, furthering the personal, social, and knowledge connections between and among all of these individuals.
- Much of the students' work focused on studying and understanding the neighborhood surroundings and investigating their own questions and interests about their local environment, thus connecting school learning to everyday life.

- A university ECC Project staff member (called a third party) worked closely with teachers and administrators during their three-hour dialogues and in the classrooms with teachers during the week, advancing more collegial and collaborative relationships between the university's and the schools' faculty members and ensuring ongoing attention to critical issues.
- Connections between parents, the neighborhood, and the school became strong and positive.

The teacher preparation that occurred at the three ECC Project sites also purposefully questioned previously unexamined traditional structures. Eleven seniors in the Teacher Education Program at the University of Arizona volunteered to enter one of the three schools as novice teachers. They knew ahead of time that their preparation would be very open-ended—that it was not clear what was going to happen during the year or how the year would end ten months later. They were also told that they would be a part of and contribute to the ongoing renewal and second-order changes under way at the site where they would serve as full-time novice teachers for the entire year. Several of the novice teachers joined different teacher teams working with multiage groups of children in the three ECC Project schools.

Throughout the year, the novices were involved in a cognitive apprenticeship in learning to become teachers.[22] They did not have methods classes or a separate student teaching experience. Instead, they engaged with their teams in teaching and learning activities, including exploring, examining, and questioning their thoughts and actions. They also pursued alternative and perpendicular ideas about learning and the subject areas in their teams. In these apprenticeship relationships, they built a foundation for developing into competent and caring educators with dispositions for examining and questioning all that was being done, old and new, in their classrooms.

From the first day of their involvement in these school sites, the novice teachers also participated in the weekly dialogue sessions. They joined their more experienced teaching colleagues from their team and those from other teams throughout the school in describing and examining together with ECC Project staff from the university what was happening in teams and in classrooms with children. The novice and experienced teachers also participated in weekly team meetings where more inquiry took place. One of the project's third parties who was at the school every day encouraged team members to examine and question the work that they undertook together in their classrooms. This same third party also met daily and individually with the novice teachers. Here, too, the novice teachers involved themselves in relationships with their other teaching colleagues who were also learning and developing shared understandings of what and how to examine and question everything that they did in their classrooms. Together they sought alternative ideas about learning and the nature of the subject fields. Novice and experienced teachers learned from and with each other in these reciprocal relationships.

What benefits accrued to each of those involved in this pilot? How do those benefits provide enhanced understandings of what is meant by a positive, symbiotic relationship; simultaneous renewal; and the three principles that we have suggested as guides?

Benefits to the School, Practicing Teachers, and Children

As was the case in the PDS programs described earlier, the numbers of adults working with children increased significantly, thereby increasing adult interactions with students. Novice teachers began early in their involvement to work with small groups of students in various activities. Eventually, they took on the same responsibilities for working with larger groups of students as did their more experienced colleagues. These changes by themselves, however, could easily remain at the level of first-order change. Doing more of the same may look different but may serve merely to harden the existing assumptions about teaching and learning.

Also similar to findings from the PDS study, the presence of the novice teachers—and their ongoing questioning of why work was done as it was—provoked an increase in everyone's reflections on teaching and learning. The novice teachers were able to point out more easily contradictions between what was said and what was done. They added new perspectives, insights, and questions that would not have been put into the mix or addressed by the experienced teachers and ECC Project staff; their newness to teaching benefited the renewal process.

One difference between the ECC Project and many PDSs was that with more adults available in the ECC Project, efforts purposefully intensified to elicit from students what they knew and were interested in. The teachers and novice teachers built personal and trusting relationships with each student in order to draw out prior knowledge and interests. The presence of additional adults on each team facilitated deeper relationships. The already-in-place structure for weekly, three-hour discussions and for teacher teaming brought the various groups of educators together on a regular basis to consider and plan for new and more engaging student learning activities.

One other difference between the project and the studied PDSs was critical: ECC Project novice teachers were expected to point out contradictions and were provided encouragement and a safe environment in which to do so.

Benefits to the Novice Teachers

The novice teachers developed insights about and commitment to the potential for renewal and for second-order reinvented thoughts and practices. In subsequent interviews a year after the pilot ended, these teachers reported that they were easily making the adjustment to teaching in a "regular" school. Colleagues of several of the ECC Project novice teacher graduates reported that the first-year teacher in their school was a leader in their school's renewal processes. For example, one first-year teacher, Brian, had initiated team teaching with a colleague. He and his teammate worked with a multiage group of students (a two-year span), an unusual arrangement at their school. He and his colleague connected to children's interests, working with children in ways that Brian had learned during the one-year ECC Project apprenticeship. Powerful learning, it appeared, could transfer to a new context when that context was open to new ways of teaching and learning.

The novice teachers learned what is involved in challenging taken-for-granted ideas and, when called for, creating new ones to take their place. They also learned how to survive the anxiety that arises when trying out something that has not been done before. Most importantly, they saw and embraced the intelligence and insightfulness of economically poor children who attended their apprenticeship schools. They rejected and defied the stereotypical depictions of economically poor children as unmotivated and unskilled. They also comprehended what it meant to engage students, to value and act on what students know, and to follow students' interests in investigations of the children's world.

Benefits to the ECC Project Staff

The ECC Project staff gained insights into creating conditions that encourage experienced teachers, parents, and novice teachers to examine and question what predictably happens in schools. The staff also better understood the necessary support for educators to entertain, struggle with, and embrace new guides for action that are based on the literature about human cognition and learning.

In several cases, again similar to the situation in stronger PDS collaborations, the teachers from the ECC Project sites and those from the university staff gathered data and descriptions of the new work and then collaboratively analyzed these data and published pieces about what they were learning. The university side of the world learned of the indispensable insights that teachers have to offer about their work and their students. Teachers learned that they could write about their experiences and that other people found what they wrote to be worth reading.

Collaborating with a school site where renewal was embraced created a powerful apprenticeship for novice teachers, demonstrating that ongoing renewal was indeed possible. The novice teachers were satisfied with their preparation to become teachers, and the teachers and university educators were pleased with what the prospective teachers were able to do. The collaboration provided benefits to the teachers, the children, and the school, as well as to the university.

Connections to Simultaneous Renewal and the Three Guiding Principles

The ECC Project school–university partnership provides us with a concrete example of the three principles described earlier. The participants—including the schools' teachers and administrators, the novice teachers, and the university staff—agreed that a primary purpose of their partnership was to challenge and alter long-held beliefs that did not hold up in the face of today's knowledge. They further agreed that everyone was responsible for raising questions about theory and practice. And finally, they all engaged in altering their work based on their inquiries into beliefs and assumptions about teaching, learning, and schooling in general.

The ECC Project illustration underscores the importance of second-order renewal in the preparation of new teachers. Learning to teach in a school that is satisfied with mediocrity or with serving only some students well will only further entrench ineffective practice. One of the conditions that challenges the old culture of schooling and forwards a new culture is the intimate involvement of an outsider seeking new cultural guides inside of a school with those educators who work every day in that school with students. In the ECC Project example, the outsider concept advanced new ways of working for university faculty and staff, which in turn encouraged new ways of working for teachers, students, and prospective teachers in the school. To fulfill the role and encourage second-order renewal, university personnel had to involve themselves in schools that had committed to the kind of renewal we have been discussing. This involvement calls for a relationship of equals. Furthermore, the outsiders have to understand what is going on inside of the school. Their interpretations of events and the guides for them must correspond at least somewhat to the meanings of those from the inside, ensuring that talk about events can eventually create shared understandings.

In order to effect simultaneous educational renewal that is second-order in nature, all partners must share the same intentions: questioning what is going on in school and teacher education classrooms; interrogating their own thoughts about their practice and the guides for that practice; and, when warranted, seeking new guides for their actions so that what manifests itself yields unique structures, activities, and practices. These intentions go well beyond the regularities of schooling and teacher education that have become so predictable in schools and in universities. But second-order renewal cannot happen simultaneously in schools and universities unless those involved in universities renew conceptions of their work as well.

University personnel engaged in teacher education and school improvement must spend less time at the university and more time in schools, understanding schools from the inside out without becoming an insider, and comprehending what it will take to renew schools from the inside. Such an inside–outside role strengthens investigations aimed at figuring out the conditions and features required to renew precollegiate schooling and teacher preparation.

Finally, the curricula and program development of the school and of teacher preparation should go hand-in-hand as well. As conventional beliefs that guide existing regularities of schooling give way to more compelling ideas about human learning and cognition, their meanings will be enhanced in practice and will provide the basis for continued exploration of even more compelling ideas for novice teacher education programs. Conventional practices and ideas are challenged by alternative and more powerful conceptions about learning. This interplay between what *is* and what is *possible* advances the necessary questioning and exploration in renewal of both schools and of teacher education programs.

SUSTAINING RENEWAL

Traditional school culture, which includes teacher isolation and maintenance of the status quo, can be transformed into a culture of second-order learning and change through vital and renewing interactions, as can the prevailing culture of teacher education programs. Both, however, need each other's differences to serve as catalysts, pushing each to think and act differently about and in their work. If everyone comes together intent on learning and renewing, and committed to examining, questioning, creating, and acting in new ways, children and youths in our nation's schools will benefit. So will their teachers, both those who are preparing to teach and those experienced in teaching in our nation's schools.

The PDSs referred to early on had created vital relationships between school and university personnel. The participants did not, however, all share the intention of examining and renewing their teaching and their learning. The ECC Project personnel took the important next step of intentional examination and renewal of their work. They all agreed that everyone's role was to question practices and assumptions and then to act on newly formed insights. Neither the PDSs nor the ECC Project, however, had determined how to sustain the intensive work of partnership that creates ongoing second-order renewal. Thus, the three principles that can serve to guide simultaneous educational renewal may be necessary to create such change but insufficient to sustain it. The conditions for renewal have to be sustained and attended to so that second-order learning and change are possible.[23] That is what educational renewal calls for. Furthermore, neither the PDSs nor the ECC Project had programmatically accepted responsibility for creating bridges from the new teachers' preparation—which is responsible for instilling many of the new teachers' sense-making guides for teaching—to the schools where the new teachers began to teach, each with its own cultural structures of sense-making. There is always more to do.

If schooling is ever to engage all children in learning that matters to them and that instills in them a desire to continue their learning, then strong partnerships between schools and universities must be sustained over time. For that to happen, the culture of each institution must change, and conditions that sustain the cultural changes must be supported. Additionally, partnership work must move from the fringes to the center of each institution, and it must extend beyond institutional borders to include parents and the communities themselves. Policymakers, top-level administrators, politicians, and leaders of philanthropic organizations can play important roles in this work by supporting simultaneous educational renewal and by understanding that the hard work of renewal, by definition, will never be complete.

NOTES

1. Robert L. Linn, "Assessments and Accountability," *Educational Researcher* 29 (March 2000): 4.

2. Richard A. Schweder, *Thinking through Cultures: Expeditions in Cultural Psychology* (Cambridge, Mass.: Harvard University Press, 1991), p. 5.

3. Paul Berman and Milbrey McLaughlin, *Federal Programs Supporting Educational Change* (Santa Monica, Calif.: RAND Corporation, September 1974, RAND Report No. R-1589/7-HEW).

4. Bradd Shore, *Culture in Mind: Cognition, Culture, and the Problem of Meaning* (New York: Oxford University Press, 1996), p. 47.

5. Goodlad actually suspected that this stasis was the case much earlier. In the mid-1960s, he and his associates explored what was happening behind the classroom doors of teachers who were being encouraged to undertake innovations and changes in their schools. Teachers and administrators certainly talked about innovations that they believed they were implementing. Their actions in classrooms, however, did not correspond to their rhetoric about innovation. Practices that had previously characterized activities in classrooms remained in place in these "innovative" schools. This work is described in John I. Goodlad, M. Frances Klein, and Associates, *Behind the Classroom Door* (Worthington, Ohio: Charles A. Jones, 1970; revised and reissued as *Looking Behind the Classroom Door*, 1974).

6. John I. Goodlad, *A Place Called School: Prospects for the Future* (New York: McGraw-Hill, 1984). See especially Chapter 4 (pp. 93–129).

7. See John I. Goodlad, *The Dynamics of Educational Change: Toward Responsive Schools* (New York: McGraw-Hill, 1975); Paul E. Heckman, "Understanding School Culture" in John I. Goodlad (ed.), *The Ecology of School Renewal: Eighty-sixth Yearbook of the National Society for the Study of Education* (Chicago: NSSE, 1987), pp. 63–78; and Seymour B. Sarason, *The Culture of the School and the Problem of Change*, 2d ed. (Boston: Allyn & Bacon, 1982).

8. John I. Goodlad, *Teachers for Our Nation's Schools* (San Francisco: Jossey-Bass, 1990), p. 155.

9. This finding was not consistent in the small liberal arts colleges included in the study.

10. See Goodlad, *Teachers for Our Nation's Schools*, especially Chapters 4–7.

11. See Kenneth A. Sirotnik and John I. Goodlad (eds.), *School-University Partnerships in Action: Concepts, Cases, and Concerns* (New York: Teachers College Press, 1988).

12. The Holmes Group and the Carnegie Forum were also calling for closer collaboration between schools and new teachers' preparation during this time. See Holmes Group, *Tomorrow's Teachers: A Report of the Holmes Group* (East Lansing, Mich.: Holmes Group, 1986). See also Carnegie Forum on Education and the Economy, Task Force on Teaching as a Profession, *A Nation Prepared: Teachers for the 21st Century* (New York: Carnegie, 1986).

13. Paul Watzlawick, John H. Weakland, and Richard Fisch, *Change: Principles of Problem Formation and Problem Resolution* (New York: W. W. Norton, 1974).

14. Chris Argyris and Donald Schön, *Organizational Learning*, 2 vols. (Reading, Mass.: Addison-Wesley, 1978).

15. These data are taken from a study by Corinne Mantle-Bromley, reported as "The Status of Early Theories of Professional Development School Potential: Progress of Four Settings across the United States," in Irma N. Guadarrama, John Ramsey, and Janice L. Nath (eds.), *Forging Alliances in Community and Thought* (Greenwich, Conn.: Information Age, 2002), pp. 3–30.

16. Donald A. Norman, *The Psychology of Everyday Things* (New York: Basic Books, 1988).

17. Joanna O. Masingila, "Mathematics Practice in Carpet Laying," *Anthropology and Education Quarterly* 25 (December 1994): 433.

18. Masingila, "Mathematics Practice," p. 458.

19. This project involved educational renewal work in five schools and neighborhoods in Tucson, Arizona, during an eight-year period. It was predicated on the belief that every aspect of precollegiate schooling—its relationship to parents, neighborhood, and community and the connections between and among the university project staff and the educators, parents, and students involved in these project sites—had to be significantly altered and renewed.

20. Reinvention in this case meant that new aspects of schooling would be created so that schools did not have the old features that previously characterized them. It also meant that the new would better reflect what was known about human cognition and learning, child development, the nature of work and human activity in many areas of society, and the human resources and knowledge that existed in the neighborhoods and communities of the schools involved.

21. Goodlad has defined a productive, symbiotic relationship as one in which the various entities of a school–university partnership benefit from all partners' efforts to renew themselves. In the process, the new program features that emerge further the educational development of children, their teachers, the prospective teachers, and the teacher educators. The accrued benefits of such renewal for each partner cannot occur without the involvement and assistance of the other partners. In the National Network for Educational Renewal (NNER), a network of school–university partnerships associated with Goodlad's renewal agenda, these partners include partner schools, a teacher education program in a school/college/department of education, and members of the arts and sciences faculties.

22. See John Seely Brown, Allan Collins, and Paul Duguid, "Situated Cognition and the Culture of Learning," *Educational Researcher* 18 (January–February, 1989): 32–42; Jean Lave and Etienne Wenger, *Situated Learning: Legitimate Peripheral Participation* (New York: Cambridge University Press, 1991); and Barbara Rogoff, *Apprenticeship in Thinking: Cognitive Development in Social Context* (New York: Oxford University Press, 1990).

23. In the ECC Project example, the conditions included the weekly three-hour inquiry discussions, the inside–outside role, and the presence of novices.

CHAPTER 5

New Teacher Induction in a Culture of Professional Development

DANIEL KATZ AND
SHARON FEIMAN-NEMSER

Teachers are frequently reminded in professional development sessions that they exist for the well-being of their students. Much less mentioned, however, is the well-being of teachers. Nor are the needs and, indeed, comforts of teachers much addressed in pre-service teacher education programs. Yet schools with reputations for caring about their teachers attract and keep good ones. That these teachers will then take good care of their students is almost a given.

Creating an environment of caring attention to one another and opportunities for continued learning constitutes a down payment on lengthening a new teacher's career. Such is good business. But, more important, it is simply the right thing to do. Sustaining a supportive environment should require no neon-lit slogans or ritualistic contingencies to remind us of the behavior our society should display. John Dewey taught us that traits such as civility, compassion, respect, and the like should be routine, reflective of cultural teaching and of learning what it means to be human.

Nonetheless, the deep structure of schooling creates an ethos of isolation and individualism among adults that must be overcome by deliberate intent and action. The unrelenting demands of teaching a class or classes all day make it difficult even to arrange to observe and discuss another's teaching. The custodial role of schools mitigates against meetings of sufficient length and intensity to effect more than cosmetic change. Convening a half-dozen teachers for a two-hour meeting during the school day means making alternative educational arrangements for more than a hundred students or sending them home. Parents do not take kindly to the latter alternative.

School renewal of the kind described by Heckman and Mantle-Bromley in the previous chapter provides the professional engagement and individual renewal that sustain and rejuvenate teachers. But such does not self-start. Until recently, the educational literature was almost devoid of strategies even for beginning, largely because reports of practice did little to advance the careers of researchers, and reports of practitioners had little place in the required reading of future teachers. The tide turned a decade ago, and as a result, there is now a helpful blending of theory and practice. Daniel Katz and Sharon Feiman-Nemser provide a good deal of this blending in this chapter.

There is an essential reciprocity in individual and cultural renewal. Domi̇,
vidual behavior begets dominant cultural behavior. And the reverse is true. The p
recommended and described by the authors of this chapter plant the seeds of c̦
renewal. Involving individuals collectively in school problems that cannot be resolved
vidually then nourishes these seeds. Individual and cultural renewal become mutuȯʌ,
nourishing. Only then does change begin to break into the deep structure of schooling.

—*The editors*

"Well, thank goodness for her [my mentor teacher] because she has all this literacy expertise . . . and all those wonderful resources . . . and she taught me how to assess where a student's at, where they're stuck, what kinds of activities to use . . ."

—Kathryn, first-year teacher, Santa Cruz, California

"Those team meetings give me opportunities to share. . . . The advice would be specific to my question. . . . Any question I've asked . . . from classroom management to specific content questions . . . I've gotten responses to them all."

—Liza, first-year teacher, Cincinnati, Ohio

Despite the geographic distance between them, the two beginning teachers quoted above shared an experience in their first year of teaching. Both were supported by well-regarded induction programs that provide beginning teachers with full-time mentors who help them establish goals, observe their classes, and offer different forms of assistance for and assessment of their teaching. Both teachers expressed gratitude for their mentors and found their work together salient in their development as teachers.

From this point, however, their experiences diverge. Kathryn was thankful for her mentor teacher at least in part because her colleagues were distant and reluctant to speak with her about teaching. On her mentor's recommendation, she sought out several members of the school's English department who were skilled in developmental reading and asked if she could observe their teaching. To her disappointment, they declined, reflecting what Kathryn saw as a trend toward isolation within the school that prevented her from having meaningful contact with colleagues as she learned to teach.

Liza, a secondary mathematics teacher, also appreciated her mentor teacher's assistance but had an entirely different experience with colleagues. Cincinnati's team initiative meant that Liza worked with col-

ə /mathematics department as well as with teachers on an
ıry team who shared responsibility for selecting instruction-
⟨ tracking student performance, and administering discipline
ₒⱳup of students. Although teams spent considerable time on
ⱥistrative duties, the increased contact with colleagues enabled Liza
to develop connections that went beyond their official time together.
These colleagues were interested in how she approached her teaching and
were willing to answer her questions. In time, they even sought her ideas
and advice about new teaching techniques. For Liza, colleagues were at
least as important as her official mentor teacher in her learning to teach.

We met Kathryn and Liza as participants in the Beginning Teacher
Induction Study, a study of programs, policies, and practices in three well-
regarded induction sites: the Santa Cruz New Teacher Project (SCNTP),
the Cincinnati Peer Assistance and Evaluation Program (PAEP), and
Connecticut's Beginning Educator Support and Training (BEST) program
as practiced in New Haven.[1] The research combined case studies of programs with longitudinal studies of beginning teachers in each site. Our
research goal was to detail the character, quality, and impact of induction
practices and the experiences of beginning teachers in each site.

All three programs are referenced in the literature on beginning
teacher induction as places where the learning needs of beginning teachers are taken seriously, and all three put substantial resources into play for
the benefit of beginning teachers. Two work with novices over a two-year
period, and two offer mentors who are released from classroom teaching
so they can work with beginning teachers full time. All three provide a
variety of professional development opportunities, mostly workshops
and seminars, in addition to a mentoring relationship. Two frame their
work around state teaching standards, while the third program focuses
heavily on district standards for students.[2]

Given their prominence in the literature and the array of resources
these sites offer beginning teachers, we entered them assuming that
induction was a serious programmatic initiative. We recruited a sample of
six to eight beginning teachers in each site and, over a two-year period,
examined their experiences within their schools, districts, and induction
programs. The longitudinal study included background interviews with
participants about their previous education, professional preparation,
and learning needs, and interviews in the fall and spring of their first and
second years of teaching about their experiences with mentors, colleagues, and principals. We also observed their teaching and interactions
with mentors on four separate occasions.

What emerged from our interviews and observations was a portrait of
novice learning through serious and sustained standards-based mentor-

ing as well as through regular interactions with supportive colleagues willing to discuss teaching across experience levels. Like Liza, some beginning teachers nominated colleagues as important sources of ideas and support in their teaching even when they had full-time mentors. Others, like Kathryn, wanted and sought out substantive work with their colleagues even in schools where such opportunities were rare. We also found significant cases of mentors who lacked either the tools or the time to provide meaningful, educative support for new teachers.

Our participants' experiences in places that take induction seriously challenge conventional thinking about the resources and support that new teachers need in order to learn to teach well and to find satisfaction and success in their work. In particular, they raise questions about the widespread tendency to equate induction with mentoring and to rely on mentor teachers as the sole source of support for beginning teachers. While formal induction programs matter, is it possible to treat beginning teachers as learners if their learning is solely the province of one-on-one mentoring? Who else needs to take responsibility for beginning teachers and their development?

In this chapter, we explore issues most pertinent to a broad understanding of quality induction. First, we consider the learning needs of new teachers and why they are rarely taken seriously. Next, we consider the role of formal induction programs and mentoring in addressing these learning needs. Finally, we consider the importance of school structures and cultures in creating conditions for new teacher development. Our discussion is informed by the experiences and insights offered by the beginning teachers we met in Santa Cruz, Cincinnati, and New Haven. Their voices speak eloquently about the need to embed quality mentoring in school contexts that promote not only beginning teacher learning but also teacher learning across experience levels.

TAKING IT SERIOUSLY: BEGINNING TEACHERS AS LEARNERS

It may be comforting to invest full confidence in beginning teachers, but this confidence is seldom justified. No matter what kind of preparation beginning teachers have, some of the most important things they need to know can be learned only on the job once they face a real group of students. A good preservice program can help new teachers understand what they need to be learning and help them develop the tools to do so. Still, new teachers face a learning agenda that goes beyond what we typically assume.

Beginning teachers often get hired late and arrive a week before school to set up the classroom and prepare for students. Everything in the environment is new. They must deal with where to put the desks; what to do on the first day and every day after that; who the students are; what kinds of families they come from; and what interests, resources, and backgrounds these students bring. For the novice, the questions are unending: What am I supposed to teach? How will my students be tested? What will their test scores say about me as a teacher? What does the principal expect? Am I supposed to keep my class quiet and move it through the halls in straight lines, or do my colleagues appreciate that lively learning sometimes means messy classrooms and active students? And after the first weeks of school, how can I find out what my students really know, deal with their diverse learning needs, and ensure that everyone is learning?

This is a major learning agenda. It touches on issues of curriculum, instruction, assessment, management, school culture, and the larger community. It goes beyond maintaining order, generally viewed as the primary concern of beginning teachers.[3] It underscores the need for regular support and guidance situated in the daily work of teachers, focused on problems of teaching and learning, and oriented toward helping new teachers develop an effective practice. The daily, complicated demands of teaching challenge all beginning teachers, even those with extensive preparation. As more and more teachers enter the field through alternative routes, the need for thoughtful induction support and guidance becomes even more pressing.

The promise of new teacher induction lies not only in easing the transition into teaching and breaking down the isolation that separates teachers, but also in providing the conditions for teacher development. The resources and working conditions that we offer new teachers determine whether the early years of teaching will be a time of constructive learning or a period of coping, adjustment, and survival. In response to these challenges and to both projected and real teacher shortages, many states and districts have turned to formal induction programs as the solution.

WHAT THREE WELL-REGARDED PROGRAMS OFFER NEW TEACHERS

To date, more than thirty states have adopted various induction programs and policies, and most urban districts offer some kind of induction support, usually in the form of mentoring.[4] Despite the increase in induction activity, however, programs vary widely in their scope and quality. Some are little more than the assignment of an "in-school" mentor with no meaningful responsibility for teacher learning, while others are sophisticated efforts to connect novices with substantial and sustained learning opportunities.

We chose our three study sites because of their reputation as strong induction efforts supported by state and/or district policy. While the literature is full of descriptions of "sink or swim" beginning teaching,[5] we wanted to know what it is like to be a new teacher in places that take induction seriously. What learning opportunities and resources are available to new teachers in these contexts? How do beginning teachers assess the relative salience of different forms of support and guidance?

In this section, we describe the formal learning opportunities available to beginning teachers in our three study locations and examine the responses of new teachers to these opportunities. Although the programs we studied are not typical, they are widely touted as models of beginning teacher induction and make serious efforts to address beginning teachers as learners. Together, they represent some of the current possibilities in beginning teacher induction.

Besides the usual in-service activities available to all teachers, beginning teachers in all three sites experienced three common program elements designed specifically for them: ① an orientation before the opening of school, ② seminars and workshops across the school year, and ③ one-on-one mentoring. In a real sense, these learning opportunities reflect the beliefs of different groups of people—state and district officials, program leaders, and mentor teachers—about what new teachers need to know or be able to do and how they can best learn. Based on observations, interviews, and document analysis, the descriptions below highlight some of the distinguishing features of these activities.

Orientations

In all three sites, beginning teachers attend an orientation before the opening of school. Ranging from one day to four, these official beginnings vary in tone and sponsorship. Two of the orientations we observed were presented by staff from the district. In one case, mentor teachers attended and explained their role; in the other, they were not present. The third orientation, presented by the mentors themselves on behalf of the district, was the most personal in tone.

Common topics across all three orientations included classroom organization and management and preparing for the first days of school. In one site, the message was delivered by classroom management guru Harry Wong via videotape. In another, a union-sponsored team of teachers presented a daylong interactive workshop, and a professor from a local university gave a two-hour lecture. In two orientations, beginning teachers met in grade-level groups to talk about getting ready for students and to get practical advice and resources.

The district-sponsored orientations introduced new teachers to local administrators as well as district policies, curriculum frameworks, and rubrics. The mentor-presented orientation introduced new teachers to the terminology and procedures of the induction program (for example, how to complete a collaborative assessment log) and concluded with a ceremony in which first-year teachers read "words of wisdom" from second-year teachers in the program.

Seminars and Workshops

Throughout the school year, all three programs offer a variety of seminars or workshops on general and subject-specific topics, including effective classroom management, planning, curriculum frameworks, content standards for students, and innovative teaching methods. In Santa Cruz and Cincinnati, mentors ran these seminars for the new teachers in their charge. In New Haven, both the state and the district sponsored a variety of seminars and workshops, but mentor teachers were not involved in these sessions. In some cases new teachers were required to attend. In most cases, attendance was recommended but voluntary.

Mentoring

Although all three programs rely on one-on-one mentoring as the primary vehicle of induction, mentors' roles vary across the sites. According to their training, Connecticut mentors are supposed to function as cognitive coaches. Cincinnati mentors are mainly performance evaluators. Santa Cruz mentors serve as standards-based teacher developers. These different role orientations, combined with differences in accessibility, affect the character and quality of mentoring in each site.

Santa Cruz mentors, called "advisors," are veteran teachers released from classroom teaching to work full time with a cohort of new teachers across the district. Advisors form close, supportive relationships, visiting novices on a weekly basis, observing teaching, providing material resources, doing demonstration teaching, and offering affective support over a two-year period. Formative assessment activities based on the California Standards for the Teaching Profession inform ongoing assistance. The SCNTP has developed a number of sophisticated tools and protocols, such as the Developmental Continuum of Teacher Abilities, the

Collaborative Assessment Log, and the Analysis of Student Work, to help advisors assess beginning teachers' progress and orient their work toward specific goals and a shared vision of good teaching.

Cincinnati's "consulting teachers" are also full-time mentors. Recruited from among experienced teachers in the district, they work with new teachers for a full school year. Consulting teachers act primarily as performance evaluators. At the beginning of the year, they establish job performance targets with beginning teachers that provide a framework for six formal classroom observations spread across the year. After each observation, consulting teachers meet with novices to review a written report containing recommendations for improvement that new teachers must act on. At the end of the year, consulting teachers make recommendations about contract renewals to a district review panel. Despite this high-stakes evaluation process, consulting teachers emphasize their supportive relationship with new teachers, which includes offering material resources, doing demonstrations in the classroom, and meeting informally at the new teachers' request. In fact, consulting teachers construe their support activities as a professional responsibility: they must help their new teachers meet the goals set in job targets and recommendations.

Connecticut's BEST program trains mentor teachers in the use of state teaching standards and in a form of "reflective conversation" meant to facilitate new teachers' examination of practice during their first two years of teaching. In practice, however, mentoring in New Haven looks far more directive than the mentor training might have indicated. For one thing, BEST mentors are still full-time classroom teachers. Furthermore, because of personnel constraints, many mentors do not work in the same school or grade level or content area as their assigned novices, making meaningful interactions almost impossible. For these reasons, we found that mentoring in New Haven was an inconsistent experience for the beginning teachers, dependent largely on the availability and commitment of the mentor and the support of the school principal in making time and space available.

Table 5.1 on the next page summarizes the features of the three common components of the induction programs.

NEW TEACHERS' ASSESSMENT OF LEARNING OPPORTUNITIES

New teachers at all three sites found little of importance in orientations before the opening of school. At their best, orientations gave key information about the induction program and/or district policies and man-

Table 5.1. Common Induction Elements and Differences in Operation

	Santa Cruz NTP	*Cincinnati PAEP*	*New Haven BEST*
New Teacher Orientation	• One-day program run by mentors • Introduction to SCNTP • Grade-level/subject-matter sessions • Community building	• Two-day program run by district • Mentors in attendance • Introduction to district standards and administrators • Grade-level/subject-matter sessions on standards and rubrics • Session on organizing early school year	• Four-day program run by district • Mentors not in attendance • Major session on organizing early school year • Sessions on management and district standards
Seminars	• Run by mentors • Monthly meetings with other new teachers • Curriculum organized around state teaching standards • Standard format: community-building and problem-solving activities	• Run by mentors • Twice-monthly meetings with other new teachers • Sequence and topics selected by mentors • Sometimes involved attendance at district-sponsored workshops	• Run by state and district • Most recommended but not required • State sessions on teaching standards • District sessions on management and curriculum

Mentor Teachers	• Full-time mentors released from teaching
	• Two years with new teacher
	• Weekly support and assistance visits:
	  ➢ Materials
	  ➢ Demonstration teaching
	  ➢ Informal feedback
	• Formative assessment:
	  ➢ Based on state teaching standards
	  ➢ Variety of tools for mentors' use
		• Full-time mentors released from teaching
		• One year with new teacher
		• Evaluation cycle:
		  ➢ Job targets
		  ➢ Observations
		  ➢ Recommendations
		  ➢ Final Evaluation
		• Classroom assistance and support:
		  ➢ Classroom materials
		  ➢ Demonstration teaching
		  ➢ Informal feedback
			• Mentors still classroom teachers
			• Two years of mentoring available
			• Idiosyncratic, episodic mentoring supports based on time and proximity
			• Not consistently placed in same school, grade level, or subject matter as new teachers in New Haven BEST

aged to foster a sense of community among new teachers; however, almost none of the new teachers in our sample believed they learned anything meaningful beyond a few practical suggestions. A Santa Cruz new teacher remarked: "I'm sure part of it was useful. Introducing how the new teacher–advisor relationship was going to work was useful." A Cincinnati new teacher was more blunt in his assessment of PAEP's orientation: "It was required." Several new teachers in Cincinnati went on to say that they would have preferred more time to set up their classrooms instead of discussing it at orientation.

Seminar meetings and workshops met similar assessments by new teachers. Although individual sessions introduced important ideas and concepts, the overall influence of seminars on teaching was rather weak, and some new teachers regarded them mostly as a chance to connect personally with other novices. One Santa Cruz teacher commented, "They would talk forever about classroom management or how to do something that I pretty much knew . . . and to spend two and a half hours when you're really tired on a Monday afternoon. . . ." For her, detailed, specific sessions mattered the most, but she often felt bogged down in general discussions of topics she already felt confident about. This perspective was mirrored in other sites. For example, a Cincinnati novice was helped by a practicum meeting dealing with the use of district standards to assess student portfolios, a task she was doing for the first time. A New Haven teacher who had not learned the Connecticut teaching standards in her undergraduate preservice program rated a state-run standards clinic as very important. Orientations and seminars appeared to be matters of "one size fits some."

Compared to these formal program opportunities, one-on-one mentoring lived up to much of the faith placed in it. In sites and situations where mentors worked closely with beginning teachers over an extended period of time and on matters of significance for their teaching, the impact of mentoring was substantial. New teachers in all three programs found a combination of emotional support for the difficult transition to teaching and professional support for their learning as teachers. Perhaps most significant, many of the new teachers reported spending considerable time examining their students' learning and thinking about the use of standards, challenging the popular belief that new teachers are mainly preoccupied with survival and classroom management.[6] Although the practice of mentoring varied greatly from site to site, two salient themes emerged from new teachers' responses.

First, mentors were able to provide meaningful and supportive relationships. There is no doubt that beginning teaching is a confusing and personally challenging time in a teacher's career, and the ability to foster emotional support and trust that mediates the transition is no small matter. In Santa Cruz, a middle school language arts teacher appreciated her advisor's willingness to meet above and beyond: "We've met many, many times outside of school. The first time we met for a really serious focus on literacy instruction, we met for three hours on a Saturday afternoon."

A Santa Cruz elementary school teacher summed up how many of the new teachers viewed their advisors: "Time with my teacher advisor: that's probably one of the most helpful [things]. . . . Between just keeping [me] from tears or letting me cry . . . to just listening and letting me talk out all that stuff. . . . She is always pointing out the things that she's noticing that I'm doing well and really insisting that I celebrate them." Like many of her peers, this teacher was gratified that her advisor helped her focus on positive accomplishments throughout the difficult work of her first year of teaching.

Another teacher in the same school expressed gratitude for having a confidante who listened to her concerns and frustrations and who was willing to help her with her own "bad habits." "I'm a procrastinator," she confessed, "and my advisor kind of kept me in check and reminded me that this deadline is coming up." For these beginning teachers, advisors offered professional support that made beginning teaching easier to manage.

In Cincinnati, supportive relationships grew from mentoring even though the consulting teachers' evaluative function added some tension and confusion. One elementary school teacher explained how she changed her management style during observations because she mistakenly assumed that her consulting teacher wanted to see her act more "patient" with student disruptions. When her consulting teacher suggested that she act more firmly with student disruptions in class, she reverted to her typical, more forceful management style. New teachers were aware of the assessment process, but they also acknowledged the emotional support they received from consulting teachers.

Assistance was not limited to emotional support, and new teachers reported that their consulting teachers provided important resources and ideas, especially in difficult situations. One new teacher was originally hired to teach third grade, but she was switched to fifth-grade science, a subject in which she had little experience. Throughout the year, she struggled with management and felt out of place with the grade level and content. Her consulting teacher offered her material resources to develop her curriculum: "She gave me a lot of helpful materials. . . . I was really lacking in resources. I had to go out and find things, and she gave . . . monthly packets to help . . . either extend a lesson or reinforce a concept and ideas of how to do it." This teacher experienced what consulting teachers themselves say they strive to accomplish: meaningful support within the context of a trusting relationship that helps new teachers to improve.

Mentor support in New Haven functioned well under circumstances that allowed for frequent contact between the novice and mentor. A third-grade teacher was originally assigned a mentor in a different school. Taking the initiative, she requested a change in this arrangement and was grateful that her new BEST mentor was located both in her school and at the same grade level. Under different circumstances, she might not have had the ability to work with him on a regular basis: "I guess I'm pretty lucky that he is in my school and he is in my grade level. . . . I never talk to the first- or second-grade teachers because they're at the other end of the building, and I just don't have the opportunity to talk to them. So I am always talking to him . . . especially with the reading—we have each other's kids. So, . . . he's been helpful." With such close proximity and close connections in their work, she was enthusiastic about her mentor's ability to support her and help her understand the workings of the school.

However, a secondary school teacher whose assigned mentor was in another department and was located on the other side of a large building provided this capsule summary of his experience: "She's not someone from my department. She's not someone from my floor. She's not someone I see as a part of my regular teaching duties. She's not someone who knows what courses I'm actually teaching." Under these circumstances, even the affective potential of mentoring is severely limited.

Another theme of effective mentoring is its focus on substantive matters of teaching and learning. Across our sites, there was evidence that mentors either kept their novices' attention on student standards or worked with them on tasks that directed their attention to student learning. In Santa Cruz, new teachers credited their advisors with a wide range of teacher learning influences. Twice a year, for example, advisors and new teachers analyze a set of student work, sorting samples according to different levels of performance, analyzing representative pieces for evidence of student understanding and confusion, and deciding on specific ways to help students at different levels move forward in their learning. The process is complex and time consuming, but new teachers were enthusiastic about the results. For one elementary teacher using a writers' workshop approach, the analysis of student work helped her see significant changes over the course of the year: "The analysis of student work was huge this year. . . . Looking at the writing samples across the year, . . . I was focusing on the writers' workshop and seeing how the writers' workshop had changed the students' writing. That was just great, and being able to plan my curriculum around it."

Despite overall positive responses to advisors' assistance in learning to teach, some new teachers in Santa Cruz had concerns or doubts about what their advisors could do. A new mathematics teacher starting a second career after many years in industry was concerned that her advisor did not have direct experience as a mathematics teacher, and she was not sure how to talk to him about mathematics content. When asked at the end of her first year if her advisor could help her understand how to break content into manageable units for her students, she replied, "I don't know how to talk to him that way."

New teachers in Cincinnati took the observation and recommendation process very seriously, understanding the stakes attached to it. Taking it seriously did not mean that they were always enthusiastic, however. For example, a third-grade teacher spoke about her consulting teacher's recommendations in very matter-of-fact terms:

> I guess it has shaped the way I've been teaching and ways I've done things. . . . When she would observe, and with the comments that she would make, by the next time she came back I had to be . . . working on those things, or else I would not get another satisfactory. . . . So, it wasn't exactly great, but I was like, "Well, I gotta eat; I have to do it."

Other new teachers reported that their consulting teachers' recommendations helped them work on their management skills, their use of the district standards, and their interactions with students. Two secondary school teachers specifically referred to the importance of using another person's observations of their teaching to understand what goes on in their classrooms. So while the assessment aspect of consulting teachers' recommendations was not universally embraced, new teachers agreed that the observations and recommendations had positive influences on their teaching. This was especially true in helping them use the district's student content standards.

BEST mentoring in New Haven was uneven in the time and proximity of its mentors; however, those new teachers who enjoyed sustained and close relationships with their mentors reported significant support for their teaching. A middle school English teacher in an arts-based magnet school had frequent contact with his mentor who taught next door to his classroom. He reported frequent interaction with her around his teaching, especially since she spent a number of hours each week in his classroom: "She's in my eighth-period class . . . so she's constantly giving me feedback. . . . She'll slip me a note or something in the middle of class, or she'll remind me to look at somebody or, you know, show attention to somebody. . . . She never interrupts . . . or anything like that. She's really good. She's very professional." This New Haven teacher had a particular advantage: the principal arranged the schedule so that every teacher spent several periods a week in another teacher's classroom. Besides having his mentor in his eighth-grade English class on a daily basis, he got to observe her teaching as well. This unique schedule, the brainchild of the principal, provided regular opportunities for modeling and feedback.

As an induction strategy, educative mentoring can be a powerful influence in new teacher learning. At its best, it offers an individualized form of professional development, situated in a particular context, oriented toward shared goals and standards, and aimed at helping new teachers create an effective instructional program for their students. Thoughtful mentoring goes well beyond giving advice and "feel-good" support. It takes time and focus. When new teachers have regular opportunities to learn with and from experienced teacher–mentors, they not only grow as teachers, but they also experience the power of collaboration and joint problem solving.

Learning to mentor a beginning teacher is itself a form of professional development for experienced teachers. Mentor teachers need more than a few days of training before they take up their new responsibilities. They also need regular opportunities to discuss questions and problems that arise in the course of their work with new teachers and to extend their knowledge and skills as teachers and mentors. Investing in the professional development of mentors produces a cadre of teacher leaders who can help foster a culture of collaboration and accountability in schools and districts.[7]

EMBEDDING MENTORING IN A SCHOOL CULTURE

Induction does not occur in a vacuum. The local professional culture of a school and opportunities to work with colleagues matter significantly. In New Haven, for example, we found beginning teachers whose mentors did not work in the same subject area or building. These arrangements prevented significant mentoring from occurring. In Cincinnati, new teachers were placed in interdisciplinary and grade-level teaching teams, which met frequently to discuss student progress and in which new teachers developed significant relationships with experienced colleagues. For all of the strengths of mentoring in Santa Cruz, some new teachers in our sample struggled to make meaningful contact with colleagues in their own buildings.

As we analyzed our data, it became clear that colleagues were often powerful resources for beginning teachers in addition to their assigned mentors and the formal learning opportunities provided by the program, the district, or the state. It also became clear that most new teachers, regardless of their school environments, wanted colleagues who did more than offer social support and instructions for the copying machine. They wished to discuss curriculum implementation, to find ideas for meeting specific student needs, and to gain insight from colleagues with many years' experience in their subject areas. The universality of these wishes comes through in other studies of beginning teachers. Summarizing results from interviews with fifty new teachers in Massachusetts, researchers Susan Moore Johnson and Susan Kardos write: "What new teachers want in their induction is experienced colleagues who will take their daily dilemmas seriously, watch them teach and provide feedback, help them develop instructional strategies, model skilled teaching, and share insights about students' work and lives."[8]

In the following section, we present two vignettes that illustrate new teachers' working closely with in-school colleagues who provided significant, educative support. This provides the basis for discussing the need to embed mentoring and formal induction within a culture of professional development.

Fern: Collegiality under Pressure

Neighborhood School is an elementary school in the Cincinnati Public School District facing redesign. Because of consistent low performance and administrative troubles, the district planned to dissolve the school's organization, bring in a new administration, and rehire the faculty from across the district. Our year of data collection on site was the last year the school was to operate under its existing administration and faculty.

Cincinnati's team-based school initiative is a districtwide effort to place more responsibility on interdisciplinary and grade-level teams of teachers. According to the district's strategic plan, teaching teams:

- Keep students until they meet the exit standards for that level
- Are led by a lead teacher (according to district's Career-in-Teaching scale)
- Select instructional materials and learning activities
- Track each child's progress and keep parents informed
- Share responsibility for each child's learning
- Purchase the services of support staff and instructor assistants
- Are responsible for achievement gains of students from the beginning to the end of the level.[9]

As a team-based school, Neighborhood School was organized into grade-level teams that met far more often than typical department meetings were held. More importantly, all of the new teachers in our study who worked in team-based schools frequently spoke about colleagues and team members as significant influences on their learning to teach. Even Neighborhood, with its impending reorganization, demonstrated this.

Fern was a novice third-grade teacher in Neighborhood School. Although Neighborhood's teacher community was close knit, the school was not an easy place to begin teaching. First, the redesign process was stressful and uncertain. Second, Fern was anxious about her classroom-management skills. New to the district and placed suddenly at Neighborhood near the beginning of the school year, she was not sure how to establish herself in the classroom, and she felt that her students' behavior was out of control: "I didn't have time to get . . . adjusted to it. It was just like *boom*, and I had to deal with it."

Fern's consulting teacher offered her material resources for her curriculum and affective support to bolster her confidence: "She did tell me that I was doing a good job as the year went on. . . . It just helps to have somebody else tell me, too, so that I didn't feel like I was beating my head against the wall." Still, Fern's consistent management difficulties undermined her sense of effectiveness.

For several weeks, however, Fern received direct help from a colleague. During an evaluation conference for a special education student, the speech teacher assigned to her team noticed Fern's stress and offered to help. Several times a week, she came to Fern's classroom, where she worked directly with students who were having difficulty and quietly intervened when student behavior was too disruptive. While Fern focused on moving her lessons forward, the speech teacher helped her maintain order by intervening with individual students as needed.

Fern credited the intervention, which continued for over a month, with a marked improvement in her students' behavior: "The kids really enjoyed it, and they started acting better with that." Eventually, the speech teacher stopped coming on a regular basis, but the assistance had an effect on both Fern and her students. As the year progressed, Fern felt comfortable seeking assistance and input from other teachers on her team, especially a long-term veteran third-grade colleague who had much more experience working with parents. With her team members' ideas about a variety of management and instructional topics, Fern felt less in survival mode and more able to concentrate on developing her lessons.

Sandy: Surrounded by a "Broad System of Support"

Sandy was hired to teach second-language learners in a fourth/fifth-grade multiage classroom in a Title I elementary school. Riverside is a professional development school affiliated with the University of California at Santa Cruz. As a UCSC graduate of the teacher certification program, Sandy was already familiar with the school, having completed a semester of student teaching there. Moreover, Eileen, her student teaching supervisor, was Riverside's professional development coordinator and Sandy's advisor.

At Riverside, Sandy enjoyed what she called "a broad system of support." Her grade-level team consisted of a mix of veteran and novice teachers whom she regarded as "comrades, great critical thinkers." Every teacher on the team was committed to multiage grouping, looping, and teaching second-language learners. Sandy relied on them for support and guidance. She also participated in schoolwide professional development initiatives in addition to one-on-one mentoring with Eileen.

Eileen met regularly with Sandy's grade-level team. During Sandy's first year of teaching, Eileen helped the team rewrite the state's language arts standards in their own language and prioritize them, given the needs of their second-language learners. Next, they examined best practices for teaching to the standards and considered what would count as meaningful evidence that students had met them. Finally, they developed curricular units that integrated quality literature and expository texts.

Eileen's weekly sessions with Sandy occurred against the backdrop of her work with the grade-level team. When the team developed writing units around different genres, Eileen helped Sandy refine individual lessons informed by ongoing analysis of student writing. When the team decided to use literature circles, Eileen showed Sandy how to get students to talk about books in rich, substantive ways, as Sandy explained: "Eileen's modeling has really been crucial—being able to watch her facilitate a discussion. She's really helped me keep the big ideas in mind to focus on what's crucial to know."

Typically, Sandy and Eileen divided their weekly meetings into two parts: discussing the lesson Sandy had just taught and planning for upcoming lessons. The latter included both "big-picture planning," where they clarified and strengthened Sandy's content knowledge and long-term goals, and more specific lesson planning, where they worked through the details of particular learning activities. This involved clarifying difficulties that students might encounter, thinking of ways to address those potential confusions, deciding how to sequence the learning activities, and developing clear language for giving students key explanations.

Eileen and Sandy regularly engaged in detailed, subject-specific work focused on planning and refining Sandy's instructional moves and understanding her students' learning. Their interactions reflected a shared sense of responsibility and professional accountability that comes through in Eileen's comment: "We are engaged in trying to figure this out so that it really works for kids. I'm very interested in how the students are doing. I'm not just looking at the teacher; I'm definitely looking at the students in relationship to the teacher. We're working together to advance the academic achievement of kids."

CONCLUSION

In their similarities and differences, these vignettes offer considerable food for thought about what it means to take new teachers seriously as learners and what it takes to make induction a constructive learning experience. In both cases, the new teachers have access to official and unofficial mentors and to intentional and unintentional mentoring. In both cases, school structures and professional cultures play a critical role, though here the differences are instructive. Without local leaders who appreciate the importance of teacher learning across all levels of experience and who understand the special learning needs of beginning teachers, the most promising structures in the world will not achieve their potential. Table 5.2 presents some of the similarities and differences in the vignettes that we highlight here.

As beginning teachers, Fern and Sandy each had regular contact with an assigned mentor responsible for ongoing assistance and assessment of their teaching within the framework of content and teaching standards. Fern's consulting teacher carried out her official duties (conducting formal observations and writing reports with recommendations for improvement). What Fern valued most, however, were the emotional support and curricular materials that she provided. Sandy's in-house advisor offered positive regard and individualized coaching in the design

Table 5.2. New Teacher Induction within a Supportive School Culture

	Official Mentor	Unofficial Mentors	Orientation of Professional Culture
Fern	Consulting teacher	Grade-level team	Shared responsibility for student learning
Sandy	School-based advisor	Grade-level team	Shared responsibility for student *and* teacher learning

and enactment of a language arts curriculum responsive to the needs of her second-language learners. Both Fern and Sandy were treated as responsible beginning teachers with legitimate learning needs who deserved regular attention from an officially designated mentor who had time to do this important professional work.

Besides their official mentors, Fern and Sandy had regular interactions with other teachers through grade-level meetings. The teaming structure enabled Fern to develop relationships with colleagues that led to supportive interactions outside of team meetings. While Fern was not placed on a team for the purposes of being mentored, the opportunity for regular work with colleagues allowed for the possibility of indirect learning and unofficial mentoring. We can only speculate about what might happen if teams were accountable not only for student learning, but also for teacher learning.[10]

In the case of Sandy's school, teacher learning was an explicit function of grade-level meetings. Led by the on-site professional development coordinator, these weekly sessions provided substantive learning opportunities for teachers at all levels of experience. By working together on the central tasks of teaching—clarifying standards, designing curriculum, developing rubrics, and analyzing student work—all teachers strengthened their professional knowledge and skills in the service of improved student learning. For new teachers like Sandy, one-on-one mentoring was a natural extension of or supplement to this collaborative work. She had the benefits of individualized mentoring tailored to her developmental needs as well as regular access to the experience and insights of other colleagues. This occurred in a school where teacher development is a defining characteristic of the professional culture and a built-in feature of the organizational structure.

Beginning teachers are newcomers to a school community and novices to the practice of teaching. In mediating their entry into classroom teaching, we need to take seriously this reality. This means providing them with access to timely information and assistance on short notice. It also means building into their regular teaching assignments opportunities to observe and be observed, to get help with curriculum and student assessment and to strengthen their subject-matter knowledge.

The current interest in new teacher induction creates an opportunity to consider how to meet the learning needs of new teachers in ways that foster a culture of collaboration and learning for all teachers. Any responsible system will probably include some combination of individualized support and guidance from thoughtful and available mentors or mentoring teams with regular opportunities to work with colleagues on substantive issues related to teaching and learning. Such a combination reflects an understanding that induction is both a unique stage in learning to teach and part of a larger continuum of teacher development.

Until schools become good places for teacher learning as well as student learning, we need advocates for new teachers and serious induction efforts. Shared leadership will be required to develop responsible professional cultures and to create the conditions for educative mentoring. The way we treat beginning teachers says a lot about how we value teachers and how we understand teaching. As we strengthen the quality of beginning teaching through serious induction efforts, we will strengthen the case for ongoing professional development as part of the work of all teachers.

NOTES

1. The research was originally sponsored by the National Partnership for Excellence and Accountability in Teaching with funds from the U.S. Department of Education's Office of Research and Improvement. Subsequent funding came from the Walter S. Johnson Foundation.

2. Cincinnati has recently adopted a teacher standards framework based heavily on PRAXIS III. During our study, the district still relied on a general framework outlined in the Peer Appraisal Manual. Connecticut recently changed its state teaching standards from the Connecticut Competency Instrument to the Common Core of Teaching, but during our study, most personnel referenced the CCI. The Santa Cruz New Teacher Project uses the California Standards for the Teaching Profession to inform its work with new teachers.

3. Simon Veenman, "Perceived Problems of Beginning Teachers," *Review of Educational Research* 54 (Summer 1984): 143–178.

4. Elizabeth F. Fideler and David Haselkorn, *Learning the Ropes: Urban Teacher Induction Programs and Practices in the United States* (Belmont, Mass.: Recruiting New Teachers, Inc., 1999).

5. See, for example, Willard Waller, *The Sociology of Teaching* (New York: Russell & Russell, 1932); Frances Fuller and Oliver Brown, "Becoming a Teacher," in Kevin Ryan (ed.), *Teacher Education: The Seventy-fourth Yearbook of the National Society for the Study of Education*, vol. 2 (Chicago: NSSE, 1975), pp. 25–52; and Dan C. Lortie, *Schoolteacher: A Sociological Study* (Chicago: University of Chicago Press, 1975).

6. See, for example, Frances E. Fuller, "Concerns of Teachers: A Developmental Conceptualization," *American Educational Research Journal* 6 (March 1969): 207–226; Veenman, "Perceived Problems"; and Dona M. Kagan, "Professional Growth among Preservice and Beginning Teachers," *Review of Educational Research* 62 (Summer 1992): 129–169.

7. The Santa Cruz New Teacher Project does an exemplary job of supporting and developing mentor teachers through weekly staff meetings and the assign-

ment of experienced advisors to mentor new advisors. The project regards advisor development as an investment in capacity building for schools and districts.

8.   Susan Moore Johnson and Susan M. Kardos, "Keeping New Teachers in Mind," *Educational Leadership* 59 (March 2002): 13. For more information on the Project on the Next Generation of Teachers at the Harvard Graduate School of Education, visit www.gse.harvard.edu/~ngt. For a full account of the project, see Susan M. Kardos et al., "Counting on Colleagues: New Teachers Encounter the Professional Cultures of Their Schools," *Educational Administration Quarterly* 37 (April 2001): 250–290.

9.   These requirements are spelled out in the Strategic Plan, Cincinnati Public Schools, 1997.

10. Since teams are headed by a lead teacher according to the district's Career-in-Teaching scale, one could also speculate on the possibility of making lead teachers responsible for the support and guidance of new teachers with the help of other team members. This would mean giving lead teachers time during the day to observe and confer with new teachers.

CHAPTER 6

Effective Recruitment and Induction into the School District

SHELDON BERMAN

Perhaps it is because schooling is so deceptively complex that proposals for improvement are deceptively simple, especially when they are made in the name of reform. When research revealed that principals can make a significant difference, getting rid of some, moving them about, and hiring new ones became the routes to betterment in many school districts. The necessary conditions were reduced to an inadequate few.

Just what good principals were supposed to do was rarely made clear. "Site-based management" became the politically correct maneuver. Support for breaking schools loose from district controls increased. Freed-up schools suddenly found themselves overwhelmed with administrative responsibilities and paperwork formerly handled by the district. The prospects for districts' providing the context for schools to become good reemerged on the school improvement agenda.

When it became glaringly obvious that the high dropout rate of teachers during the first three years of practice had sweeping implications for school improvement, it also became obvious that the causal factors were many: inadequate preparation, isolation in the workplace, limited instructional resources, absence of a supportive school culture, diffident principals, burdensome district and state requirements, and more. Many of the most promising teachers were found to be among those departing. But those were not factors impinging solely on teacher retention. They cloaked and influenced every part of the schooling infrastructure.

The district may well be both the smallest and the largest entity encompassing the wide range of conditions that determine the nature of the bottom line in the schooling enterprise: the instructional learning relationship between teacher and student. We nod our heads in agreement regarding the critical importance of teachers' moral and intellectual grounding, the careful selection of candidates for teaching, the depth and balance of theory and practice in the preparation program, supportive collegial relationships, ongoing school renewal, and more. But no one of these conditions is sufficient unto itself, even though we often conduct improvement as though concentrated attention to just one will suffice.

What follows in this chapter is a rarity. The conceptual span of the district's infrastructure embraces virtually all of the elements put forward as the solution but favors none as sufficient. There is no way for state or federal interventions to conceptualize, let alone manage, this diverse array of local circumstances. Nor is it possible for local districts to purchase and install prefabricated models. Hudson is not the kind of suburban, upper-middle-class community that is so often thought of as supporting a premier school district. What is unique is the long tenure of Superintendent Sheldon Berman.

Superintendents and districts like this attract good teachers—teachers looking to long careers. The word gets around. Nonetheless, school boards are prone to seek out saviors, superintendents who shake up the district for a few years and move on to larger ones and bigger salaries. Superintendents such as Sheldon Berman have many such opportunities but are grounded in the knowledge that significant change takes time and in the satisfaction of doing good work. They attract, support, and keep principals and teachers similarly grounded.

—The editors

There is no more important long-term strategy for improving schools than hiring and retaining talented teachers who share their district's mission and vision. Because the instructional relationship between teacher and student is critical to the success of the learning process, effective recruitment and selection of new faculty members must be a key, well-thought-out aspect of a district's renewal effort.

However, effective recruitment and selection are not sufficient to ensure the success of the new teacher. Sustaining a high-quality instructional relationship between teacher and student requires school and district cultures that support the development and recognition of that relationship. Talented teachers will not last long in a culture that undermines or is neutral to their needs and interests, leaves them isolated, or fails to promote their growth. In addition, new teachers need to experience a sense of compatibility with the district's vision and mission, which, in turn, must be meaningful and compelling in order to inspire and orient them and give them a context in which they feel they can make a difference.

Hudson, Massachusetts, is an industry-based community thirty-five miles west of Boston, with a multicultural, multilingual, and socioeconomically diverse population. The Hudson Public School District comprises six schools, 2,800 students, and 250 faculty members. In my eleven years as superintendent in Hudson, I have had the opportunity to hire 70% of the current faculty and will hire at least another 20% within the next five years. Clearly, the hiring decisions we make and the ways we foster the development of new faculty members will define the district's instructional capabilities for decades to come.

Over the past eleven years, we have worked hard to improve teaching and learning through significant restructuring efforts, the implementation of new curricula, the expansion of districtwide professional development, the pursuit of innovative instructional strategies, and a conscious effort to recruit and nurture teachers with significant potential. Our efforts in Hudson may serve as a case study in effective practice, lessons learned, and issues that continue to challenge us. Because we believe that the vision and mission of the district provide the starting point and compass for this journey, this is where I will begin.

VISION AND MISSION

Vision and mission are critical to the success of any district in the process of renewal. They guide the district through the political, financial, and personnel challenges that will surely face the renewal process. They guide the faculty and administrators as they design or select curricula, develop new instructional practices, and make the daily decisions that ensure that the mission is embodied in the culture of the school. And they inspire faculty members by giving them a sense of both the larger purposes that education serves and how they can make a difference for children and our society. As superintendent, I am responsible for articulating the district's vision and mission and ensuring that they are embedded in policy, culture, and practice. Nowhere, however, is clarity of vision and mission more essential than in the selection of new faculty members and in the induction process.

Through the selection process I want to make sure that the people we hire will not only share our vision and mission but will be leaders in achieving them. Therefore, it is essential that the district clearly let candidates know what the vision and mission are. It is equally essential that we assess to what degree candidates already share them. I have found that this clarity has attracted teachers with strong potential to our district and has enabled us to support their growth and development as professionals.

We all seek a sense of meaning in our work and a sense of affiliation with a larger purpose. For teachers, the profession is often so isolating that this sense of meaning comes only from the positive interactions they have with children, which give them an important sense of satisfaction. But these interactions do not ensure the quality of instruction or that teachers are pursuing appropriate goals and strategies. For these, teachers need to orient themselves to something larger, usually a commitment to a particular philosophy of education, a vision of how education can impact society, or a mission as defined by their school or district. It is this sense of larger social purpose that often makes it possible for teachers to remain in their challenging profession with a commitment to continuous growth and improvement.

Currently, with so much of the national educational agenda focused on testing and accountability, districts have begun to define themselves and their mission in terms of improving test scores. In an environment of standards, testing, and accountability, we often forget that public education serves a larger public purpose: to help young people develop the convictions and skills to shape a safe, sustainable, and just world. Preserving and promoting a democratic society was the founding precept of our public education system, and if we are to continue to preserve our democracy, this goal must remain central to our efforts. Teachers who start with a vision of an equitable society and social change and understand that the development of a critical perspective is essential to democracy will become different teachers than those who are more narrowly focused.

In Hudson, we define our vision in terms of teaching young people to make a positive difference in the world around them so that they can be effective, participatory citizens who enter the world with an ethic of care and service and a capacity for thoughtful questioning and investigation. It is within this context that academics and school culture take on a new meaning for both faculty and student. We define the challenge for all of us as creating an instructional community that lives up to that ideal.

In addition to this vision, we articulate a consistent educational philosophy that guides our instructional and administrative decision making. Hudson's vision, mission, and guiding principles represent an effort to reclaim the power and effectiveness of progressive education. We believe that the core principles of progressive education will enable us to create the most productive and powerful learning environment for children. However, what we truly represent is an experiment in adapting and expanding upon progressive education principles based on the new knowledge we have gained through research and experience and the new challenges we face in the 21st century. Because we frame our work in terms of an open-ended search for best practice, the faculty is engaged in organizational learning, continuous improvement, and innovation. In fact, "innovation and excellence" is the phrase that has come to symbolize our efforts. It appears as the subheading for our website and on the Hudson Public School shirts for faculty and staff members.

We have tried to embody this larger sense of purpose, our consistent educational philosophy, and the concept of innovation within our mission, guiding principles, and vision. Hudson's mission statement reads: "Our goal is to promote the intellectual, ethical, civic, and social development of students through a challenging instructional program and a caring classroom and school environment." This embodies the progressive concept of teaching to the whole child and the necessity of balancing intellectual development with ethical, civic, and social development. It also embodies the concept of community, in that classrooms and schools must be caring, nurturing environments as well as academically rigorous ones.

We have articulated a set of guiding principles that build on this mission and form the common core for the changes we have put in place:

- Focus on depth versus breadth for both students and teachers
- Promote inquiry-based learning and constructivist teaching
- Enhance learning through the integrated use of technology
- Enable *all* students to meet a higher set of standards and expectations
- Intervene early to identify and address student needs
- Create a caring, collaborative, and professional culture for students, staff, and parents
- Inextricably interconnect social, emotional, and ethical development with intellectual development
- Enhance civic participation through authentic experiences in the social/political world

Finally, this larger sense of purpose is embodied in the vision statement that we have developed (see Figure 6.1). Communicating this vision and mission then becomes a critical aspect of the hiring process; support-

Figure 6.1. Hudson's Vision Statement

We won't stop until . . .

Our schools are havens where children reach their potential.

Each child's strengths are valued.

Each child's learning style is supported.

Each child is given opportunities to demonstrate what he or she knows in a number of ways.

Each child learns to acknowledge the worth of every individual, and all students know they make a difference in the world.

Our community's cultural diversity is celebrated.

Parents are partners, and home and school are synonymous.

The entire community is involved in the education of our children.

Our students and their parents know we care about children.

The success of each child is a commitment, not just a concept.

There is truly equal educational opportunity for all.

ing teachers' professional growth, in turn, becomes a critical aspect of the induction process.

RECRUITMENT

The first step in strengthening and sustaining new teachers is giving them the opportunity to know the direction the district is taking and to assess whether that direction is one in which they can invest themselves. We begin to lay this out in our advertising for teaching and administrative positions. With the limited space available in a major newspaper advertisement, it has become critical to state as simply and directly as possible who we are and the kind of candidates we are looking for. The following are sample advertisements we have placed recently.

Teachers: The Hudson Public Schools is a leader in educational innovation. We are looking for creative, student-centered, and technologically literate teachers committed to working in a culturally and economically diverse community. We are interested in teachers and administrators who engage students in cooperative learning, critical thinking, service learning, alternative assessment, and other innovative instructional approaches.

Curriculum Director: The Hudson Public Schools is looking for a curriculum director who is committed to working in a culturally and economically diverse community and interested in promoting innovative approaches to instruction. We are interested in an individual who is familiar with the leading innovative curriculum programs; has demonstrated an ability to work with teachers to implement student-centered, inquiry-oriented, and problem-based approaches; has experience with alternative assessment; integrates the use of technology into the curriculum; and is familiar with current research on effective professional development and systemic reform strategies.

Principal: The Hudson Public Schools is seeking a collaborative, innovative, and technologically proficient elementary school principal committed to working in a culturally and economically diverse community. We are interested in an individual who:

- is familiar with instructional innovation and the research on school change;

- has demonstrated an ability to work collaboratively with teachers and parents to implement instructional improvement;
- has familiarity with alternative assessment and student-centered, inquiry-oriented instructional approaches;
- is interested in promoting student responsibility through service learning and social development programs;
- is able to create a caring and supportive school culture; and
- can provide dynamic, positive leadership.

These types of ads have been highly effective in bringing to the district educators who want to work in a setting that is both progressive and creative. They have also been effective in helping new teachers orient themselves and feel a sense of affinity with the direction that the district is taking.

The rest of the hiring process continues to provide candidates with more information about the system so that they can make a good choice for themselves. When feasible, we have used screening committees composed of curriculum directors, teachers, and parents, with students joining the committees at the high school for our initial screening of candidates and our initial interviews. At the beginning of the process, screening committees receive a briefing on the selection process that includes a set of criteria for reviewing candidates. Although it is clear that no teacher, especially a beginning teacher, can meet all of the criteria, we ask the screening committees to look for candidates they believe are aligned with our approach and have the potential to grow. The criteria set out in more concrete terms the practical representations of our approach and vision (see Figure 6.2 on the next page).

Screening committees recommend four or five candidates to the principal who, in turn, recommends two or three candidates to the superintendent. Usually the principal and curriculum director join the superintendent for the final interview. At each step of the way, the candidate is given material on the school and district. In the final interview, I talk with candidates about our philosophy and direction. I indicate that we are looking for teachers who will create the instructional scaffolding for students to achieve higher expectations, who are interested in pursuing innovation within the context of a progressive approach to education, and who are interested in creating caring classroom communities to support the social, emotional, and ethical development of children. I also share the set of criteria used by the screening committee so that the candidate can get a more concrete sense of what we value and what we are looking for.

One final aspect of the hiring process that makes a difference in the long-term success of new teachers is the teaching assignments they are

Figure 6.2. Hudson Public Schools' Criteria for Selection of
New Teachers

1. Communicates well with students, parents, and colleagues.

2. Able to provide sufficient structure to maintain effective and positive discipline.

3. Sets high expectations for all students.

4. Instructional methods engage students in active learning with a focus on thinking and problem-solving.

5. Understands issues related to child and/or adolescent development and developmentally appropriate educational approaches.

6. Technologically literate.

7. Aware of current trends in education and willing to explore new teaching strategies and methods.

8. Interest in and/or experience with such strategies as cooperative learning, thematically organized and project-based instruction, alternative assessment, community–service learning, character education, inclusion, etc.

9. Uses rich teaching materials, for example, first-hand experiments in science, primary source material in social studies, literature in reading and language arts, manipulatives and spreadsheets in math, etc.

10. Values diversity and multicultural understanding and builds this into instruction.

11. Accounts for diverse abilities, needs, and learning styles in planning instruction.

12. Works effectively and compassionately with more difficult and less-motivated students.

13. Interest in the development of social skills, character, and social responsibility (that is, helping students develop the skills and aptitudes to make a positive difference in the world) and in linking curriculum with issues in the larger world.

14. Willing to work in a team and to participate in peer support/supervision.

15. Willing to participate as a member of school community outside the classroom and to work with students in extracurricular activities.

16. Interest in interdisciplinary or cross-grade efforts.

17. Expertise in an area that would add to the range of skills and talents of the faculty and academic and life experiences that add diversity to the system.

18. Shows evidence of thoughtfulness, enthusiasm, caring about children, dedication, and industriousness.

offered. All too often new teachers are seen as the lowest in the pecking order of seniority and given the most basic levels of classes and/or the most challenging students. Instead of these types of assignments, Hudson administrators try to create teaching assignments for new teachers that are well balanced in terms of the heterogeneity of students within the classroom or, at the high school level, in the types of classes the new teacher will teach. At the secondary level, we have no department heads and do not assign classes based on seniority. Instead, we have full-time, nonteaching curriculum directors who have multiple subject assignments, such as math and science or English and social studies. These curriculum directors collaborate with the principal to create assignments that utilize the strengths and interests of new faculty members, including having them teach advanced-level courses. At the elementary and middle school levels, our emphasis is on well-balanced classes, often giving senior teachers the more challenged students so that new teachers will have a greater chance of having a successful first year. This assignment policy is a relief to new teachers and gives them an early feeling of support and acceptance within the faculty.

We have found that our hiring process is generally effective in giving new teachers a thorough understanding of what we are trying to accomplish. Many leave the interview process with a sense of excitement about our direction and our approach, feeling that they are in the company of colleagues who will support their interests and development.

PRESERVICE PARTNERSHIPS

Partnerships between school districts and universities to better support the preparation of teachers can be a significant boost to a district's recruitment and induction efforts. Too often, the student teaching experience is an isolated one that acts as a test of a new teacher's endurance and talent but does not adequately support the development of a new teacher. Partnerships have the benefit of bringing student teachers into a consistent, more integrated experience in which their course preparation and their student teaching assignment are aligned and mutually supportive. In addition, partnerships provide the opportunity for university and school faculty members to collaborate for the benefit of prospective teachers.

Hudson is located far enough from local universities to make it challenging for student teachers to reach us. However, based on the leadership we have taken in implementing inquiry-oriented approaches to math and science, we have developed an important relationship with Assumption College, a small private college in Worcester. Each year,

Assumption has placed a student teacher with each of the four fourth-grade teachers at one of our elementary schools for the entire year.

This team of teachers has consistently provided leadership for the improvement efforts in math and science. One has been the president of the Massachusetts Association of Science Teachers. Another has been the president of the Massachusetts Environmental Education Society. Three of the four have completed their National Board for Professional Teaching Standards certification. Because Assumption College's elementary teacher preparation program also focuses on teaching prospective teachers an inquiry-based approach to math and science, the dean and faculty felt that Hudson and this team would provide the kind of student teaching experience that would complement their efforts. Since its inception, the program has come to involve other grade levels and teachers at our other elementary schools.

The program has been a powerful one for both the veteran teachers and the student teachers. They have collaboratively engaged in action research. All the teachers and student teachers meet together almost daily for lunch and at other times during the day. Student teachers are able to observe other members of their grade-level team. They participate in schoolwide activities and are well integrated into the school as a whole. The district's relationship with the college has also been a strong one, with university faculty working collaboratively with our teachers.

This is an excellent model to provide quality support to preservice teachers. It is one we are trying to develop with several other colleges based on our extensive community service–learning program. It is clear to the administrators and teachers who interview applicants for teaching positions that candidates who have benefited from collaborative school–university partnerships are generally stronger and more experienced than other prospects. In fact, Hudson has hired several of the Assumption College student teachers; one even replaced one of the fourth-grade team members who retired.

ORIENTATION AND INDUCTION

Induction is a multilayered process that supports and nurtures new teachers over an extended period of time. In Hudson it begins with the immediate opening of all professional development opportunities to newly hired faculty members. Many take advantage of our summer institutes and other programs that give them specific training in particular areas as well as an opportunity to get to know their new colleagues in an informal atmosphere.

For example, the middle school is moving forward on building a positive, caring environment for students through a social–emotional development program entitled Responsive Classroom. Responsive Classroom, developed by the Northeast Foundation for Children in Greenfield, Massachusetts, is designed to enable teachers to work with students to create respectful, caring communities in classrooms through class meetings and a variety of other strategies. In summer 2002, twenty-five middle school teachers participated in a weeklong training session. Our middle school hired eight new teachers in spring 2002, six of whom were first-year teachers. Seven of the eight new faculty members were able to join a large group of other faculty, the assistant principal, and the principal in this training. This not only brought them into the school community in a positive way, but it gave them added confidence and support as they started their teaching careers. Because this was a whole-school program, new teachers were able to learn about and participate in strategies alongside more experienced faculty members, thus helping to bridge the gap that is often felt when new teachers enter a school.

We also structure a two-day orientation program in which new teachers get a chance to meet each other, tour the district and town, spend time with the superintendent reviewing the current work toward the district's goals, and meet other members of the administrative and support team who will assist them. On the second day, they receive a half day of training in service learning to enable them to explore how they might integrate this important district program into their curriculum. New teachers spend the remainder of the second day with mentor teachers they have been paired with for the year. The mentors accompany them to their classrooms and assist them by touring the physical plant, sharing classroom strategies, ensuring that they have the necessary items for their first week, and offering support and guidance. During this time, they plan their weekly meetings and discuss future nonevaluative observations. This begins their mentor–mentee relationship for the year.

As part of the orientation, each new teacher receives a notebook with important information about the district compiled collaboratively by the teachers' association and the administration. In the notebook are samples of all of the forms teachers need to use, a list of important dates, contact information for various resource and administrative personnel, and important policies from the School Committee policy handbook. The notebook contains the answers to many of the questions new teachers will have throughout the year, organized in an easy-to-access format.

Support for new teachers continues beyond the orientation. New teachers are assigned mentor–teachers in their schools, meet monthly in a seminar led by administrators, receive in-class support from full-time curriculum directors and staff developers, participate in a new teachers' course, often have common preparation or planning time with other teachers at their grade level or on their team, and are invited to participate in an extensive range of professional development opportunities. Each of these components is designed to support the growth and development of new teachers. However, there is much that we have learned about improving our efforts in these areas.

Our mentoring program has evolved over time. For many years, each principal would ask one experienced teacher at the grade level or in the subject area of the new teacher to serve as a mentor. The arrangement was informal and largely effective in acquainting teachers with the procedures of the school and district. It also worked to a degree as a vehicle for new teachers to ask questions about classroom and instructional issues. At times a mentor might observe a class, although more frequently a new teacher would be able to observe experienced teachers. This informal system worked well, but it did not create a program with the kind of coaching and support relationships embodied in many mentoring programs.

Four years ago, we began a formal mentoring program, with teachers taking training as mentors through a state-supported program. We also formed a Mentor Committee to provide leadership and direction for the program. The training was valuable and gave experienced teachers effective tools and strategies for working with new faculty members. However, because there was an insufficient number of trained mentors, and principals preferred to maintain the one-on-one system of mentoring, it created two classes of mentors in the system: informal and formal mentors. This limited the productivity of our mentoring program and raised questions about who should be permitted to mentor. Did training qualify *anyone* to be a mentor? What if a mentor was not effective? What were the appropriate roles for the principal and the Mentor Committee in the selection process? The issues of who assigns the mentor, what that assignment entails, and what level of stipend a mentor receives became matters for contract negotiations but remained unresolved even at the conclusion of those negotiations.

Eventually, through a series of discussions with the Mentor Committee, union leaders, and the administrative team, we were able to reformulate the mentoring program. The primary focus is now on supporting new teachers through peer-coaching relationships, with opportunities not only for the mentor and new teacher to visit each other's classrooms, but also for released time to discuss their observations. In addition, we provide monthly meetings for mentors and for new teachers so that they can share their experiences. Although this is more intensive than our previous model, it has added a greater level of depth and professional growth for both the mentors and the new teachers.

We were also able to clarify the mentor selection process. In the spring, faculty members interested in mentoring submit their names to one of our curriculum directors, who serves as the mentor coordinator. As we move through the hiring process, principals can draw mentors from this list, but they can also identify other faculty members whom they feel would best support the new teachers. The principals make the final selection. Those mentors who are selected then attend a two-day training session and begin the year-long process of coaching and supporting the new teacher. They also serve on the Mentor Committee with other interested faculty members to continue to refine the program. This system ensured a greater level of compatibility between mentor and new teacher, eliminated the issue of having both an informal and a formal mentoring system, and eased the tensions that had emerged in the initial development of the program.

In addition to mentoring, we provide a range of other supports that have been highly effective. One of the most fruitful has been in-class assistance by curriculum directors and staff developers. As indicated previously, we have broken with the more traditional curriculum supervision structure. We have established four full-time, nonteaching positions for curriculum directors in the four core subject areas, all of which combine disciplines. One of the primary responsibilities of these individuals is to spend time with new teachers, coaching them, modeling lessons, and meeting with them to discuss curricular and classroom management issues. These individuals are in the schools and available when an issue emerges and a teacher needs support. This structure for new teachers continues well beyond the first year of teaching and has worked well to support the development of new teachers.

In addition, we believe that there is a great deal of value for both new and more senior teachers in meeting together to plan, discuss student performance, and exchange ideas. For this reason, we have structured our elementary specialists' schedules so that teachers at each grade level in each elementary school can have forty minutes of common preparation time on a regular basis. Where we have teachers partnering in multiage classrooms, we have scheduled common preparation time so that they can meet for forty minutes on a regular basis as well. At the middle and early high school level, grades 6 to 9, we have created teams of four subject-area teachers who have both common preparation time every day and common planning time almost every day. We are currently restructuring our grade 10 to 12 program and dividing the high school into four thematic clusters of 150 students each with approximately twelve to fourteen faculty members assigned to each cluster. Again, we will try to provide common preparation time for as many of these teachers as possible. We have found that this structure can provide important assistance to new teachers, as it gives them opportunities for support from other colleagues and can build a strong sense of community among teachers.

Finally, we provide teachers with a range of professional development opportunities. New teachers are offered a variety of courses, institutes, and workshops through the department of education, private consultants, state college and university partnerships, and partnerships with other districts that have geographic proximity to Hudson. Two of our curriculum directors provide leadership for monthly meetings with new teachers, covering such topics as administrative procedures, classroom management, differentiating instruction, and special education. We have worked hard to provide extensive professional development opportunities for all staff and encourage new faculty members to participate in courses and workshops that are appropriate to them. Some of this professional development occurs during the school day, and teachers are released to participate. For example, we have a K–8 math and science initiative to enrich our inquiry-based approach in both areas and to build linkages between the two subjects. All teachers are released by grade level three times a year to work with colleagues on developing stronger content knowledge and on examining student work to better understand where we are successful and where students are misunderstanding the material. These sessions enable new teachers to work closely with more senior teachers in a highly professional and engaging dialogue about instructional practice and understanding student work.

The combination of orientation, mentoring, in-class support, common preparation time, and focused professional development have created an effective induction program for new teachers.

THE LONG TERM

Each year, the eighteen members of the Hudson district's administrative team—principals, assistant principals, curriculum directors, and central office administrators—meet in a weeklong summer strategic planning meeting. Several years ago the administrative team focused on the question, "How do we support and challenge the faculty members who have been with us for three to six years so that they sustain their excitement, continue to feel that they are growing, and want to make a long-term commitment to Hudson?" We chose this focus because we believed that sustaining commitment over the long term required a different approach than the one we had taken in our induction program. Our success with induction set a positive beginning, but we needed to ensure that we would meet the needs of many teachers who were now at this second stage of development.

Our discussion focused on four areas we believed were critical to a teacher's long-term interest and professional growth. These included providing new teachers with sufficient resources to perform well, supporting their professional and personal growth, providing opportunities for them to participate in district decision making, and ensuring that school culture was collaborative and collegial. The administrative team identified a number of ways that we currently provide support in these four areas and additional ways we could improve our work in each.

Sufficient Resources

The first area we identified was having sufficient resources to perform well in one's work. Teachers in this stage of growth want to have resources at hand to enable them to enhance their instructional capabilities. These resources include computer technology, library collections, materials to differentiate instruction, and high-quality texts and instructional materials. However, having sufficient resources entails other needs as well. Teachers at this stage appreciate having curricular consistency so that they can confer with colleagues and build upon a solid curricular base. They continue to be interested in classroom support from expert teachers, in-class support from staff developers, special education assistance in integrating students with special needs, and general curricular support and advice, although now they use these resource people to explore more advanced instructional terrain. In essence, teachers at this stage may be less focused on the basic need of managing the classroom and becoming good teachers and more focused on the larger coordination of curriculum and services that can advance and refine their professional practice.

This is not to say that all teachers will move from poorer districts to wealthier ones if they become frustrated with the lack of resources and support for their work. In fact, some teachers continue to work in the most adverse, high-poverty situations out of a deep commitment to their values and a desire to make a difference with children who most need quality instruction. There are many in our inner cities who carry the torch of equity every day into the classroom. However, for others, the lack of resources and support leaves them feeling less effective professionally, and they seek opportunities to advance their craft in schools where these resources exist. This is one of the most important reasons that equity in school funding is such a critical issue. Teachers in all environments require and deserve the resources necessary to be professionally effective.

Although Hudson is not a financially well-off district, we have been careful to address teachers' needs for quality resources. The administrative team felt that we also needed to provide better support in addressing the needs of teachers of behavior-challenged students. We felt that we could strengthen our support through quick administrative response to problem situations, equitable class placements, adequate preparation for teachers who have problem students placed in their classes, and alternative programs in which to place students if other avenues failed.

Professional and Personal Growth and Fulfillment

The second area of need at this stage of development that our administrative team identified was professional and personal growth and fulfillment. Teachers with three to six years of experience have developed some stability and confidence as classroom teachers. Many want to explore refinements that advance their classroom practice and take advantage of professional leadership opportunities. They are no longer as satisfied with the simple "make and take" kinds of professional development workshops in which they simply look for new ideas to enliven their classrooms. Rather, many are interested in a deeper level of dialogue—one that is reflective and analytical—among colleagues. Others, however, do not have experience with or mental models for this kind of professional development. Resolving the tensions surrounding these different expectations is part of our ongoing work in crafting professionally sustaining work with teachers. As a result of the number of teachers at this stage of development in Hudson, we shifted our professional development program from a focus on implementation of new methods and materials to reflective dialogue among peers about their practice and about student work. This type of professional development involves the use of classroom videos, case studies, action research, and studies of student work to encourage reflective practice and collegial dialogue about teaching.

One of the best examples of this type of professional development was the involvement of five middle school and high school English teachers in a two-year seminar examining their own process of development as writers and applying what they were learning about themselves to the teaching of writing. The team from Hudson also had the opportunity to work with teams from other districts and interact with university professors who taught writing. All five teachers found the experience to be a powerful influence on their attitudes about writing and their skill in teaching it. These teachers came back to the district and led a series of seminars for other English teachers that deepened the proficiency of the entire department.

At this stage of development, teachers are also beginning to look for leadership roles. Offering workshops for other teachers, presenting at state and national conferences, being recognized by the district for leadership roles, and having the opportunity to visit other schools to review programs and teaching methods are all positive ways to support this desire to express oneself professionally beyond the classroom. One way we have tried to address this need is through our elementary math and science initiative. As part of a five-year, grades K–8, National Science Foundation-supported Local Systemic Change initiative in both math and science, we have created opportunities for teachers to become grade-level teacher–leaders. There are at least two teacher–leaders at each grade, which provides ample opportunity for new teachers to participate, advance their own practice, and support other teachers through consultation and workshop leadership. Our work in this area has highlighted the power and challenge of overcoming the prevailing closed-door culture of schools and moving toward more open peer support and critical-friends dialogue.

Another example has been our work with Responsive Classroom at the elementary level. Most of our elementary teachers have voluntarily attended training in Responsive Classroom. The program has been received so enthusiastically by our faculty that this is becoming a consistent social–emotional development program across all elementary schools. To develop an internal training and support capability, we asked if any teachers would be interested in becoming our internal Responsive Classroom-certified trainers. Interestingly, the two individuals who volunteered were in the range of four to six years of experience. Enabling them to take this kind of leadership role has solidified their commitment to Hudson and is providing them with a powerful and enriching learning experience.

Yet another way we have involved teachers at this stage of development in professional growth is through participation in innovative grant projects and pilots of new methods and materials. There are few professional development opportunities as good as getting involved in original research. Several years ago, when the federal government was offering technology challenge grants to states and districts, Hudson applied for and won two large grants. One was to create a Virtual High School (VHS) on the Internet in collaboration with other high schools across the country. The two teachers who volunteered to try teaching one course each in the Virtual High School had been with us a short time. Not only did they learn something new for themselves, but they became, in essence, educational pioneers. These two teachers have continued to teach one course for VHS as part of their daily schedule and are still excited about what they are learning through this ongoing experiment and about what they have contributed to others in the field. VHS is now a private, nonprofit collaboration of high schools supporting each other in offering courses that could never be provided within a single school. One of the most notable results of the pioneering efforts of the many teachers involved in VHS has been the excitement of launching into a new area and producing a successful virtual learning environment. It has sustained many new teachers through a critical period in which they decide whether or not to continue in the field of education. It has also given a renewed sense of excitement to many veteran teachers.

The other grant involved providing a group of teachers in grades 4 through 6 with laptops and scientific equipment and helping them engage students in real field science. Although this project was less successful than our Virtual High School effort, it was a profound learning experience for teachers. Not only did they advance their skills in the use of technology and their knowledge of field research, but they were able to be part of testing and refining an innovation never tried in a school setting and to share the results of their pilot effort with others. Both this grant project and the Virtual High School were collaborative efforts that enabled our teachers to work closely with researchers, consultants, and university faculty. In many cases, these relationships proved to be rich learning opportunities for our teachers.

Our curriculum directors continue to look for opportunities in which teachers are partnered with researchers in such educational research and development organizations as the Concord Consortium, the Lawrence Hall of Science, the Education Development Corporation, TERC, Earthwatch Institute, and others. They continue to write grants that allow teachers to test the cutting edge of innovation. Not all of our innovative projects are successful, but they establish an ethos of experimentation and risk taking that helps new teachers feel safe in their professional exploration. The excitement we have been able to generate among faculty members and the professional development opportunities we have been able to provide have sustained and nurtured new teachers. We believe that these types of engagement have helped our teachers choose to continue in the field of teaching through the excitement they experience in exploring new terrain and the opportunities they have to be part of projects that advance the quality of education we offer children.

Another aspect of encouraging professional growth at this stage involved a shift in our teacher evaluation process. We have moved from evaluation as an accountability tool to one focused on the continuous professional growth of the faculty. Although we still retain the option to pursue a comprehensive evaluation or to place a teacher on an intensive support plan that requires that he or she address deficiencies in his or her practice, the vast majority of our teachers move to a professional growth model of evaluation at the fourth year in the district. This professional growth model of supervision and evaluation relies on teachers' self-assessing their professional skills; setting realistic and meaningful goals for professional growth; identifying and implementing strategies for achieving that growth; having multiple options for pursuing, documenting, and reporting on professional growth; and maintaining ongoing dialogue with their supervising administrators about their growth. We believe that this strategy respects teachers' professional judgment and provides them with the ongoing support and encouragement to reach higher.

After three years in the district, a teacher is able to move to this different model of evaluation. Instead of the standard administrator-led comprehensive evaluation, teachers develop professional growth plans that focus their improvement efforts for the year. Although goal setting is part of the evaluation process during the first three years, during the fourth year the increasingly experienced teacher enters a six-year professional growth cycle with the standard evaluation representing only one of the six years.

Each year, the teacher develops a set of goals and a plan for achieving these goals. He or she meets with an administrator to review and refine the goals and professional growth plan. In years 2, 4, and 6 of the six-year cycle, the new teacher pursues his or her plan, communicates with the supervising administrator about the progress being made, and writes up a report on what was achieved. This report is discussed with the supervising administrator at the end of the year, and new goals are set for the following year.

In years 3 and 5 of the cycle, teachers have a variety of options for pursuing and documenting growth. These options provide flexibility and allow for teacher creativity. As Figure 6.3 shows, teachers can develop their own individual growth plans and document their growth in a variety of ways. Alternatively, they can work together, observing, coaching, and supporting each other's teaching. Or they can work collaboratively

Figure 6.3.

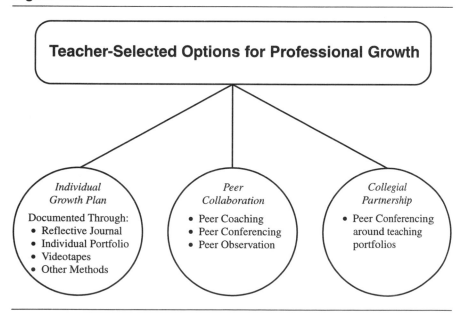

with a group of teachers to develop and share teaching portfolios. Whatever the option, the goal is for teachers to have the opportunity to reflect on their practice, set goals for growth, and pursue those goals in consultation with their supervising administrators.

This model of evaluation has been far more productive in promoting professional growth than our previous system. However, it is also more time consuming on the part of administrators. As an administrative team, we still struggle to find adequate time to spend with each teacher so that the system fully realizes the goal of professional growth. Each year, as we have revisited evaluation, we have identified a need for additional administrative staff to reduce our supervisor–teacher ratio so that we could provide better support and feedback to teachers.

Underlying our professional development, leadership opportunities, innovative projects, and evaluation system is a belief that engaging teachers in professional dialogue and reflection with colleagues, researchers, and university faculty will not only advance their practice, but also create a positive learning environment that will nurture their growth and development and sustain their interest in teaching over the long term.

Teacher Voice and Participation

The third critical area identified by the administrative team for teachers in the fourth through sixth years is teacher voice and participation. Teachers at this stage have developed sufficient expertise to participate in discussions that provide direction for the school, the curriculum, and the district. Therefore, they need to be able to participate in forums on school and curricular issues. They also need to be able to serve on committees or task forces that take active roles in moving the district forward. Because there is a tendency for teachers with only a few years' experience to defer to more senior faculty members, it is important to provide encouragement for them to join committees and then to support their entry into the dialogue through effective facilitation.

For example, we have convened literacy teams at each elementary school and actively encouraged teachers at this stage of development to join these teams. We also make sure that these teachers know that they are welcome on school councils and on all the district committees. In fact, we are very careful to ensure a balance of newer and more senior teachers on decision-making committees so that newer teachers gain experience in taking an active leadership role in the district.

Another example of increasing teachers' voice and participation has been the development of the cluster model of organization at the high school. During the three years that it took to produce this model, numerous in-service days were devoted to consideration of such issues as whether to have heterogeneous or thematic clusters and what model of student governance would enable us to build a strong sense of community and involve all students in decision making about school issues. A committee of teachers worked to steer the process, and the dialogue involved both newer and more senior faculty members.

Collaborative, Collegial Culture

All of the previous areas culminate in the final and most critical need we identified to support teachers at this second stage of development: having a collaborative, collegial culture in the school that facilitates teacher interaction and growth. The sense of connection to other teachers and administrators and the depth of conversation about teaching itself are powerful forces in helping teachers improve their work and enjoy their jobs. Karen Seashore Louis and Sharon D. Kruse found that schools that performed well had strong professional cultures characterized by reflective dialogue, collaboration, shared norms and values, the deprivatization of practice, and a collective focus on student learning.[1] Developing a professional culture requires leadership on the part of the principal and curriculum directors. They need to become facilitators and community builders as well as instructional leaders and managers. This collaborative, collegial culture is supported by professional development opportunities and an evaluation system focused on dialogue and reflection about practice. Providing common preparation or planning time for teachers to communicate is essential, but equally essential is the way that communication is facilitated.

Consciously developing a culture that supports the open exchange of ideas and honest reflection on practice requires that we think carefully about all the elements that influence the culture of a school. For example, the way a principal runs faculty meetings makes a profound statement about the culture of the school. Are serious issues discussed? Do all teachers get a chance to participate? Most often, faculty meetings are procedural updates on administrative matters. As a result of the administrative team discussion about how school culture can sustain and strengthen new teachers, we have redesigned faculty meetings. We deal with administrative matters in memos to the faculty and focus the meetings on professional practice in a particular area or on an issue of concern to the faculty. The teachers' association contract allows only one hour for these meetings, so we often frame an essential question for the meeting, break the faculty into small groups for dialogue, and bring back the ideas of these small groups to the entire faculty. We are also applying the concept of promoting dialogue and reflection to all our meetings with teachers: professional development workshops, in-service days, curriculum coordination meetings, teacher leader meetings, and teacher–administrator meetings dealing with evaluation.

In addition, we are in the process of developing the capability to use technology to further the dialogue among teachers. All teachers have e-mail and access to the Internet. We have enhanced the capabilities of our system by establishing listservs and dialogue groups for each grade, subject area, committee, and task force so that the conversation does not have to stop when the meeting time runs out. We will be establishing facilitated on-line discussion groups about various issues as well as on-line professional development programs. We are also creating individual virtual work spaces for teachers through a state initiative called Virtual Education Space that will significantly enhance the technology tools that teachers can access and the ease with which teachers can exchange information and ideas. We believe that over time our virtual communication will complement our face-to-face communication and support our work on dialogue and reflection.

Finally, developing a collaborative, collegial culture requires a common appreciation for and understanding of the mission and vision of the district. This brings us full circle back to where this chapter began. As mission and vision are key to recruitment, they are key to sustaining teachers over the long term. Too often, districts have a focus of the year. One year it is differentiating instruction. The next it is multicultural education. The next it is something else. Although all are viable initiatives, change does not take place in a year or even two. Our mission, vision, and goals must be long term so that teachers can go deeply into gaining proficiency in an area. Teachers, particularly new teachers, need to feel that the district is focused on a meaningful goal and that this goal is shared by all. This creates a sense of cohesiveness and coherence that will help sustain new teachers.

As an administrative team, we continue to look for better ways to support our newer teachers. We believe that the efforts we have made to provide new teachers with sufficient resources, support their professional and personal growth, provide opportunities for them to participate in district decision making, and ensure that the school culture is one that is collaborative and collegial have been effective in sustaining and nurturing teachers with three to six years of experience. Teacher development moves through other stages as one gains more experience. However, the effort made during these formative years will set in place basic attitudes about the profession and one's capabilities that are critical for a teacher's long-term commitment to teaching.

CONCLUSION

In Hudson, we have used our mission, vision, and guiding principles to provide a frame of reference for all that we do. We believe that teaching is a profoundly important profession that is making a difference for children and for our society and world. We try to embody this belief in our recruitment and induction efforts and to inspire new teachers with the sense that they, too, make a difference. We believe that school culture must reflect this vision and mission and create an atmosphere where teachers feel safe to take risks and grow. We have tried hard to provide the resources, professional growth experiences, and engagement in decision making that enable teachers to develop skill and confidence in their work and in the goals of the district.

None of this is easy. The traditional private universe of teaching is one that is hard to overcome. Developing a collaborative culture, changing the nature of meetings, putting in place new evaluation systems, redefining professional development, and creating innovative initiatives for teachers to participate in takes time and consistent leadership. In spite of the eleven years over which I have provided this consistent leadership for Hudson, we are still a work in progress with many areas that could be further enhanced. We believe that our induction strategies and our efforts to meet the needs of teachers in their second stage of development have sustained teachers through the tests and trials of their early years in teaching. However, there is much more that can be done, and I hope that this chapter serves as one element of the conversation within the field about strengthening and sustaining new teachers so that we can all learn from each other.

NOTE

1. Karen Seashore Louis and Sharon D. Kruse, *Professionalism and Community: Perspectives on Reforming Urban Schools* (Thousand Oaks, Calif.: Corwin, 1995).

CHAPTER 7

The Union Role in Teachers' Careers

THOMAS GILLETT AND
ADAM URBANSKI

Union leaders have long recognized the importance of aligning unionization with the public good. The opportunity in teacher unions is quite clear. The public good is served by drawing attention to union actions that strengthen teachers' roles in improving student learning—strengthening preparation programs, providing support during the early years, sustaining professional development environments, and more. These activities in turn nurture both the teachers' self-perceptions and the public's image of teaching as a profession. Gillett and Urbanski nicely phrase the first half of this desired outcome as follows: "It is now possible for teachers to expect unionism and professionalism to be mutually supportive rather than mutually exclusive."

The candor of the authors, both union leaders, in addressing the difficulties in moving from rhetoric to reality is refreshing. And the work of the Teacher Union Reform Network (TURN) representing both the NEA and the AFT is seeking to effect what the rhetoric proclaims is encouraging. In turning attention to close collaboration with other major stakeholders in the career line of teachers, unions inescapably share accountability for school improvement. This will not quickly change the convenient villain label to one of advocacy, but it does challenge the accuser to be specific.

Chapter 3 illustrated that it is difficult to change longstanding perceptions and relationships. But it also illustrated the power of stakeholders coming together to address a theme, too long neglected, on which all deliberate change in schooling depends: namely, the quality of the teaching force. Unions have had a long but little-known history of providing supporting environments for workers—often the only source of sustained congeniality in drab circumstances, going far beyond the conventional perception of addressing only bread-and-butter issues. Novels centered on teachers of past eras and studies of teaching in the present reveal frequent circumstances of isolation and loneliness. Some of these arise out of deep structures of schooling that continue to defy change. An enlightened union role and work such as that represented by TURN add power to the necessary renewal.

Critics of teacher unions have done a rather effective job of pointing to them as the primary obstacle to school improvement. State and federal policymakers have been strong proponents of this view. But recent years have seen politically driven uniformity invade the entire system of public schooling. As a result, policies and practices tradi-

tionally within the purview of local districts have been squeezed out. As Richard Wisniewski insightfully points out in the concluding sentence of Chapter 9, "The harder we work to improve the system now in place, the more we guarantee that the system will remain essentially the same." Inadvertently, excessive state and federal intervention in the practices of local schools may have provided the necessary stimulus for unprecedented collaboration of a long-divided educational establishment on overdue fundamental change.

—The editors

The broad public perception of teachers and their unions continues to be shaped by critics like Myron Lieberman, who voices popular attitudes toward the American Federation of Teachers (AFT) and the National Education Association (NEA): "The unions are an obstacle to reform; the task is to persuade them to change their anti-reform policies. The unions are an obstacle to reform because their obstruction is inherent in the nature of public sector unionization; the task is to weaken their power to block reforms."[1] Many current union leaders would just as strongly argue precisely the opposite: that the best chance for deep, systemic educational reform is through the unions by means of collective bargaining.

In local school districts and in individual schools, most parents—and teachers, to a considerable extent—are unaware and unconcerned that the national unions serve as a collective whipping boy for critics of a public school system that fails so many children. Although individual schools, school calendars and schedules, course offerings and curricula, and almost every other aspect of American public schooling have remained remarkably constant over the last fifty years, teacher unions are in the midst of major changes in focus and strategy. Teacher unions arose through one of the most successful organizing campaigns in history. In just a few decades, teachers went from being "spoken for" by administrators to representing their own economic interests.[2] The current struggle is being defined in the next stage of organizing, which brings teachers representation as educators and professionals.

THE NEED TO CHANGE

The commission reports of the 1980s (*Teachers for Tomorrow, A Nation Prepared,* and the like) set the stage for reform in unions as much as in schools. The 1996 report, *What Matters Most: Teaching for America's Future,* further articulated the professional interests of teachers and their unions.[3] A number of factors have enabled teacher unions to redefine themselves.

The standards movement, new forms of student assessment tied to more rigorous learning standards, general improvement in teacher salaries, the availability of national certification for teachers, attention by policymakers to teacher recruitment and retention, and an acknowledgment of a potential teacher shortage, among other influences, have brought attention to the direct relationship between teacher quality and improved student learning. It is now possible for teachers to expect unionism and professionalism to be mutually supportive rather than mutually exclusive.

In *The Changing Idea of a Teachers' Union,* Charles Kerchner and Douglas Mitchell accurately forecast the current labor–management détente and the emphasis of more and more unions on teacher quality and related professional issues: "Labor relations will need to recognize that teachers must be involved in conceptualizing and planning their work as well as in building a system for assuring fair and equitable supervision of their performance."[4] Kerchner and Mitchell underscore the need for "professional unionism" to move union leaders away from the industrial bureaucracy and the "old" union model lodged within. "Rethinking unionism," they argue, "is a requirement for reworking teaching"[5]—and, we would add, for reforming schools.

The Teacher Union Reform Network (TURN), composed of about two dozen AFT and NEA locals across the country,[6] is a prime example of this new brand of unionism. TURN began with the premise that teacher unions in America must be reformed. Founding members believe this can best happen if teacher unionists themselves recognize not only the need for change, but also that it is in the interest of their unions to welcome the next logical stage in their unions' evolution. Certainly, forces and threats from the outside can play a role. In fact, much hinges on the capacity of teacher union leaders to understand the changing environment and to interpret it for their members. Such a proactive mode may ensure that changes are not merely a begrudging accommodation but rather a purposeful fulfillment of a union's vision for the organization and its members. In a February 2000 *Education Week* article about TURN, Ann Bradley noted, "Bashing teachers' unions never goes out of style in education."[7] In TURN, however, it is voices from *within* the teacher union movement that are calling for reform.

Unions are more likely to change if the unionists themselves are *agents* of reform. If they are not, they will remain *targets* of reform. A persuasive case for teacher union reform can be made only in a manner that is sensitive to the experience and culture of unions. This, after all, is not a matter of abandoning what teacher unions are; instead, it is a matter of building on the foundation that has been laid.

The industrial union model that emerged from years of struggling for parity with management was a good match for the industrial-style school organization. It mirrored the institution in which the teacher unions existed, and the effectiveness of this approach brought it both legitimacy and loyalty. Indeed, industrial unionism served teachers well. It helped them to achieve middle-class status and to launch college- and university-fueled professional careers for their children. It also improved the terms and conditions under which teachers worked and, in many instances, democratized the workplace.

Recognizing all of this as an important foundation for building the next stage of teacher unionism is indispensable. Whatever is to become part of the "new unionism" must be built on the essential commitments of what teacher unions have always stood for and must always retain: a commitment to democratic dynamics, fairness, and due process; to self-determination; to unity without unanimity; to social justice; and to valuing the dignity of all work and workers.

There is no reason to believe that reforming unions will prove any less difficult than renewing schools and education. Nonetheless, teacher unions must change in tandem with the changes that are so obviously needed in schools and in education in general. Reinventing both is necessary for maintaining public support and confidence in the institution of public education.

Just like schools, most of today's unions have changed little from yesterday's. They still expend most of their energy and resources on defending a very small minority of troubled members, they still define their mission narrowly as pertaining only to bread-and-butter issues, and they still confine themselves to reacting to management's actions and provocations.

Change is inevitable, and although it is possible to change without improving, it is not possible to improve without changing. So it is futile to agonize over whether or not to change. The only choice for unions is whether the changes will be the kind that truly improve our institutions and increase the chances that more students will learn. The strong unions that have been built, therefore, must now help deliver a more genuine profession for teachers and more effective schools for all students.

This will not be easy. Even in states that allow teachers to bargain collectively, many professional issues are either outside the scope of collective bargaining or, at best, are "permissive" items of bargaining. Thus, the collective voice of teachers is often muzzled on the very matters that can best ensure improvements in education and engender confidence in schools. Professionals in higher education have achieved the right to negotiate professional issues and thus to maintain their professional status. Unfortunately, that right has been denied to elementary and secondary school educators.

In essence, teachers have a so-called profession, but the nominal professionals have little or no voice in professional matters. Precisely because there is a connection between what teachers *do* collectively and what they *are* professionally, the scope of collective bargaining must be expanded to permit negotiations on professional, pedagogical, and instructional issues.

As it happens, this is a good fit with what new teachers now expect from their unions: to invest no less in meeting their professional needs—including access to new knowledge; professional development; opportunities to plan, design, and implement new programs; and opportunities for continuous learning—than in the traditional union priorities such as contract negotiations, grievance processing, health, and other benefits.

But teacher unions have additional reasons to seek union reform and school reform: to help diminish the isolation among teachers, thereby improving collaboration, communication, debate, and learning about reform; to encourage initiatives from teachers and their unions that take the lead in reform and promote the kinds of initiatives that make sense to practitioners in education; to help ensure that reform goes beyond rhetoric; to increase prospects and pathways for translating good ideas into practical local realities; and to create, articulate, and actualize their own vision for unions, the profession, and their schools.

ENVISIONING THE POSSIBLE

What might be the vision that teachers and teacher unionists wish for themselves in the future? Here is a glimpse of what might be possible only a few years hence:

- Instead of two major teacher unions, there is one merged organization that acts not only as an advocate for all of America's educators but also as a lobby for all of their students.
- Union members, like guild members hundreds of years ago, share responsibility for the induction of other teachers; every new teacher has a mentor to guide his or her entry into the profession. Teachers not only serve as gatekeepers to the profession, but also ensure that members maintain high standards of practice throughout their careers.
- Features of industrial unionism have yielded to changes that offer the promise of making public education more effective. The scope of collective bargaining has been extended to include negotiations on professional issues in addition to wages, benefits, and working conditions.
- The union promotes such practices and dynamics as peer review, differentiated staffing and pay, public school choice, professional accountability, the transfer of teachers based on cri-

teria other than seniority alone, and the involvement of parents, students, and peers in teacher evaluations.

- The union not only considers itself the voice of teachers, but it also sees itself as *giving* voice to teachers. It spends as much energy and resources on the professional needs of its members as it does on collective bargaining, contract enforcement, economic benefits, and other basic traditional union functions.
- Recognizing that the welfare of the union and its members hinges on the effectiveness of the profession, the teachers union has formalized its commitment to reform.
- This new teachers union considers unionism and professionalism as complementary and not mutually exclusive. It views the negotiated contract as the floor and not the ceiling for what union members are willing to do for students, and it acts as the guardian of professional and educational standards.

BUILDING ON PAST ACCOMPLISHMENTS

Any vision is only a pipe dream unless it is created twice: first in the mind and then in the real world. But whatever unionists can envision, they can also achieve. In Rochester, New York, for example, members of the teachers union learned over the last decade and a half that the more they promote educational reforms and professionalism, the stronger and more credible the union becomes. The stronger the union grows, the more it is able to promote the needed changes in education. Through collaboration and a willingness to rethink traditional postures, the union achieved a substantial number of changes; namely, it:

- Altered the traditional teacher evaluation process by developing the Performance Assessment Review for Teachers (PART), a portfolio-based system that includes peer evaluation and parallels the principles and criteria of the National Board for Professional Teaching Standards
- Negotiated a school-based planning process that involves teachers, parents, high school students, and school administrators in making decisions about each school's instructional program
- Negotiated a "professional day" provision that eliminates the teachers' dismissal time so that the teachers' workday ends when their professional responsibilities (as determined by the teachers) are completed
- Introduced aspects of pay for knowledge, skills, and additional service into the teacher compensation system

- Negotiated an annual Classroom Resource Fund to support effective school practices and to invest in what works for student learning
- Created and published a pedagogical journal that features articles by teachers and paraprofessionals themselves
- Supported public school choice as a way to empower parents and students while providing additional incentives to schools
- Negotiated the Career in Teaching program, which includes differentiated staffing and differentiated pay
- Developed "lead teacher" positions for accomplished teachers who assume additional responsibilities and roles in exchange for additional pay and different job descriptions
- Negotiated a formal role for teachers in the annual evaluation of their supervisors and other administrators
- Negotiated a role for parents in the teacher evaluation process
- Designed and negotiated an internship program for new teachers and a peer intervention plan for tenured teachers who are experiencing difficulty with their classroom teaching
- Adjusted teacher seniority provisions for teacher assignments and transfers
- Initiated and continues to support a hot line for students to help them with homework and school-related matters

By placing a premium on what teachers stand *for*, not just focusing on what they are *against*, unionists begin to bridge the gap between unionism and professionalism. And although this has been a rocky and scenic route, TURN members and others remain determined to continue on this path in collaboration with school management.

The Rochester Teachers Association's commitment to union and school reform is not unique. In fact, the new leaders of both the National Education Association (NEA) and the American Federation of Teachers (AFT) champion the very same impulses and directions. Former NEA president Bob Chase's outspoken support of peer review and AFT president Sandra Feldman's position on not tolerating low-performing schools are examples of this. And there are local teacher unions within the AFT (in Toledo, Cincinnati, etc.) and the NEA (in Columbus, Seattle, etc.) that have been pursuing similar goals and implementing similar changes.

THE TEACHER UNION REFORM NETWORK

Founded in July 1995, the Teacher Union Reform Network began with the express purpose of redesigning teacher unions so that they could become more effective partners in the effort to improve education in America's public schools. Supported by an initial grant from The Pew Charitable Trusts, and in collaboration with UCLA's Graduate School of Education and Information Studies, TURN works toward fulfilling the promise of the following statements of principles:

- Teacher unions must provide leadership for the collective voice of their members.
- Teacher unions have a responsibility to students, their families, and the broader society.
- Teacher unions are committed to public education as a vital element of American democracy.

What unites these responsibilities is the commitment to help all children learn.

TURN affirms the unions' responsibility to collaborate with other stakeholders in public education to:

- Improve continuously the quality of the teaching force
- See consistently higher levels of student achievement
- Promote in public education and in the union democratic dynamics, fairness, and due process for all
- Improve on an ongoing basis the terms and conditions under which both adults and children work and learn

Including teacher unions as partners in transforming public education is essential to achieving the ultimate goal of improving student learning. Progressive union leaders have begun to recognize that fundamental cultural change in their own organizations is a precondition to broader reforms that will culminate in better education for students. As industrial trade unions have recently begun to discover, rapid and unpredictable changes in the social and economic environment now demand the rethinking of the roles and structures of unions. AFT and NEA locals participating in TURN embrace this conclusion and seek ways to recreate themselves to meet the needs of this new environment.

TURN's goal is to explore, develop, and demonstrate workable models of restructuring that enable teacher unions to meet the needs of members and to become agents of school and educational reform. That restructuring will ultimately improve student learning. To develop the desired models, TURN relies on lessons drawn from research, internal initiatives, and the experience of industrial trade unions that have begun to transform themselves. Critical to the process of creating high-performing

unions is developing a network of reformers to share ideas, create mutual systems of support, and participate in the evaluation of progress to
build organizations committed to taking on broadened responsibility for
educational quality. Because teachers are closest to students and to the
learning process, they are in a unique position to play a powerful role in
stimulating the necessary changes.

TURN has already delved into specific work in three initial projects:

- In conjunction with the National Commission on Teaching and
  America's Future, TURN locals pursue the goal of ensuring
  teacher and school quality.
- In partnership with Brown University's Center for Leadership
  and Professional Development, TURN participants explore how
  teacher unions can become facilitators of professional development for their members.
- In collaboration with Allan Odden and the University of
  Wisconsin's Consortium for Policy Research in Education,
  TURN locals seek to develop alternatives to the current prevailing teacher compensation model.

EFFECTIVE STRATEGIES FOR UNION-DRIVEN REFORM

In his last speech to the AFT Convention in 1996, the late AFT president
Albert Shanker reminded the assembled teacher unionists that "It is no
less the responsibility of a teachers union to preserve public education
than to negotiate good contracts." To achieve this, teacher unions will
have to change their traditional orientation. They will have to seek not
only the job-related interests of their members but also the success of education writ large. They will have to recognize that teachers will do well
financially only if their students do well academically. Thus, school productivity must become central to the mission of teacher unions.

Collaborating with Colleges and
Universities to Prepare New Teachers

State and local unions have paid increasing attention to the concerns
and needs of new members in the last several years because so many baby
boomer-generation teachers have retired and the ranks are refilling. In
districts with mentor teacher arrangements that support the induction of
new teachers, the data show that programs preparing teachers, by and
large, do an inadequate job of preparing teachers for the classroom.

Data from the Rochester Mentor Teacher–Intern Program (MTIP) have been consistent over the sixteen years of the MTIP's existence in that district. As part of a comprehensive survey of first-year teachers (interns) administered each year, new teachers are asked a series of questions on how well they thought their college experiences prepared them for their teaching careers. Although more than 80% thought that their college experiences had adequately prepared them to handle teaching in their *content* areas, only 59% felt that their college experiences had adequately prepared them to establish an effective classroom management system, and just 42% of the new hires felt adequately prepared to address the diverse needs of urban youths.[8]

Colleges and universities have developed cooperative programs with local school districts in many cities, primarily to ensure that their own students have access to a variety of student teaching placements and preservice experiences. But collaborative arrangements involving teacher unions are rare, despite the unions' sharing with institutions of higher education and school districts an interest in quality teacher preparation. This shared interest might point logically to increased partnership work in the future, particularly since all three parties endorse the concept of a continuum of teaching that begins long before the first solo class is taught. Colleges improve teacher preparation by providing more and better practice teaching experiences for their students; districts enhance their recruitment and hiring efforts by investing in potential teaching candidates before they enter the applicant pool; and unions participate in renewing the profession by providing both the best training for "apprentice" teachers and professional growth opportunities for the experienced practitioners who guide prospective teachers.

Districts, unions, and colleges would do well to start by systematically asking beginning teachers—both student teachers and first-year practitioners—about their backgrounds and experiences, and then adjusting policies and programs based on these data. Alternative teacher certification programs should also be collaboratively developed and informed by data derived from participants as well as from college and district staff members and practitioners who support new teachers.

Establishing a Mentor Teacher Program

Properly designed and implemented, a quality mentor teacher program (MTP) probably surpasses anything else for guiding the induction of a new teacher. A brief list of the elements necessary to a "properly designed and implemented" mentor program would include *time, expertise,* and *support.* A high-quality program requires *time* for interaction between mentor and intern, for appropriate activities, for learning about teaching during the school day as opposed to after it, and for reflection on what the professional standards are and how they can best be met. It requires *expertise* on the part of the mentor: knowledge of teaching and learning matched to the intern's specific discipline, familiarity with available resources, and the ability to navigate political turbulence. It also requires *support* from other parts of the system: administrators, colleagues, community agencies, and other resources. An excellent MTP would be established by the district and the union, and both the district and the union would be committed to it as a way to ensure having the highest caliber teachers in the district and the profession.

The partners in the effort to strengthen and support teachers need to be mindful of traditional impediments to quality teacher inductions and take active steps to remove them. Beginning teachers are given difficult teaching assignments in most districts because union contracts and past practice permit more senior teachers to avoid these "undesirable" classes. Across the country, new teachers are more likely to receive dramatically different assignments from year to year—for example, teaching kindergarten one year and sixth grade the next. These practices do not lead to optimal situations for students, and they are inconsistent with the way other professions support new members. Solutions are within reach. In Rochester, the union and the district have negotiated contract language that requires split-grade elementary classes to be staffed by tenured, permanently certified teachers instead of the newest members of the faculty.

The teachers union and the district must work together to develop opportunities for teachers to advance in education without leaving teaching. Lead teacher positions (including that of mentor) belie the old saw that "all teachers are created equal . . . and stay that way." From the beginning of an internship, new teachers can participate in peer review and support and at the same time see experienced colleagues doing so. This is one way practices consistent with those found in other professions can be established and reinforced from the very beginning of a teacher's career.

With an effective mentor program as a foundation, the district and the union can address the problem of experienced (tenured) teachers who do not meet standards by creating an intervention program that is delivered by master teachers. The union demonstrates its commitment by assisting its members in their efforts to improve or by counseling them out of the profession. Ideally, correcting and avoiding harmful teaching practice is more of a concern for the union than for district management.

For unions, the influx of new teacher–members poses other challenges. As the ranks fill, a large percentage of first-year teachers have no understanding of unionism or the historical struggles of teacher unions to create a viable profession. Many "Generation X" teachers, as they have been termed by social commentators,

> acknowledge they know little about organized labor, nor do many of them care to find out more. These younger educators, who are required to join unions by law in many states, typically don't participate in the life of their teacher organizations and doubt they'll ever take on leadership roles. They often dismiss such groups as irrelevant to their teaching practice and view them as averse to innovation.[9]

Both the NEA and the AFT have launched major initiatives aimed at making sure that their newer members are aware of and involved in the profession-related aspects of the union's efforts. The demographics—a teaching force made up of approximately 40% baby boomers—demand that these organizations take steps now to provide leadership training and real engagement opportunities for the next generation of teacher union leaders.

The Minneapolis Federation of Teachers (MFT) has taken dramatic steps to involve newer members. Longtime MFT president Louise Sundin recognizes the needs these novices have, and she has developed programs in response. In Minneapolis, this response has taken the form of expanding the MFT's role beyond bread-and-butter bargaining to focus on teaching practice and other topics identified by new teachers. Working with the district, the MFT has promoted ways to appeal to the new teachers. Achieving tenure, for example, merits a bonus or laptop computer, and teachers can trade unused sick leave for fitness club memberships. Along with a collaboratively developed and operated mentor program, these measures are designed to ensure that teachers will continue working in the district and continue to be active union members.[10]

Attracting and Retaining Quality Teachers

Historically, teaching has been a profession that people entered because they wanted to do good, not because they expected to do well. Entry-level teaching salaries through the early 1970s were barely above the poverty level established by the federal government. Paying teachers competitive salaries has been an obvious and frequent recommendation in virtually every report on teaching and improving teaching quality. Even today, when top teacher salaries in some downstate New York districts exceed $100,000, teachers remain grossly underpaid in many states, and in urban and rural districts in almost every state.

Unions continue to be the best hope for teachers to improve their salaries and working conditions—that is, in states where teachers have the right to bargain their contracts collectively. It is encouraging that new proposals for teacher compensation with greater potential to impact teaching and learning are now being negotiated. Unions had almost universally rejected "pay-for-performance" schemes and merit pay plans because there was no evidence that such plans could be implemented fairly and with the stated outcome: to ensure improved teacher quality and student performance.

And it has not been only teacher unions that have been opposed to merit pay schemes. Educators and some economists have pointed out that it is nearly impossible to define all the practices that are characteristic of an excellent teacher, and as a result, administrators are often hard-pressed to justify merit awards. Those who are denied merit raises are often demoralized and bitter, feelings that make effective teaming extremely difficult to establish and sustain. Merit pay is vulnerable for other reasons also: When budgets are strained, merit pay is frequently the first place managers look to cut because it is usually structured as an add-on to base pay.[11]

Consistent with the report *What Matters Most,* Allan Odden, writing for the Consortium for Policy Research in Education at the University of Wisconsin–Madison, promotes "knowledge- and skills-based pay" and school-based performance incentives tied to student achievement. He cites the certification process offered by the National Board for Professional Teaching Standards for its development of assessments that validly and reliably reflect the knowledge and skills of experienced teachers. For midcareer teachers, the PRAXIS III assessment process, based on the work of Charlotte Danielson for the Educational Testing Service, provides a similarly authentic measure of teacher skills and knowledge.[12]

Odden points out that "Progressive unions . . . have supported fundamental pay innovations in many of their districts" and "as always happens in America, states, districts, and schools are already functioning as laboratories for policy innovation."[13] Unions are beginning to embrace the shift toward some inclusion of knowledge- and skills-based compensation systems, especially when the concept connects to improving student and school performance.

Perhaps the most daunting circumstances related to improving teacher compensation result from the divergent impulses within the economy and state and federal policy. Standards for teacher certification are being raised in states and through the federal government's most recent and largest funding bill, the reauthorization of the Elementary and Secondary Education Act (ESEA). This bill, also dubbed the "No Child Left Behind" Act, calls for "highly qualified" teachers in classrooms funded by the act. Nationally, however, there are far fewer certified physics teachers than there are school districts. The task of finding sufficient numbers of "highly qualified" teachers is impossible without major salary restructuring. In many states, property taxes remain the primary vehicle for education funding, and taxpayers will not authorize significant increases.

At a time when the teacher shortage is acute, states are raising standards and making certification more difficult to obtain. Although policymakers decry the low salaries for teachers, they are unwilling or unable to provide adequate funding for teacher salary improvements.

RECOMMENDATIONS

Prior to 1985, the most significant step in most teachers' first five years of teaching was deciding to leave the profession. For various reasons, the retention rate through the first five years seems to have improved since then. If a union, district, and college of education can work together as partners, additional gains can be made in attracting and retaining good teachers. Some of these support mechanisms are in place in many districts and will be mentioned (as recommendations) without being fully elaborated upon:

- *Establish a Mentor Teacher–Intern Program (MTIP) that is designed to retain teachers and to equip them to succeed.* In districts where a mentor program matches expert practitioners with new hires, the retention rates are markedly better. In Rochester, for example, since the mentor program was negotiated in 1986, retention rates have approached 90% for the first five years of a teacher's career. In addition, a supportive mentor program is based on promoting collegiality and reflection— aspects of practice essential in a high-quality teaching force. Even more important, those teachers who began as interns continue a professional mentor–intern connection after the first year ends. Mentors continue this contact and support, sometimes for more than ten years. Former interns are drawn into collegial support activities for subsequent cohorts of interns.
- *Reduce teacher isolation through team teaching, peer observation and review, provision of common planning time, and other strategies.* Occasions for teachers to work together and to see other practitioners at work must be structured to occur regularly rather than rarely. When Rochester moved to peer review for tenured teachers in 1991, one math teacher commented, "I've taught for seventeen years and have never been in a colleague's classroom until this year. It was a remarkable experience! I learned more in forty-five minutes than I learned in an entire methods course." Feedback from colleagues can be invaluable for causing changes in practice and for improving student performance. Districts,

unions, and colleges must commit to finding ways to reduce isolation and increase the exchange of successful teaching methods.

- *Collaborate with colleges to offer master's degree programs with significant on-the-job teaching and learning. Include financial support for a master's degree program in the compensation package for beginning teachers.* The parties in this collaborative effort need to find ways to support professional development, certification requirements, and competitive compensation arrangements. Even today, too many master's programs are disconnected from teaching and learning in a school setting. With a collaborative approach among unions, districts, and higher education, it should be easier for colleges to move more instruction into schools and classrooms, thereby creating partner schools to serve as "learning laboratories." Districts can make teaching more attractive by funding master's degree tuition payments for teachers who meet performance-appraisal standards. In this way, a district may influence professional development in major ways and provide incentives for beginning teachers to continue in their employment.

- *Make professional development* everyone's *business—unions, districts, and colleges.* Professional development is still, for the most part, something teachers sit through. It is district-directed and delivered in ways that are inconsistent with what we know about how people learn. In most districts, professional development is woefully underfunded, often representing less than 1% of district expenditures. It has been more comfortable for unions to criticize the poor efforts at staff in-service sessions than to initiate their own programs and strategies. Teachers need to design and implement activities that will better equip new teachers.

- *Adjust teacher salaries as necessary to attract and retain the highest caliber of professionals.* Teacher salaries made significant gains in the 1980s but are now falling behind those of comparable professions, particularly relative to the Consumer Price Index. It would be shortsighted to make other adjustments and revisions in the ways teachers are supported and to ignore this fundamental economic reality. Low teacher salaries cause many of our nation's most capable young people to reject even considering teaching as a career; similarly, low pay drives many excellent teachers to leave the profession early.

- *Redesign performance-appraisal systems to yield formative evaluations as well as summative ones that are completed by other practitioners.* Teacher evaluation procedures continue to be deprofessionalizing in most districts. They commonly consist of thirty-minute "snapshots" of teachers at work, usually completed by nonpractitioners. They rarely generate any useful suggestions about how practice might be improved because the evaluators are not themselves skillful teachers. As a result, most teacher evaluations are a colossal waste of resources, measured in administrators' time to complete paperwork that is ineffectual and clerical time devoted to executing and cataloging useless, irrelevant material.

Peer review is a professional's responsibility. It results in useful suggestions and observations about an individual's practice; it has the dual benefit of informing the observer and the observed. Teachers acknowledge that they "always learn something" about their own practice when they participate in peer review.

As asserted in a recent National Commission on Teaching and America's Future monograph, "Traditional evaluation plans usually assume that the purpose of teacher appraisal is to certify minimum competence, not to improve practice."[14] The analysis goes on to enumerate several positive aspects of peer review, as defined in the Rochester district: it encourages collegiality aimed at new instructional strategies; it requires documentation of practice and evidence of student learning; it is long term rather than a "snapshot"; it is formative through the first two years of an evaluation cycle, resulting in a summative rating at the end of the third year; it empowers teachers to choose the focus of the work that is assessed; it involves both peers and administrators; and it makes teachers take active roles in their own evaluations.[15]

Teacher unions, school districts, and colleges of education must come to the table and develop understandings about how they can, together, move the agenda. The task as it is outlined here and in other chapters may seem overwhelming, but lack of action is even more ominous. If teacher preparation is not reshaped, another generation of students will be deprived of the best conditions for learning.

NOTES

1. Myron Lieberman, *The Teacher Unions: How the NEA and AFT Sabotage Reform and Hold Students, Parents, and Taxpayers Hostage to Bureaucracy* (New York: Free Press, 1997), p. 245.

2. Charles T. Kerchner, Julia E. Koppich, and Joseph G. Weeres, *United Mind Workers: Unions and Teaching in the Knowledge Society* (San Francisco: Jossey-Bass, 1997), p. 61.

3. Holmes Group, *Tomorrow's Teachers* (East Lansing, Mich.: Holmes Group, 1986); Carnegie Forum on Education and the Economy, *A Nation Prepared: Teachers*

for the 21st Century (Washington, D.C.: Carnegie Forum on Education and the Economy, 1986); National Commission on Teaching and America's Future, *What Matters Most: Teaching for America's Future* (New York: NCTAF, 1996).

4. Charles Taylor Kerchner and Douglas E. Mitchell, *The Changing Idea of a Teachers' Union* (New York: Falmer Press, 1988), pp. 235–236.

5. Kerchner and Mitchell, *Changing Idea,* p. 256.

6. The local teacher unions belonging to TURN are: Albuquerque Teachers Federation (AFT), Bellevue (Wash.) Education Association (NEA), Boston Teachers Union (AFT), Cincinnati Federation of Teachers (AFT), Columbus Education Association (NEA), Denver Classroom Teachers Association (NEA), Hammond (Ind.) Teachers Federation (AFT), Memphis Education Association (NEA), Minneapolis Federation of Teachers (AFT), Montgomery County (Md.) Education Association (NEA), Pinellas (Fla.) Classroom Teachers Association (NEA), Pittsburgh Federation of Teachers (AFT), Rochester (N.Y.) Teachers Association (AFT), San Diego Teachers Association (NEA), Seattle Education Association (NEA), Toledo Federation of Teachers (AFT), United Educators of San Francisco (AFT-NEA), United Federation of Teachers (New York City, AFT), United Teachers of Dade County (AFT), United Teachers of Los Angeles (NEA-AFT), and Westerly (R.I.) Teachers Association (NEA).

7. Ann Bradley, "Unions Turn a Critical Eye on Themselves," *Education Week,* 16 February 2000, p. 1.

8. Kim A. Halkett, "Teacher Preparation: A Plan and Recommended Actions," Career in Teaching, Rochester City School District, April 1991.

9. Julie Blair, "Gen-Xers Apathetic about Union Label," *Education Week*, 30 January 2002, p. 1.

10. Blair, "Gen-Xers," p. 17.

11. Dale Ballou and Michael Podgursky, *Teacher Pay and Teacher Quality* (Kalamazoo, Mich.: Upjohn Institute for Employment Research, 1997), p. 108.

12. Allan Odden, "New and Better Forms of Teacher Compensation are Possible," *Phi Delta Kappan* 81 (January 2000): 361–366.

13. Odden, "New and Better Forms," p. 362.

14. Julia Koppich, Carla Asher, and Charles Kerchner, *Developing Careers, Building a Profession: The Rochester Career in Teaching Plan* (New York: National Commission on Teaching and America's Future, 2002), p. 40.

15. Koppich, Asher, and Kerchner, *Developing Careers,* p. 40.

CHAPTER 8

An Early Look at SST: Spawning Communities of Interest

NANCY JEAN SAHLING AND
BETTY LOU WHITFORD

There is much reference in the foregoing chapters to a process we believe is necessary to the well-being of humans, their institutions, and the world they share. We call it renewal. We hear much about school reform but little about school renewal. Reform is about somebody doing something to or requiring something of someone else. We speak, for example, of reform schools—custodial institutions where incarcerated young people, presumed to have done something bad, are to be reformed. The results have not been encouraging. Nor have those of school reform.

Renewal is a quite different, more positive concept and process. Nobody is presumed to be bad or delinquent. Rather, the assumption is that people derive satisfaction from learning something new or doing it better. But perhaps the context of their daily lives is such that it mitigates against this natural desire. There may need to be some catalyst to jump-start a process of change, of getting people to believe they can and want to. Frequently, this comes from some external source—not a threatening one, but an inviting one.

Until recently, getting renewal under way and intensifying the process was little studied. Educational researchers looked almost exclusively at outcomes, usually those stated at the outset by people setting out to improve some aspect of their daily work over a predetermined period of time. How they did this, what problems and obstacles they encountered, and how they made progress was of little interest. But both the participants in efforts to change and researchers began to realize the importance of ongoing inquiry accompanying the work.

The partners guiding and involved in conducting the Strengthening and Sustaining Teachers (SST) initiative referred to from time to time in this book decided at the outset that research and development had to proceed together if they were to learn from the pilot sites the lessons likely to help others. This is the work in progress that Nancy Jean Sahling and Betty Lou Whitford share with us in this chapter. In their narrative, they nicely balance the assumed interests of both researchers and those educators whose satisfactions stem from the renewing process itself.

—The editors

THE STRENGTHENING AND SUSTAINING TEACHERS INITIATIVE

Launching and sustaining a new educational initiative requires visionary leadership and commitment by the participants. In the case of the Strengthening and Sustaining Teachers (SST) initiative, experienced educators in Portland, Maine, and Seattle, Washington, are enthusiastically demonstrating such leadership and commitment.[1] SST brings together nationally prominent educators with two urban communities that have formed local partnerships to enhance the preservice preparation and continuing professional education of teachers for the schools of their cities. An SST partnership consists of a school district, its teachers union, and the local university's colleges of education and of arts and sciences—the professional stakeholders in teacher education and teacher professional development. The work of these SST collaboratives spans institutional boundaries and cultures long held in place by disconnected and often conflicting norms and interests.

The story of SST shines a light on the intersections of the cultures and attitudes of disparate educational institutions intentionally brought together into a new professional community. After just a few years, SST's partners have coalesced into distinct and high-profile entities in their cities. These energetic educational innovators and leaders have bonded into a professional "community of interest"—to use the term advanced by Gary Griffin and Patrice Litman[2]—with essential educational and societal goals: to sustain a quality workforce of teachers for their community and to demonstrate to others new possibilities for nurturing and instructing those individuals who aspire to become teachers.

SST has reframed the traditional paradigm of "teacher educators," expanding it to include a constellation of professionals from many types of educational endeavors. They are members of the teachers union, university professors, and K–12 school district educators such as teachers, principals, and vice principals. The result is a visionary reconfiguration of "teacher educators" into an inclusive team of educational specialists with broad responsibility for teacher professional learning. In their community of interest, SST's participants are "working together to bring greater power and authority to the experience of learning to teach."[3] Together, they have formed a crucial infrastructure for improving schooling in their cities.

Overarching Goals of SST

The Strengthening and Sustaining Teachers initiative's goal is to develop articulated systems of teacher preparation and job-embedded supports for beginning teachers, starting with preservice university programs and extending into the workplace through the first five years of teaching. This ambitious agenda calls for the stakeholders to create a new culture for working with each other. Through this collaborative culture, the project predicts, SST will rejuvenate the manner in which the profession prepares teachers for today's schools. The underlying premise of SST is that with "seamlessness" of the teacher preparation curriculum and coordinated support during the first five years of teaching, new teachers will more often taste success and experience the deep satisfactions and rewards of teaching and working among children and youths, especially in urban settings. As a result, project leaders posit, greater numbers of new teachers will sustain a commitment to teaching as a career, thereby combating attrition and ultimately enhancing the quality of public education.

Governance Structure

The governance structure of the SST project was conceived as follows: Nationally, the Coordinating Council—a confederation of prominent educators—regularly and sometimes strenuously gives voice to the vision and purpose of SST. The Coordinating Council includes one or two members from each of the partner institutions: the University of Washington, Bank Street College of Education, the National Commission on Teaching and America's Future (NCTAF), the Teacher Union Reform Network (TURN), and the Institute for Educational Inquiry (IEI). The Coordinating Council sets the broad direction for the initiative and provides expertise and counsel to the site partnerships. Council members visit the local sites, offer technical assistance, follow the progress of the local sites, and assist in problem solving and accessing resources. They also read and respond to the sites' seasonal progress reports and provide critiques on the sites' annual reports and proposed plans for the next year of the project. The council's responsibilities also include obtaining project funding, overseeing research and evidence collecting, planning for and developing dissemination of project findings to funders, dispensing funds, and providing accountability to funders. Through this structure, the members of the Coordinating Council become the project grantors and extend a broad reach over the project.

A project director serves an essential role in providing cohesion to the national SST initiative. She is the liaison between the Coordinating Council and the local sites, routinely reinforcing core values of the national partners and conveying nuances of local context to the council as well as assistance to the sites. In this vital integrative role, the project director matches needs and resources, organizes and facilitates meetings, and nudges and prods both leaders and participants, all with tenacity and quiet grace.

Each local urban site has its own SST Site Council and project coordinator. The Site Council consists of prominent leaders from each partner organization: a teacher union representative, a school district representative, and a college of education representative. In Seattle, there is also a representative from the University of Washington's College of Arts and Sciences. The local Site Council, also known as the Steering Committee, guides the project with attention to its underlying purpose, reports back to the national Coordinating Council, and engages with and informs constituents. The Site Council members meet regularly as equal partners, shaping and monitoring their local initiative.

SST's Early Impact

Early in the project, SST leaders in Portland and Seattle followed deliberate processes to determine the initial direction of their respective initiatives. Portland's project leaders devoted a planning year to collecting data on the existing practices and programs for educating and supporting prospective, new, and veteran teachers in their schools. They probed for the opinions of Portland's rank-and-file educators, and their grassroots approach resulted in a widespread commitment to the project among Portland's educators. Seattle's leaders took a "professional inventory" of the strengths and weaknesses of each partner's institution with respect to teacher development. Both processes led the participants to formulate programs that were meaningful to their communities, given their local contexts, needs, and goals.

Each site's program is unique and involves new and different configurations of educators from each of the constituencies. While some participants in the sites have significant local partnership experience, the SST decision-making and program-design configurations have created new roles and relationships among both the individuals and the organizations. For example, since it is often the case in higher education that teacher preparation faculty members do not themselves work at the schools with experienced educators, new alliances are needed across the continuum, even within collaborating partner organizations.

Already, SST's collaboratives have had an impact on their communities. During the first half of SST's initial five-year funding cycle, both sites have succeeded in forging working partnerships and can point to several significant accomplishments:

- Leaders of the entities agreed to accept the challenges of SST's ambitious agenda. This process alone involved untold meetings, deliberations, and decisions. As SST partners, they were a new and unique group of highly visible leaders in the community with an urgent purpose unifying them. They drew up formal documents, memoranda of understanding, and guiding principles to direct the work of everyone who would be participating in the local effort. To conduct the actual educational initiative, the partners drafted a full complement of educators on various committees.

- Seattle's four partners—the Seattle Public Schools, the Seattle Education Association, and the University of Washington's College of Education and College of Arts and Sciences—have created and are piloting an alternative route to teaching middle school math and science that includes a year-long internship and induction mentoring in six middle schools. Formally launched in spring 2002, the Teaching Learning Partnership (TLP) is working with twenty prospective teachers who are on track to begin teaching in 2003.

- Portland's three partners—the Portland Public Schools, the Portland Education Association, and the University of Southern Maine's College of Education and Human Development—are focusing on a two-year induction mentoring program for novices and ongoing mentor-training experiences for veteran mentor teachers. As of the 2002–2003 academic year, fully one-third of Portland schools provided thorough induction mentoring to new teachers, and over one hundred veteran teachers were formally trained mentors.

Each site entered SST by focusing initially on one point along the continuum of teacher preparation, induction, and sustained professional development. Joining SST in 2000, Seattle began with teacher preparation, while Portland began with the induction of newly hired teachers. The plan is that each site will focus on one additional point along the continuum each year, until the seamless curriculum and support are built across all phases. At the same time, the conceptual framework of SST is intentionally fluid, so that each locality can respond to changing needs and circumstances, such as budgetary or legislative imperatives.

THEMES OF DISCOVERY

In studying SST at the Portland and Seattle sites, we collected qualitative data for eighteen months. We attended local and national SST meetings (for example, Design Team, Steering Committee, and Coordinating Council sessions), listened in on telephone conference calls as project leaders discussed issues and strategies, interviewed leaders and a sample of participants, facilitated meetings of researchers from each site, and reviewed stacks of project-generated documents.

Our data reveal the power and creativity of committed educators willing to reconfigure themselves into a professional community of interest, critique their practices, and experiment with nontraditional ways of preparing teachers in their urban settings. SST's highly ambitious renewal effort in teacher education and professional development has proved to be—as Seymour Sarason described the work of restructuring schools— "not for the faint hearted. It is for those who seek a redefinition of their professional lives, for those who want to put *their* imprimatur" on their work.[4]

Our cross-site analysis of the data reveals three themes that capture significant elements of the early work in Portland and Seattle:

1. SST is guided by a shared, compelling, and centrally articulated and reinforced national purpose, which is interpreted and enacted in local contexts.
2. Teacher union participation and power sharing are particularly salient to SST partnership building, culture change, and program design.
3. Engaging in partnership building and collaborative program design spawns collegiality, professional learning, and professional community among educators.

All three themes address professional culture building. The themes play out differently in the two sites, but their unmistakable emergence is testimony to the power of educational partnerships to engender cultures of commitment, collegiality, and professional community among educators in two urban settings. Thus far in its journey, SST is a complex story of the creation of professional cultures of community and commitment in Portland, Maine, and Seattle, Washington.

Theme One:
Shared National Purpose with Local Interpretation

A compelling, central purpose drives the work of SST. This point, deceptively simple to state, is highly complex in execution. It is an educational and societal purpose: to draw upon the considerable expertise of the partners, national and local, in order to improve ways that urban settings attract, induct, and retain well-qualified teachers. Further, SST strives to prepare, support, and nurture teachers so that they will commit to teaching and to giving all children opportunities for success, thereby enhancing our society. This purpose drives the work and sustains individual commitment. Significantly, SST is *not* about any particular "delivery system" to accomplish the goal. Instead, within broad parameters, the work is fluid, generative, recursive, and site specific.

This central purpose also brings urgency to the work. Both Seattle and Portland are experiencing increasing attrition and teacher shortages. As public schools continuously embrace the diversity of American students, educators and the public must come to understand that the mission of schooling must change from merely providing opportunity to ensuring learning. Providing opportunity assumes that learners and their families know how to access the opportunity. A mission to ensure learning places far greater responsibility on educators to be proactively attentive to each child, thus calling for more sophisticated, professionalized approaches to teacher learning and support.

In full recognition of these shifts, SST is a high-leverage strategy to prepare, support, and develop teachers so they can achieve challenging learning goals with all learners. The national SST initiative maintains that partnerships among schools, unions, and universities—especially in our urban centers—are necessary to secure new ways to provide high-quality education for our nation's youth.

Although a focus on mission—of schooling, of teaching, of democracy—is prominent in project leaders' talk, it is sometimes difficult to discern in program design and logistics. When localized discussion becomes technical and detailed—and necessarily wrapped up in logistics and contingencies—typically someone from among the national partners reframes the conversation in terms of SST's central purpose. For one national SST leader, a major tension for the work is

> making sure that everyone is on the same agenda. It takes relentlessness. . . . Even when people are willing to do the work, I find we need to keep refocusing the participants. . . . I know that I must keep on telling the SST story over and over when I attend meetings. "Help me figure this out and find a way" needs to be said . . . by all the leaders on this challenging project.

Another dimension of SST is to create a coherent continuum for new teacher learning and support over a five-year period—and to do so by leveraging the expertise and resources of the partners. In the local meetings, conversations are amalgamations of strategies for new ways of working along the continuum. But they also often veer into how schools and institutions of higher education and unions operate: their norms, structures, and roles. Embedded in these discussions is a growing recognition that although program design is important, organizing programs, schooling, and teaching to provide substantially more professional support is equally important. Hence, along with the centrally articulated purpose, each site's local context and education professionals compose a community of interest where specific needs are determined and SST directions in the local setting are shaped.

The participants' generative formation into professional communities of interest is a key to SST. Many in the Coordinating Council repeat their hope and intention that SST will generate a culture change leading to "institutionalization" of SST. They do not refer to the institutionalization of any particular SST program (because programs are always subject to change), but rather to SST's model of truly collaborative partnering and power sharing among the key constituents of teacher professional learning. In that way, SST is similar to other educational improvement initiatives. As Judith Warren Little argues, "However reform proposals are portrayed in documents or by their advocates inside and outside the school, they are subject to individual, collective, and institutional interpretations."[5] Many participants in Portland and Seattle have given expression to their unique personal and institutional interpretations of the meaning of their current SST work.

The Meaning of SST in Portland

To understand the meaning of SST in Portland, one must revisit the project's origins. Portland's SST work began with a planning-year grant to gather ideas from the rank and file of Portland's educators about a meaningful direction for the new SST project. Members of the new SST Steering Committee held a series of dine-and-discuss gatherings with groups of local educators: principals, veteran and new teachers, union members, and university faculty. Probing for their genuinely felt needs, the SST committee members asked everyone: "In Portland, where would you recommend starting an SST initiative and research project, with university preparation, new teacher induction, or teacher professional development?"

There was strong interest in and enthusiasm for beginning an initiative in new teacher induction, and Portland's educators began the long process of collaborating and developing experimental programs in mentoring and mentor training. To a lesser extent, they would also begin to reexamine the teacher education program at the University of Southern Maine (USM). The path they proceeded on proved to be tortuous.

Just what was the fundamental meaning and appeal of this work to so many educators in Portland? A Portland SST leader summed up the motivation of many: "It's the desire to help. It's the language of SST that appeals to people. People want to help new teachers." Indeed, the language of SST, its very lexicon, reads as a kind of mantra of professional nurturing of novices who will teach our children. Phrases include "strengthen and sustain," "support new teachers through the first five years," and "increase the capacity of mentor teachers to support novice teachers."

The major focus of SST in Portland—to nurture and develop new teachers as members of the profession and as teachers in the city's schools—is a winner. For many years, Southern Maine has been a hotbed of school improvement efforts. In this climate, educational renewal is a regularity of schooling. Thus, when Portland's educators received an invitation to join the national SST project, they felt at home with the work. In their regional educational culture, Southern Maine's committed career professionals already had an entrenched cultural norm of professional stewardship. The Southern Maine Partnership, based at USM, has a long history of membership in the National Network for Educational Renewal (NNER) and commitment to the Agenda for Education in a Democracy that guides the work of all NNER settings in the nation. The partnership has also been an enduring catalyst in the simultaneous renewal of the local schools and teacher education. The goals of SST fit comfortably with those of the Portland Public Schools (PPS); the University of Southern Maine, with its national reputation for teacher education partnerships; and the Portland Education Association (PEA). SST builds on the existing culture of educational innovation and continuous school improvement as well as the mission of schooling in a democracy.

A teacher gives expression to the "fit" between SST and teacher professionalism in Portland. She sees SST as enhancing educators' professionalism through opportunities to develop young teachers *and* veterans: "I see great potential in training new teachers and sustaining them and helping them through those first difficult years. I really see it equally as helping all our teachers come to their understanding about what it is to be a career professional, and it's in that arena that I think this project offers us lots of opportunities."

Another SST participant, a school administrator, enthusiastically shares her belief in the many professional benefits of the project and its job-embedded mentoring:

> It is incredibly valuable for the teacher. There are so many benefits professionally. We are building the cultural piece in the building. We are building efficacy. Just the opportunity to talk about practice is so valuable. . . . It's just crucial to stretch and grow as a professional and to confirm that what you are doing is a great thing. There are so many possibilities.

Many others expressed their interpretation of the value and meaning of SST to teachers in Portland. By helping to develop the talents of their new teachers, veteran teachers also feel valued and are given opportunities for professional growth.

Portland's educators expressed another reason to be in SST and to focus their energies on new teacher induction. SST provides an avenue for developing "in house" those provisionally certified teachers hired to fill shortage areas—namely, math, science, special education, and second language learning. Portland is a highly desirable school system in which to work. It pays teachers well, and it receives many applications from experienced educators for each new position. Consequently, Portland has a staff of well-established career professionals, and in the past it has hired very few new teachers. This is starting to change, however, as shortages experienced nationally are beginning to hit home in Portland. SST is helping to deal with those shortages by creating sustained, mentored induction for all novice teachers. In this way, new teachers will help maintain the high-quality educational program for which the Portland schools are nationally recognized.

Portland's principals, teachers, SST leaders, union representatives, and university faculty members all attest to the importance of SST. There are subtle differences in their individual takes on SST. That SST allows for such individuality is significant because the broad agenda of the work touches on many fundamental professional interests. In so doing, it stimulates a broadly based "buy in" by the various partners, which is critical to the achievement of the collaborative structure defining SST. For everyone in Portland, though, SST boils down to a fundamental desire to help new teachers succeed in this vital profession. And that is the core SST objective.

Since its inception in Portland in January 2000, SST has designed, piloted, and brought to fruition several activities. Presently, over thirty new teachers in seven schools are being nurtured and supported in their challenging beginning years. In 2002–2003, fully one-third of Portland's schools signed on to SST. In addition, SST is sponsoring mentor training for virtually all of Portland's mentors. At last count, over one hundred mentors had gone through SST workshops called Foundations of Mentoring, and many are doing more professional development in the mentoring and inducting of new teachers. Educators from the university and the public schools continue to engage in ongoing discussions to refine SST's efforts and coordinate them more effectively with both USM's teacher education programs and the goals and learning standards of the Portland Public Schools. Two pilot programs have been introduced into experimental sites: an initial mentoring pilot and a pilot in teacher professional development, which is the next phase of teacher learning along SST's developmental continuum.

Other activities are in the works, as SST goals extend to institutionalizing the initiative as a collaborative way of doing the work of schooling in Portland. SST has proved to be a major undertaking, played out amid the rocky terrain typical of any new partnership. Many in Portland have dedicated themselves tirelessly to the work of SST. Their next steps for years 4 and 5 will be equally ambitious: Portland has a whole new consciousness about the needs and requirements of the beginning teacher. SST has instigated a coherent approach to supporting and developing new teachers and training their mentors through a professional mentor training program. The bottom line in Portland is that participants in SST are setting up their professionals for success.

The Meaning of SST in Seattle

In Seattle, SST began with an honest professional inventory among the partners. With the guidance of the national director, Seattle's SST leaders consented to critique each other's work in teacher education, new teacher induction, and teacher professional development. In a direct face-to-face encounter, they took their own "professional inventory." They charted what was right and wrong with each institution's full array of programs, and they assessed their respective strengths and weaknesses. The university's teacher education program was critiqued, as was professional development in the school district, including the existing mentoring program.

SST in Seattle has struck a responsive chord among its partners by addressing the persistent problems of unequal access to quality public education in the urban community. Union leaders voiced a strong concern about teacher attrition and shortages—not only in math and science but also in special education and second language learning. "The shortage situation . . . was a real catalyst," remarked a union official. She added that she feels hopeful that the SST partners can all work together to confront this problem.

After taking their professional inventory, the SST leaders held lengthy planning meetings at which they reached consensus about their point of entry into SST. They would address a shortage area in Seattle by creating an alternative certification route at the university to prepare career changers to become middle school teachers of math and science.

As the program unfolded, there was an unmistakable air of excitement about bringing career changers into the profession in Seattle. One Steering Committee member offered her perspective:

SST has broad-based support in the community. Anyone who is anyone in education knows about SST. In Seattle, everyone is involved! The Alliance for Education, a high-powered business group, has lots of interest in SST, as do the superintendent of schools and the chief academic officer. . . . In addition, . . . we're embarking on William Sanders's "value-added assessment," . . . which has taught us that there is a significant difference in the quality of teaching at the middle school or high school when it values the strong content knowledge of the teacher. In education, we are in a situation where valuing the generalist versus the content specialist has become an interesting debate.

A member of the SST leadership team explained the excitement: "Hook number one was getting well-qualified people in math and science. It's a winner because there is a vast hole there. And hook number two is the chance to do this collaboratively. There's a growing realization that you need people with different knowledge areas and expertise." Another participant commented that the Seattle SST project is succeeding in "getting the various entities, in particular the College of Education and the College of Arts and Sciences faculty, to understand the mission about new teachers."

With enthusiasm, another participant talked about valuing the "incredible opportunity for the union to work for the first time with the College of Education and the dean"—and the university's valuing the timely opportunity to forge a relationship with the union. SST is allowing everyone to get to know each other as professionals and to increase understanding of what each organization is about. According to a union official, SST is a promising vehicle for the union in Seattle to collaborate with all the partners in teacher professional development as well as other areas of professional endeavor. Within the union reform movement, there is a trend of thinking that values opportunities for teachers to take on more leadership roles and differentiated professional roles. SST affords occasions and structures for Seattle's teachers to work as mentors and building-level coordinators of mentoring.

Seattle's local initiative was born, then, out of a combination of powerful motivations: professional, educational, and societal. In a very tight time frame, the SST collaborative launched a pilot program known as Teaching Learning Partnership (TLP). In fall 2002, as faculty and students were returning to the University of Washington for the new quarter, the TLP interns were starting their school-based internships. They were changing careers and were, indeed, on track to be certified as math and science teachers by June 2003.

Theme Two: Saliency of Teacher Union Participation in Partnership Building, Culture Change, and Program Design

By design, SST requires collaboration among a school district, a teachers union, a university college of education, and a college of arts and sciences. SST's national leaders on the Coordinating Council reinforce this requirement. As they provide frequent feedback and critiques to the local sites, they ask routinely, "Are all partners represented in this decision?" While the schools and universities in both Seattle and Portland have partnership histories—and thus relationships and experiences to draw upon—in both places, involving the union as a partner is a new development. Indeed, it is SST's very intentional power sharing with the union that is one of its visionary aspects. Educational renewal partnerships bring together functionally independent entities in order to focus on their interrelated work. Such arrangements both facilitate and complicate the work done together, but when the mission is institutionally shared, the partnership is more likely to withstand tensions.[6] There is evidence in Seattle and Portland to support this claim, particularly regarding the union as a partner.

Before SST, neither the Portland Education Association (PEA) nor the Seattle Education Association (SEA) had worked with its nearby major university in matters of teacher education and professional development. Now the project is prodding everyone in Portland and Seattle to grapple with the implications of an enlarged role for the union, extending beyond contractual compensation, job security, and benefits. In effect, SST asserts that unionism and professionalism are mutually *inclusive*.

The national SST initiative assumes a stance toward teacher unions that recognizes contemporary movements in unions' focus and strategy. Increasingly, members of teacher unions are taking on influential roles as educators and professionals. As Teacher Union Reform Network (TURN) codirector Adam Urbanski explains, "Teachers must be involved in setting high and rigorous standards for their profession."[7] To help meet these standards, Urbanski continues, a "professional accountability system" should be put in place "to ensure responsible and responsive practices that are knowledge-based and client-oriented."[8]

SST has configured a paradigm that positions the unions to share power and thus to share in conceptualizing and designing educational policies, programs, and accountability systems alongside the college of education, the college of arts and sciences, and the school district.

The Portland Education Association and SST

In just a few years, SST in Portland has grown dramatically. All of the local partners—the university, the school district, and the union—have contributed substantially and unselfishly. The success of the project has resulted from the complex, layered, overlapping efforts of the people involved. Each institution has contributed its endowment of expertise, resources, and knowledge. And each individual has contributed from his or her own skill set, professional and interpersonal, to bring SST to fruition in Portland.[9]

The historical and current role of the PEA in Portland's SST project, however, deserves particular attention. Explaining the local context and culture surrounding the union in Portland, Richard Barnes writes in Chapter 3:

> In this brief history of the partnership between the PPS [Portland Public Schools] and USM, the teachers union is conspicuously absent. . . . It never occurred to those involved with the partnership that the PEA could or should have any formal role in establishing or implementing policies for recruiting teachers in developing projects and activities in partner schools. University-based partnership members assumed that the PEA was uninterested in the teacher professional development in which the university was engaged. The PEA was seen as the voice of the teachers on contractual matters; its activities were largely regulatory and part of the bureaucratic culture that characterized much of the university's work in Portland. As SST started, USM participants soon learned how mistaken they were in this belief. PEA leaders had many questions and concerns about how USM implemented its programs and defined partnership in teacher education matters, and they welcomed SST as an opportunity to enter the stage.

And enter the stage the union surely did. The national Coordinating Council had invited the PEA to become a partner in SST in Portland, and in response, the PEA has actively sought recognition as an equal with the university and the school district. To this end, the PEA has stepped up and taken on the leadership that such a role requires. Some view the union's effectiveness in bringing people on board SST as being among the key outcomes of the project in Portland. For example, in their case report about SST in Portland, Julie Canniff and Melody Shank conclude, "One of the most significant outcomes of the implementation year was a subtle but profound shift in the perception of the union as a true ally in the professional development of all teachers."[10]

After an initial year-long pilot in mentoring, which involved only six mentors and six new teachers, the SST mentoring program has expanded markedly in Portland. By 2002–2003, seven schools engaged in mentored induction of their more than thirty new teachers under SST. In addition, SST's Foundations of Mentoring training program is preparing *all* teachers who mentor in Portland, whether they mentor in SST's target schools or elsewhere in the district. This groundswell of interest in mentoring affects one-third of the schools in this midsize urban district. As Portland looks ahead to the professional development phase of SST, the project leaders have tapped another school willing to do a pilot.

The Portland Education Association has demonstrated keen interest in SST and has played an active and effective role in the initiative. The union's insider knowledge of its own teachers and schools amounts to a particular savoir faire for effecting change within its own rank and file and specific schools in the district. The union's understanding of the importance of timing and its ability to identify those particular schools and individuals most receptive to reform work cannot be stated emphatically enough. As one SST participant explained it, the union leadership's keen eye and ability to select effective individuals and willing schools "have been essential to the success of the early work of SST."

A high school mentor teacher drives home his interpretation of the union's vital professional interest in participating in SST:

> The importance of the union's being a part of it is that it brings a balance to who's looking out for the quality of the educators that we grow in Portland . . . that it isn't just an evaluation process, but that it's something everyone has ownership in. We are all looking out for quality teachers, and we are trying to develop them through joint ownership in mentoring them. It isn't just three people's role, it's everybody's role. That's what I see as the benefit of the union's being in SST.[11]

Throughout SST, the union's role has been noteworthy. Remember that heretofore in Portland, the union was conspicuously absent from participation in developing projects and activities of partnerships between the schools and the university. From the outset of SST, however, the PEA president has represented the union on the powerful three-member SST Steering Committee. Through the union leadership's new role of sharing equally in policy and program development, the union has established an ethos of teacher leadership in Portland. That is, the PEA has parity with the other partners, and a new climate of professional power sharing characterizes the work of their growing initiative.

SST, it bears emphasizing, is a totally *voluntary* program among the faculty of Portland. Indeed, SST's entire program of mentored induction rests in substantial ways on the shoulders of veteran mentor teachers who wish to take on the challenging, time-consuming work of mentoring a

new member of their school's faculty. Such early and widespread acceptance could not happen without the enthusiastic support of the teachers
and their union.

During the three years of SST in Portland, issues have surfaced and
resurfaced concerning the extent of the union's power and its role in
program development and decision making with respect to new teacher
education, mentoring and induction, and teacher professional development. Again, this power sharing is a new situation in Portland, and as
the union has gained footing, some people in traditional decision-making roles are in the process of adjusting to SST's collaborative process.
For example, very early in the project, there was a dispute over the policy of including only union member teachers on SST planning committees. In the view of some principals and others in Portland, nonunion
teachers are as well qualified to mentor as teachers who are union members, and they believed it was appropriate and fair to tap them for the
job as well. The situation was serious enough to create a rift, and one
principal withdrew his school from the project. Subsequently, the partners have turned to mending fences, but the issue resurfaces at different
junctures.

More recently, another issue developed over criteria for the selection of
mentors. The matter has complicated the making of mentor/mentee
matches in at least one school, and it has brought to the surface more differences between principals and the union. In mid-October 2002—well
into the school year—two new teachers were still without mentors, pend-
ing the resolution of SST policy over qualifications of mentors. Taken individually, each situation has been solvable, but tensions inevitably accompany problems that arise during the reconfiguration of power sharing in
any organization.

As the participants' traditional roles expand, change, and overlap, a
different paradigm is operating in Portland's SST. The project has been a
catalyst for everyone to expand the definition of his or her work and to
assume new roles and new learning as "teacher educators." In particular,
the union's new and visible role in the professional domains of SST has
stimulated different ways of conducting the business of education in the
project. The PEA leadership has welcomed and embraced the opportunity to work alongside the other partners in establishing and implementing
professional policies and programs.

The Seattle Education Association and SST

Like its counterpart in Portland, Maine, the Seattle Education
Association (SEA) had never before worked with a local university in

preparing teachers. The SEA had partnered before with the Seattle Public Schools, but it had never partnered with the major public university right in its midst. The SEA welcomed the opportunity presented through SST to work on issues of new teacher preparation with the University of Washington's College of Education and its College of Arts and Sciences. The union identified several good reasons to join the SST collaborative, as one SEA union leader explained:

> Nowhere else in the state of Washington is the union in such a partnership with a university. This is the first time that the union has been able to establish a relationship with the University of Washington, which we should have had a really intimate relationship with maybe a decade ago, so we could have started figuring out how we're going to address the shortages and do it in a way that we grow our own teachers. We never had a visible relationship or partnership with an institution of higher learning that produced teachers until this. . . . And we have been able to understand each other now that we are together. It sets the groundwork for other collaborations in the future. So we see it as a critical partnership.

In this leader's view, then, there are three significant reasons for the union to have joined the SST partnership: (1) to establish a relationship with an institution of higher education that produces teachers, (2) to work on the teacher shortage crisis, and (3) to lay the groundwork for future professional collaborations.

A leader in the SEA noted that the union is keenly interested in the prospect of developing a districtwide, collaborative model for alternative certification in other shortage areas, particularly in special education, where there is a serious shortfall, and in second language learning:

> We're hoping to learn enough from this that we can move to institute a broader kind of alternative route. We have to tread very carefully, however, because our members are not sure whether this is wise. They know it's wise to deal with the shortage problem, but . . . we have to convince them that the standards [of teacher preparation] are rigorous. Our leadership role in this is to provide oversight and ensure that this is a quality program. But I see that it could serve as a model—and that is very, very exciting to us.

In addition, the union's teachers will play an active role in mentoring at the building level. For example, the SST project in Seattle calls for one-on-one mentoring, as well as departmental mentoring of intern teachers by each school's math and science teachers. For its mentoring program, then, SST relies to a great degree on the expertise of Seattle's classroom practitioners. These teachers are assuming new roles as mentors, as program designers, and as leaders in school governance, and a few are teaching the interns at the university alongside the Teaching Learning Partnership's professors.

Many in Seattle, especially leaders in the public schools, have emphasized that these new roles are powerful pathways of professional development and a welcome responsibility for teachers, whose deepening knowledge and broadening experience can translate into advanced learning for children. At the same time, these new roles raise issues about working conditions, incentives, and rewards—areas of vital importance to the professionals involved. As one teacher participant observed, "There is no quality time to manage new roles well." All kinds of structural, logistical, and working-condition issues that affect teachers will have to be worked out, school by school, in Seattle's decentralized, large, urban district.

The union and its teachers have a vital interest in the SST project. A university partner discussed his awareness of the union's key professional role in educational renewal efforts: "If the union hadn't been involved in this from the beginning, that would have been the first thing I would have asked for. It's a no-brainer. You are there operating with the teacher union people. Usually, people just don't ask [the union to participate]. They make assumptions that the union is about compensation only."

Looking ahead, a leader of SEA views SST as an opportunity for teachers to assume differentiated professional roles. For instance, in the current SST initiative, Seattle's teachers work as mentors or building-level "chief worriers" to coordinate the individual and group mentoring program within a particular school. Both the school district and union leadership recognize the merit of these kinds of expanded professional roles for classroom teachers. Differentiated roles increase job satisfaction and provide additional compensation for teachers by building a "career ladder," a valuable means of enhancing the professional career of teaching. And enhancing the profession is the raison d'être of the national SST initiative.

There is another rationale for the union to embrace the SST partnership: SST is affording the union a voice and a role, along with the other partners, in teachers' professional learning. In the effort to certify career changers in middle school math and science, Seattle's teachers play vital roles. They function as cooperating teachers, one-on-one mentors, departmental mentors, and teachers of teachers; they are also Design Team members and adjunct university instructors in the TLP program. Along with the other SST partners, the union has entered the project's ongoing dialogue about the design of teacher professional learning experiences occurring over the five-year period of the initiative.

The significance for the union is the potential for future collaboration in an area of great import to its teachers. As one union leader explained it, SST has provided SEA the opportunity to work in tandem with its district and university partners and be a part of the important, ongoing conversation about teacher professional development. The union official continued, "We can help by selecting our premier educators," to collaborate with the SST partners in the professional development of Seattle's new teachers. Infusing all of the work is a desire to be stewards of their own profession and to participate as partners in developing and "growing their own" high-quality teachers. In Portland, it was the same refrain.

SST is a visionary, forward-looking initiative. Through the inclusion of the union in its educational partnerships, SST has broken through a wall of crystallized educational practice in Portland and Seattle. The result in both sites is that teachers in the unions are positioned now as true partners in the process of renewal in their own schools. The evolution of this structure, which values collaboration and shared responsibility for supporting new teachers, is inevitably driving cultural change within the educational communities of Portland and Seattle.

Theme Three: The SST for Building Collegiality, Professional Learning, and Professional Community

A third theme emerging during the initial stages of SST, therefore, is that collaboration such as we have witnessed in Portland and Seattle spawns a culture marked by collegiality, reveals professional learning needs, and builds professional community. Building professional communities in Portland and Seattle has been a social process that has taken time. Thus far, our early look at SST reveals a clear image of committed community building among the professionals in the initiative.

Building Trust in Portland and Seattle

A prerequisite to building a new culture of professional community and commitment is establishing trust in one another. Aware of the importance of building a climate of trust, and mindful that there are no shortcuts to the process, the partners have devoted themselves consciously to this aspect of their new partnerships, arranging regular opportunities to have direct and collaborative experiences together. Two and three years into the work, SST team members continue to underscore "trust among the partners" as one of their biggest accomplishments. In Chapter 3,

Richard Barnes noted that building and earning trust require commitment and skill, stating: "Partners in the Portland, Maine, SST project built trust and collaboration by paying careful attention to group dynamics and ensuring that dialogue was open and inclusive. The 'forming, storming, norming, and performing' stages of organizational development were present in the key events." In his account of the formative stages of the Portland SST partnership, Barnes described several critical incidents and their resolutions, which ultimately resulted in establishing increasing levels of trust among the partners.

An example of one such interaction revealing the respect and openness that have settled into the Portland participants' way of conducting business comes from the June 2002 "tuning" meeting, where participants were refining their next steps. The local partners differed openly over a sensitive issue—what to do in a situation where a newer teacher, who had an SST mentor, needed "a different kind of help." A central office administrator stated with emphasis that her bottom line is helping each individual teacher who needs it. A union partner responded that she, too, was concerned for the teacher, but she did not want SST to give the impression that it is at all heavy-handed with any teacher or that it is in any way an imposed program. The union's perspective, she explained, is that the individual buildings, which have site-based management, need to find out the best ways to handle these questions. She emphasized that SST is a partnership, and the union has a voice. A university partner agreed that the union's voice is critical, and that [the project] "can't be causing problems for the union" or "fanning any anti-SST fires." Finally, the union representative urged everyone to consult the SST framework as a source of guidelines for what to do for the new teacher.

During this honest and respectful exchange, we witness the three partners stating their perspectives but also considering their partners' views, validating one another's positions and trusting each other and their collaborative process to settle the question. This is the level of professional discourse that has characterized Portland's participants at every meeting of the project.

Likewise, in Seattle, many SST participants highlighted the human dimensions of becoming trusted partners. A Seattle Steering Committee member described the social process and stages of coming to know and trust each other: "From the initiation, it was planning, planning, planning. We spent a lot of time trying to get the partners to agree on what they wanted to do. They weren't meshing well. Everyone had different ideas." The local SST leader continued, noting several issues that surfaced, such as competing for each other's turf, tensions over resources, and whether or not they each really valued the project: "There were suspicions about each other's motives. . . . Once all these issues could be aired and our not-always-positive perceptions of each other could be vented, we could build tight-knit, honest relationships."

In project interviews in Seattle, many participants reflected high regard for their colleagues. They routinely credited others for their accomplishments and communicated an energetic esprit de corps. "There are some phenomenal people who make things happen!" said one participant. Another reported: "The projects rest on the shoulders of one or two key people who are the fulcrum." Yet another professed, "If there weren't key faculty members, it couldn't happen. No program like this could ever succeed without them." Still another admired a colleague "with the intellectual clout to get this through the faculty."

Another key participant in Seattle cited trust as also among the important accomplishments of the project at this stage. After two years of working in the partnership, she reported: "The level of trust between the partners is that their intentions are good, are clear. It's messy to figure out the responsibilities. The people involved are really committed to the process now."

In this last comment, we hear a hint of some internal tensions. There are, of course, myriad challenges and tensions in both of SST's new partnerships. To bolster themselves, the participants are drawing upon their collective fund of interpersonal and professional resources, their experience in school renewal work, and their commitment to the project and its purpose. The problems of partnership building and school improvement are well documented in the literature. Portland's and Seattle's encounters with those problems are edifying and instructive parts of the story of SST and the creation of professional communities.

Tensions and Difficult Issues

Difficulties are inevitable when autonomous institutions join together as partners to build new educational structures that value collaboration and shared responsibility. In the case of SST, these new structures involve the education and preparation of professionals entrusted with the care and education of our nation's young people. High expectations and high standards are important to everyone—and therein lies the rub.

As discussed previously, Portland has been working out a collaborative process to design and implement a mentored induction program for new teachers, as well as a mentor training program for veteran teachers in the district. The project's problems and tensions have revolved around the new power-sharing structure among the union, the school district, and the university. Seattle's difficulties likewise stem from issues of

power sharing and center on the collaborative efforts to introduce a new
alternative certification program in middle school mathematics and science. As one participant characterized it, the project has been a "humon-
gous undertaking."

Seattle SST has four partners: the Seattle Education Association, the
Seattle Public Schools, and the University of Washington's College of
Education (COE) and College of Arts and Sciences (A&S). Thus, there are
four institutional cultures and mindsets. In addition, they all work under
the jurisdiction of Washington's state education department, replete with
its requirements and regulations.

The challenge for SST in Seattle has been primarily the ongoing tension between A&S and COE about what is "enough" content versus pedagogy in the university's course requirements for the Teaching Learning
Partnership (TLP) program. The partners are consciously designing a preservice internship program that has less "frontloading" of university
course work and that focuses a core of courses on the "essentials" for a
teacher to get started in the classroom. A&S and COE faculty are having
a hard time figuring out what these "essentials" are. In their debate, they
are struggling over how and where to reduce the amount of information
gathered up front by preservice teachers and how to spread out their
learning over the first few years on the job.

Seattle's TLP alternative certification program design was based on
the assumption that the career changers who were brought into the program already had baccalaureate degrees. Nevertheless, among the
University of Washington faculty members there are strong feelings that
in spite of these preservice teachers' prior knowledge in science and
mathematics, they need additional course work so they can begin to
learn how to access appropriate content knowledge in order to teach it
well. There is also concern that once preservice teachers are hired as
beginning teachers, providing continuing support (for example, formalized experiences to deepen pedagogical content knowledge) is difficult,
since time and cost interfere.

In addition, that the TLP interns receive endorsements in both middle
school math and science complicates the SST efforts in Seattle. Many of
these students entered the program with better knowledge in one discipline than the other, so the partners have struggled with what experiences
all interns must have. Should they differentiate? Given the federal funding received by the TLP program and the state's guidelines for alternative
certification, the university was required to design a competency-based
program that was somewhat individualized. The competencies are very
general in identifying the critical content knowledge necessary for middle
school math and science teaching. Also, the partners were required to

design a program so that an individual who met all the competencies could graduate early. These issues forced compromises and caused some of the partners to question their involvement and support for SST.

There has been another problem as well. The University of Washington is a Research I university, and tenure-track faculty members in the College of Arts and Sciences are actually penalized for spending too much effort on K–12 schooling. In 2002, in fact, the individual who initially represented A&S on the SST Steering Committee was denied tenure and departed. This left a vacancy on the committee, which was an understandably difficult slot to fill.

Building SST: A Problem of Professional Learning, a Problem of Implementation

Judith Warren Little states that "long-term observers of educational innovation and school reform have argued that reform *might more productively be seen as a problem of learning than as a problem of implementation*."[12] This construct provides a perspective on the nature of the challenges inherent in the creation of the specific partnerships and professional communities in Portland and Seattle.

In both sites, SST participants have identified evolving needs for expanding and deepening their professional learning and knowledge about many aspects of new teacher education, organizational development, and partnership building. Their demand for and openness to new learning stems from two sources. First, by virtue of being a part of the SST initiative, all participants are involved in various specialized fields of teacher preparation and teacher professional development. The participants acknowledge that in their newly configured approaches to new teacher learning, they are deepening their own professional knowledge, and they are learning from each other and from outside specialists. And second, by requiring a collaborative process for decision making, the project asserts participants' ability to identify their needs and problems accurately as well as to develop strategies for dealing with them constructively. Achieving substantive professional learning and developing positive group dynamics take time. In the case of SST, the partners' learning typically emerges from sustained and deep inquiry into their own practices.

Various modes of professional inquiry learning have been evident in Portland. At one juncture, the partners ran into problems that required them to seek help on collaborative group dynamics. Portland asked for outside assistance from representatives of the Teacher Union Reform Network (TURN), who provided extensive and ongoing consultation regarding the union's role in SST. Similarly, during the course of their SST work, many individuals and groups have made their own requests for assistance. Partners have pinpointed helpful resources, or upon request, the national project director has identified outside assistance—for example, a consultant on formalizing partnership agreements or an expert on various aspects of job-embedded induction of new teachers. Additional support has come from inside the partnership. In some schools, the governance boards have asked for support with the broad field of mentoring. Some work groups are collaborating with an inside team, consisting of a Steering Committee member and the project co-coordinators, which facilitates sessions with them. One individual on the Steering Committee who has extensive experience as a school district leader and policy expert has met with school leaders, including some principals and the superintendent, who have requested assistance. In short, Portland's participants are building their own capacity to do the broad renewal work of SST.

Judith Warren Little identifies three kinds of teacher–professional learning demands that restructuring projects typically entail, a list that corresponds well with the experiences of both Portland and Seattle:

- Restructuring requires specific professional learning.
- Restructuring calls for "teachers and others to engage in *collegial work*" and in a decidedly "collective and public" forum around issues that prove to be "complex and contentious."
- Restructuring initiatives bring teachers into "new forms of *governance and decision making*," thereby changing their relationships with each other, breaking through some traditional boundaries, and making those relationships less predictable.[13]

SST educators in Portland and Seattle are experiencing exactly these effects. According to Little, one of the paradoxes of reform work is that the process "intensifies professional bonds *and* foments professional con-flict."[14] Above all, our study of SST reveals how the partners' work togeth-er has spawned communities of interest and communities of commitment despite the occasional conflicts.

Spawning Professional Communities of Interest

SST initiatives in Portland and Seattle are expansive, multilayered col-laborations composed of design teams and decision-making configura-tions that overlay and intersect existing governance and programmatic structures. In each partnership, committed individuals tenaciously work through the barriers and tensions surrounding their nascent collabora-tions. As we have discussed, the barriers can be especially rigid when the institutions are complex social organizations such as public universities, school districts, schools, and unions. As one college of education professor commented: "It's a good idea to have internships, etc., in schools [for preservice teachers]. It all sounds fine until the university and the school districts try it. There are major obstacles on both sides."

In studying the hard work of both SST sites, we have witnessed a particular phenomenon transcending the many obstacles and tensions: namely, the professional, intellectual commitment that characterizes the work of the SST participants. Through their collaboration and their creation of new possibilities, SST's educators are bonding into professional communities of interest.

SST's conceptualization of learning to teach revolves around a community endeavor of educational entities within urban settings—a school district, its teachers union, and a university's colleges of education and arts and sciences. In SST, the goal is for the constituencies to mesh their work together, creating synergy to improve teaching and learning in the community. Their work together promises to be stronger than their work apart, as Griffin and Litman characterize good partnerships.[15]

Thus far in their evolution, the SST projects in Portland and Seattle present many phenomena associated with the process of becoming a community of interest. In their respective professional communities, the partners are creating their own new cultures. And they are generating new approaches to preparing teachers for their schools and students of today—and tomorrow.

In their lively community exchanges, the partners freely ask questions, reveal that they have something to learn, share knowledge, confront issues, and offer help. College of education professors provide information about their preservice courses on teaching and learning. Based on their "on the ground" experience and classroom expertise, school district faculty members, union representatives, and school administrators give their views on effective teacher professional development. In Seattle's SST, faculty members in the arts and sciences and those in the school of education have broken through a longstanding boundary within research universities. Further, career-changer interns have requested a voice in the professional community, and the Design Team has welcomed their representation. Thus, SST as a community of interest in Seattle will evolve to be inclusive of another important voice in new teacher education: the teacher interns in the new TLP program. From their critical perspective, these twenty adult learners who are in the act of becoming new teachers stand to contribute many insights to the SST initiative in Seattle.

CONCLUSION

Through ongoing collaboration on design teams, work groups, and committees, SST's participants are coalescing into identifiable communities of interest. Elucidating the SST vision of creating a solid culture of professional practice, a key project leader summed up progress in Portland:

> SST is building into a solid entity, not as a project, but as a way to structure professional practice. SST's framework is that it's not a way to support beginning teachers in the first few years and then "freeze" them. We need an ongoing culture [of teacher learning]. SST's vision, then, is about developing an ongoing culture of structuring professional practice. We can say that our Steering Committee is focusing on one particular piece of SST, but it's part of the systemic change underlying the SST schematic framework. . . . And, in addition, now that [we] are a solid structure and an identifiable entity, we are a vehicle for other agencies, such as the National Science Foundation, to approach us . . . and for us to approach others.

Partly accounting for the emergence of this new community of interest is the distinct openness of the professionals to new learning and new structures, despite the tensions and difficulties of the collaboratives. As we interviewed and observed SST's educators, we heard them sounding a constant theme: Just by "sitting next to" another practitioner and learning about another's field of endeavor and experience, SST participants enrich their own knowledge. Over and over, the participants testify to the value of their own professional learning and enrichment as vital means of advancing the work of the project. As John Goodlad notes in Chapter 2, these "testimonials reveal the powerful symbioses of simultaneous cultural and individual renewal" that accompany genuine educational improvement. Through SST, we are learning how professional communities of interest are responding to the critical and changing demands of schooling in the new millennium.

NOTES

1. Albuquerque, New Mexico, was a third SST site, but it is no longer in SST.
2. Gary A. Griffin and Patrice R. Litman, "Teacher Education on the Leading Edge: Learning With and From One Another," in Gary A. Griffin and Associates, *Rethinking Standards through Teacher Preparation Partnerships* (Albany: State University of New York Press, 2002), p. 6.

3. Griffin and Litman, "Teacher Education," p. 11.

4. Seymour B. Sarason, Foreword to Ann Lieberman (ed.), *The Work of Restructuring Schools: Building from the Ground Up* (New York: Teachers College Press, 1995), p. viii.

5. Judith Warren Little, "Professional Development in Pursuit of School Reform," in Ann Lieberman and Lynne Miller (eds.), *Teachers Caught in the Action: Professional Development That Matters* (New York: Teachers College Press, 2001), p. 28.

6. Phillip C. Schlechty and Betty Lou Whitford, "Shared Problems and Shared Vision: Organic Collaboration," in Kenneth A. Sirotnik and John I. Goodlad (eds.), *School–University Partnerships: Concepts, Cases, and Concerns* (New York: Teachers College Press, 1988), pp. 191–204.

7. Adam Urbanski, "Teacher Professionalism and Teacher Accountability: Toward a More Genuine Teaching Profession," *Educational Policy* 12 (July 1998): 450–451.

8. Urbanski, "Teacher Professionalism," p. 453.

9. Julie G. Canniff and Melody Shank, "Strengthening and Sustaining Teachers: Portland Evaluation Report" (Portland, Maine: SST, 2002); and Barnes, "Learning to Walk and Talk Together," Chapter 3, this volume.

10. Canniff and Shank, "Strengthening and Sustaining Teachers," p. 44.

11. Canniff and Shank, "Strengthening and Sustaining Teachers," p. 44.

12. Little, "Professional Development," p. 31. Emphasis added.

13. Little, "Professional Development," p. 32.

14. Little, "Professional Development," p. 25.

15. Griffin and Litman, "Teacher Education," p. 2.

CHAPTER 9

Today Is Tomorrow

RICHARD WISNIEWSKI

Recently, one of the editors of this book was teaching a class of future teachers who had just returned from a week of visiting schools. They were depressed by the dominant attention to preparing for tests that they encountered there. The first question addressed to him was simply, "Is there any hope that this will change?"

On entering this teacher education program just a few weeks before visiting the schools, nearly all of those enrolled had said that they intended to be in teaching for the long haul. They perceived educating the young to be both uplifting and of great importance to society. Suddenly, they had encountered circumstances appearing to be unduly restrictive, not conducive to supporting the kind of classroom learning they intended to create. They had bumped head-on into the federal law mandating massive testing that provided some of the backdrop for this concluding chapter by Richard Wisniewski. And they were asking one of the major questions guiding his writing. Unfortunately, the excellent answer his chapter provides was not yet available for their reading. One might describe Wisniewski's perspective as a blend of sober realism and cautious optimism. Even in his least encouraging scenario—the first—he conveys a mild, firm optimism. He is saying, in effect, that while "these things too shall pass," do not count on their not being followed by other worrisome circumstances. Public schooling is a political enterprise pushed this way and that by diverse local, state, and federal interests.

Although he occasionally makes explicit the necessity for teachers to be grounded in moral educational belief that keeps them on a steady course, this perspective is more implicit. He himself has been sustained by adherence to moral principle, honed by the exigencies of long and varied experience. He gives the reader no false hope that circumstances conflicting with his perspective will fade away. Some will, but they will be replaced by new ones—often old wine in new bottles. He makes his disagreements clear but does not wring his hands and complain that he would do the right thing if existing circumstances would get out of his way. He leaves the reader to ponder whether his or her own beliefs and commitment are sufficiently strong to withstand the buffeting of misguided school reform eras that now appear to be a chronic condition of schooling.

Largely because of the way Wisniewski opens to the reader the moral scope of teaching the young, writers and readers of this book's chapters (in draft form) sug-

gested that his be the lead-off chapter. We considered the recommendation carefully; there is much to commend it. We finally decided that as a concluding chapter it makes the central message of the opening chapter all the more important. From the beginning, Wisniewski introduces the necessity for the individual teacher to continue throughout his or her career in the learning that accompanies a guiding credo of educational belief. Only then is one able to sustain hope and remain steadfast to moral principle when besieged by conflicting expectations. Wisniewski's message will never be out of date because there will always be circumstances that challenge one's beliefs.

—The editors

As I was writing this chapter,[1] I heard from a friend with whom I have shared many years in education. He is deeply committed to teaching and has always encouraged bright, capable people to become teachers. Reflecting on his positive memories of being a teacher and his work as a professor, he is dismayed by the damage being done to creative teaching by what he calls the standards-and-testing bandwagon. He said that he could not in good conscience encourage students to enter teaching. I share his concerns—but not his conclusion—and end this essay with my advice to those thinking of becoming teachers.

PREDICTING THE FUTURE

Predicting the future is easy for a charlatan, difficult for an expert, and usually futile. Describing the future of the teaching profession is no exception, but it is a worthwhile exercise. It is an opportunity to speculate about which aspects of one's work may endure and which may wither. Since the future is always a product of the past, it may be more vivid than one wants to admit.

The best one can do is to demonstrate the power of Marshall McLuhan's observation that we see the future in our rearview mirrors. Life conditions us to "what was" and to "what is." "What will be" is difficult to contemplate given the urgency of the present. While wisdom and age may be correlated, the relationship is not a given. The longer one lives, the more likely one's conditioning is an even greater hindrance to so-called out-of-the-box thinking.

Whether one addresses what teachers do, their preparation, or what schools might be like, the same issues and forces come to the fore. After a lifetime in public education, I have been conditioned to what goes on in schools and colleges. Everything I know about them has been reinforced in tens of thousands of ways. I believe this is true of virtually all teachers, administrators, and professors. Predicting where teacher preparation and teaching are heading is vexing when one is immersed in the mix.

Like others, I lament that teachers do not have the same intensity of training associated with other professions. Their working conditions are not conducive to reflection or to providing the individualized attention that children deserve. Research on teaching and learning is overwhelmed by ideological, political, and social factors, including a heavy dose of folk wisdom. Expectations for teachers are deeply rooted in our culture. Almost any change is viewed with suspicion. Because of the sheer mass of the enterprise, school practices are replicated and reinforced again and again. Despite variations on the theme, schools are far more alike than different, be they public or private, large or small, urban or rural.

My thinking about these matters is compromised by an optimistic bent. I believe that teaching is making progress toward becoming a stronger profession despite conflicting evidence. I have an idealistic streak that colors my perceptions of what is happening or ought to happen. I *want* teaching to become far more of a profession than is now the case. I *want* efforts to strengthen the preparation, induction, and work of teachers to succeed, and my ideals color what I see in the tea leaves. I am also enough of a realist to know that ideals are never fully achieved.

I sometimes worry that there are not many people in teaching, in schools of education, and in the educational bureaucracies who are deeply concerned with the future. It is understandable why this would be the case. Keeping the vast educational enterprise going is nearly overwhelming. Dealing with problems at every level and just getting through the day are more than enough for most of us. Many, if not most, teachers assume that the future of their profession is the kind of vague subject that superintendents might worry about, but it is not something remotely close to the world in which they work. Indeed, they would prefer that their superintendents worked harder on providing higher salaries, more supplies, or less-crowded classrooms.

Many professors would not seem to be much different in this regard, and this is not offered as a criticism. I am merely underscoring that the daily demands of one's work and responsibilities leave little time or energy for thinking about the future, even at the university level. Many teachers and professors want their profession improved, and they struggle to make their programs stronger. Their desires and goals, however, are usually limited to improving "what is" rather than offering alternatives. Small changes do not seriously influence where an entire profession might be heading except in a slow, glacial sense.

Even policy wonks are conditioned by their rearview mirrors. The formulation of a policy and its translation into legislation and regulations is a slow process riddled with compromise and political considerations. The changes offered are usually sharply focused and may take a generation to be broadly effective. Their impact is limited because so many other conditions of teaching are left untouched, and the latter will undermine that which is changed. Fixing or improving "what is" has a way of diluting visions of a more desirable future.

I do not offer these thoughts as a cynic. My observations do not apply to those struggling to alter how schools are organized and how teachers are prepared—persons who go beyond superficial efforts to improve the enterprise. Ideas such as differentiated staffing, small rather than huge schools, and alternative ways of organizing schools for learning have the potential for dramatically changing schools. My professional heroes are those who have demonstrated alternatives to the lockstep notions of schooling, teacher preparation, teaching, and assessment that characterize the profession. I weep at how often they are frustrated as they struggle to advance their visions—frustrated especially by others in the profession.

With these worries, assumptions, and convictions permeating my thinking, I offer my view on the future of teaching. I hope to demonstrate that anyone engaged in education can, to some degree, predict the future of teaching. One has but to pause and observe what one does day after day and some of the future will be revealed. It is what we do today that is the foundation of tomorrows to come. If we become more aware of the consequences of our daily actions, we are on the cusp of understanding the future of our calling. Each new course, each new requirement, each new appointment of a teacher or professor, for example, is an act that helps to determine the future in a small, incremental way. What we do now is a precursor to what we will do tomorrow.

I offer three scenarios for the future of the profession. One or more of them may come to pass, but the time frames involved are highly uncertain. In the 1960s, Arthur C. Clarke offered a vision of the world in 2001. It is a safe bet that he did not anticipate writing sequels projecting his ideas into the year 3001. In contrast, Alvin Toffler's *Future Shock* (1970) had a more immediate impact. The book appeared in an era when many were concerned with the future of our society. Courses on the future appeared at some universities. A futurist colleague of mine had taped to his office door a cartoon of a man sitting in a chair. A clock in the background shows the time to be 6:00 p.m. The balloon above the man's head shows the same clock showing the time to be 6:05 p.m. The caption reads: "The man who could see into the future."

My predictions have the limitations captured by that cartoon.

SOME GROUND RULES

Let us assume that foretelling the future is akin to playing a game or a sport. Certain rules must be followed for the game to be played. I offer ground rules that, if followed, could make predicting the future more of a game than an ideological showdown. I use the term "game" deliberately, since game theory is at the heart of analyzing trends and predicting outcomes.

Rule 1: Whatever one's biases, the most important rule is to qualify carefully any generalizations one makes about teaching.

I begin with this rule, because it is violated often and blatantly. There are about three million teachers in this country. Each of the fifty states has regulations regarding who shall teach, how they shall be prepared, and so on. There are fifteen thousand school districts and school boards, each with its own unique history, pattern of organization, and political intrigues. In these districts, administrative structures range from a superintendent in charge of one or two schools to the byzantine bureaucracies found in large cities.

There are about eighty-five thousand schools at the elementary and secondary levels. Each school has its own subculture, despite pressures toward standardized practices. Each school attempts to implement the curricula for which it is responsible. It also adapts to the socioeconomic variations among the children it serves. Because of the isolated nature of teaching, each teacher shapes what is taught and how it might fit into the overall scheme of education within a given school and system.

There are currently about thirteen hundred schools of education of varied quality preparing teachers. I believe that the past two decades have seen strengthened practices emerging on many campuses. Requirements have been raised and curricula have been altered. Partnerships with schools are now far more evident. The idea of linking preparation with the achievement of children in schools is gaining adherents. At the same time, there are alternative ways for entering the profession, also of varied quality. Some have great potential, and others undermine programs in the best schools of education.

There are hundreds of professional organizations and associations to which teachers, professors, and administrators belong, each arguing for its primacy. Federal, state, and local governing bodies, politicians, critics, journalists, judges, pundits, and others all play roles in guiding, controlling, and evaluating the educational establishment and its teachers. And most powerful of all, everyone who has gone to school has memories to determine his or her impressions of what is right or wrong about the enterprise.

I have said enough to underscore why I begin with the pious injunction that one should try to control the inevitable tendency to overstate conditions, behaviors, or remedies. Given the disregard of this fundamental injunction on the part of many politicians, critics, and even professionals in the field, it seems foolhardy to wave a cautionary flag. At the very least, statements about teachers, schools, or colleges should begin with the phrase "some teachers," "some schools," or "some colleges." Such generalizations will be closer to the truth, though even "some" covers a lot of territory. I do my best to observe this rule but am not always successful.

Rule 2: The second rule of the game is that one should offer predictions at every opportunity.

This rule may appear to be inconsistent with the injunction to be cautious. Would not a plethora of predictions make it difficult to separate the wheat from the chaff, creating a kind of Gresham's Law of predictability? This could well be the outcome, but I will argue the contrary. We can more powerfully impact the course of events by offering alternate predictions at every opportunity. Ideas are like seeds; which ones will germinate and blossom? No one knows which ideas are powerful enough to influence the future of our profession. The more ideas in circulation, the better the odds that some will take hold.

Rule 3: Predictions should include the pros and cons of what is being advocated.

Every plan, policy, or new rule is in effect a prediction of what some group wants teaching to become. Specifying outcomes, likely problems, and unanticipated consequences is part of this process. Not all consequences can be anticipated, of course. Teaching, schooling, and the careers of teachers, however, are familiar areas of knowledge. It is not difficult to outline what any given change will engender. Laying out the pros and cons of a policy will not stem controversy, but it is the honest, up-front way of dealing with divided views.

Being forthright regarding obvious pros and cons is not apparent in the federal mandate to test children as a way of "not leaving any child behind." Many states have implemented testing programs as, in their wisdom, the single best way to improve achievement. The results are mixed, and that is as neutral a statement as can be made about them. High-stakes testing has been embraced by some as *the way* to get teachers to shape up, to force children to learn, and to punish those who do not make the cut. Does such legislation have merit? Not for those convinced that teaching, learning, opportunity, and the health and welfare of children are far more important than trying to reduce all of schooling to test scores. The testing mandate has more of a punitive than positive tone.

Testing programs have well-documented functions and dysfunctions. If children fail the tests, they will be left behind. This is a dysfunctional outcome. Branding some schools as failures will not ensure that needed resources will be forthcoming. Deteriorating school buildings will not be repaired simply because tests are taken. The health needs of children will not be improved because of test results. These matters are debated, but many are apparently willing to allow the future of children to be determined by politicians imposing a wrongheaded solution. While promising the opposite, the testing mandate will likely deepen the gaps between the haves and have-nots.

This is not a screed in opposition to tests used as diagnostic tools or to measure selected forms of achievement. I advocate the use of tests in this manner as part of the teacher preparation process. Nor should my reservations be viewed as being in opposition to increasing achievement levels. Some children and teachers will work harder to prepare for the tests. Some schools will demonstrate gains in various subject areas. But these outcomes are pale substitutes for allowing children to demonstrate what they know and can do in a host of ways. A policy that reduces teaching, learning, and life opportunities to flawed tests of subject-matter mastery is not in keeping with good sense, let alone everything known about growth, development, and learning.

The testing mandate is sufficient to underscore the fact that policies are often riddled with pluses and minuses. And if there are minuses, the policies must include ways of mitigating them. Ignoring negative outcomes because of political expediency, intellectual dishonesty, or ideological fervor is not acceptable, yet this behavior is common in public life. Happily, there are groups and organizations ready to challenge those in power. The health of a democracy is dependent on persistent challenges to those who would be king.

Rule 4: My fourth rule is to "think big"—to offer predictions of sufficient scope to make a difference.

This may seem like another contradiction of Rule 1, but I am merely echoing the oft-heard injunction to think out of the proverbial box. This is especially difficult to do for some in education. I am thinking again about the standardization and routines that are so much a part of schooling.

Teachers, principals, professors, and all others associated with the enterprise are overwhelmed with the mass of details that need tending day after day, week after week, year after year. As a result, change efforts often focus on the details of schooling rather than on more fundamental parts of the process. Thinking big when predicting the future means that the ideas offered must be of sufficient scope to challenge the existing order. They have to upset and replace that which is accepted as normal and appropriate.

An example of "thinking small" is seen in endless efforts to change some aspect of the curriculum. We have had "new" reading, math, and social science programs by the bushel. Publishers and software merchants hawk the latest materials that will ensure that children will learn every subject taught in the schools. More ambitious programs may require that teachers receive specialized training to use the new materials, while others proclaim that they are "teacher-proof." Whatever the curricular change, researchers will prove that the new materials are better, about the same, or perhaps worse than what was in use originally. These mixed results are especially likely if the new materials are judged exclusively by test results.

Curricular changes that do not deal with the preparation of teachers, the induction system, the conditions for teaching and learning in schools, the evaluation process, and other aspects of schooling are simply insufficient. Piecemeal changes in curricula or any other aspect of teaching will not alter much of anything except in superficial ways.

THREE SCENARIOS

There are many possible scenarios for the future of teaching, but I can offer only three that are visible in my clouded rearview mirror. I am thinking in a relatively short-term time frame, say the next twenty-five years. I can speak with some authority about what has happened over the past fifty years, and my experiences help me to project them into the future. Twenty-five years from now, (1) teaching will be much the same but more difficult; (2) teaching will be much the same but improved; or (3) teaching will be markedly different from what we know today.

Scenario One:
Teaching Will Be Much the Same But More Difficult

Despite everything being done to strengthen teaching and to improve schools, these worthy efforts will be reduced in their efficacy by more powerful conditions outside the profession. Growth and demographic changes are a part of these trends, but they are not necessarily huge problems. These are things with which schools have grappled for decades. They are not easily solved problems, but the genius of American education is in keeping with the motto of the Statue of Liberty: Public schools have again and again taken the huddled masses of each new generation and offered an education, despite formidable internal and external problems.

I do not subscribe to the chic opinion that public education either has been or is currently a failure. It is the one institution in which all Americans should take pride. Granted, it has not served all in our diverse society well. It could be better, and not all teachers and principals are heroes. Like any institution, it has its blind spots. But at the end of the day, what a marvelous thing it is: an institution that seeks to provide an education for everyone in our society. And despite attacks on public education, the vast majority of Americans continue to demonstrate that they deeply value their schools.

The problems faced by public education are not new. What is amazing is how well it all works despite those problems. My concern in this first scenario is not with teacher preparation, induction systems, salaries, and other issues. These are matters that have confronted the profession for decades, and they will continue to do so, although we have every hope of making slow but sure progress. Rather, my concern here involves at least two powerful societal phenomena that hinder improvement.

First, our political system is failing to support our schools and far more. Throughout our history, the struggle over addressing human needs has been central to the political process. The Republican Party is devoted to the reduction of taxes and governmental services. The Democratic Party has, to a lesser degree, joined this chorus. The complexity of these bald statements need not be examined here. My concern is with the effect that rancorous political wrangling has had on schooling and all public services.

As a public enterprise, schooling is dependent on a tax base that will allow it to serve a growing and diverse population. While money alone will not change education, it is its lifeblood. Inequities in funding remain unresolved, especially given the needs of urban centers. Yet many politicians have lit the sky with one message again and again: Our taxes are too high and must be cut. We can have all the public services we need and pay less in taxes. We can even go to war and simultaneously cut taxes. All of this, we are told, can be accomplished by demanding efficiencies in government and by turning to the private sector for selected public services.

The fact that I do not agree with this view is not why I enter the morass. I do so only to assert that our society has been enervated by this ideological schism to the point that the future of all public services is less than sanguine. If funding for education, health, safety, and other public needs continues to be cut, with only occasional bursts of support, why would the next twenty-five years be much different from the present? If we as a public continue to be bombarded by the view that government is bad and that we should not expect to be taxed, how will our public services get the resources needed?

The good news, of course, is that the nation is split on the issue. Voters often pass school levies and indicate in polls that they would pay more in taxes to improve specific public services, especially schools. What is worrisome is the gap between what the majority of people say they want and the workings of the political system. The debate about campaign financing is about far more than the amounts of money that can be contributed. Those of other persuasions do not have to accept my views to acknowledge the linkage between the fight over taxation and the future of education.

Acknowledging variations often within the same state or community, schools over the next several decades will remain essentially as they are for the simple reason that the monies needed to improve them will not be available without a dramatic shift in the political scene. I am convinced that the emergence of a third political party devoted to the support of public services is the only viable hope for a better future. Catastrophic events can also influence what will happen, but a catastrophe does not have even the hint of a silver lining.

A second sociocultural factor that supports a "more of the same" scenario is the resistance to change so apparent in education. As some wag put it, if Rip Van Winkle were to awaken in this age, he would be amazed at the marvels that would greet his eyes. The one place he would feel comfortable would be in the typical classroom. The one-teacher-one-classroom model of direct teaching remains the pattern for schooling, despite 1,001 variations that coexist alongside it.

Given the power of the culture of schooling and the expectations for teacher and student behaviors embedded in that culture, arguing that things will be far more alike than different would seem to be a safe bet. Perhaps one has to live through it to truly understand, but as I participate in the educational debates of the day, I think back to when I heard the same issues and words fifty years ago. Schools have changed over those fifty years—and I would argue that they have changed for the better. But the debates within and without the profession are as predictable as the tides.

Improvements in many aspects of education have not fundamentally altered the mainstream of what most children experience or what teachers do day after day. Computers in classrooms, as but one example, have augmented but not overcome century-old routines. The new technology may take more than twenty-five years to seriously alter teaching and learning save in innovative settings. We have always had such settings, and one can only hope that there will be more to come. It is remarkable how persistent the educational mainstream is, given all of the positive examples of how things could be changed and strengthened. But it is not surprising. The culture of schooling is a reflection of what most adults, including teachers, experienced as children, and this is what most persons expect schools to be like.

The resources needed to provide rich educational experiences for all children and to better prepare and reward teachers are available in the richest nation on earth, but many have been conditioned to believe the opposite. Even more disturbing, healthcare for all children is not likely to be provided on the scale needed despite the strong correlation between good health and successful schooling.

While one need not accept this scenario as a given, it is consistent with what has been experienced for decades. Teaching will remain much as it is but burdened by ever-growing constraints and limited resources. The ideological wars will continue. Every advancement will be tempered by political and resource issues that will limit its efficacy. This scenario may cause some to despair and give up, but others will always continue the good fight to achieve the schools we say we want.

Scenario Two: Teaching Will Be Much the Same But Improved

This is a more positive prediction. It is premised on a resolution of the gloomy resource condition described above. This does not mean a political miracle will take place or that debates about the allocation of resources will disappear. It is based on the assumption that political groups more disposed to expand and support public services will be in power more often than not over the next several decades. It is further predicated on a shift in the public mood that will even more strongly support public rather than private solutions to health, education, and other public services.

I have already suggested that teacher preparation is becoming more rigorous and is stronger than it was several decades ago. I say this as one who remains critical of many established practices. Colleges have increased admission standards, have made their programs more clinical in nature, and are working more closely with schools. This cannot be said with confidence of all thirteen hundred teacher-preparing colleges, but there is good evidence that the majority have responded positively to criticisms of their practices. Many teacher educators point with justified pride to what they have done to raise standards, strengthen curricula, and respond to school needs.

Making any change in the academic environment is difficult and slow. This is why I am convinced that some teacher educators would be doing even more to link their programs to the pressing needs of schools if they could do so. Not all professors of education, of course, are eager to get too close to the hurly-burly world of public education. They work hard to slow the efforts of those colleagues ready to enter the fray. But even more powerful are those university procedures and traditions that make it very difficult to make even modest changes in programs or ways of working with schools.

University expectations and reward systems are designed to keep professors as close to their nests as possible, and this is true of all academic disciplines. The problem for teacher educators is that their work does not have the buffer zones common to other disciplines. What is happening in education is of broad public concern and on a scale beyond that with which other disciplines must deal. Despite the rhetoric of higher education that trumpets linkages to school needs, the gap between the words and practices is great. I would add that reading advertisements for new professors of education is usually a gloomy exercise. The expectations communicated to applicants seldom include working closely with public education or the opportunity to be part of innovative programs. They essentially read as if they had been crafted decades ago.

Some of the other contributions to this book are devoted to the links between teacher preparation and the induction of new teachers. Promising mentoring practices are offered as a way to support new teachers, to build career paths, and to encourage and reward teachers for enhancing student learning. While such activities require additional funding, the amounts needed are modest. Much can be accomplished by redesigning established preparation, hiring, and induction practices using available resources in redirected ways.

There are reasons to be optimistic that these efforts will eventually characterize the preparation and induction phases of teaching. The longer-term goals of career paths and changes in the reward system for teachers will likely require a longer period of transition. Even so, teaching as a profession will be strengthened because of these changes. But will it be much different from what is happening in classrooms today?

A positive response must be premised on the belief that all teachers will have the skills, dispositions, and subject-matter competencies appropriate to their responsibilities. While this is an easily challenged premise, let us assume that this will be the case. The problem remaining is that even the best-prepared, most conscientious teachers will be working in schools based on the industrial model of education that has been the norm for a century.

The key components of the factory model of schooling include age/grade groupings, a teacher for each classroom and subject, and rigid funding formulas based on the number of children per classroom. The curricula for each grade and subject are prescribed, and assuming that the testing-*über-alles* mantra remains dominant, the "learning" outcomes for each grade and subject are also prescribed. The idea is essentially that of an assembly line with teachers doling out what children must learn as they pass from grade to grade. In the classic divide between viewing children as empty vessels to be filled with knowledge, on the one hand, and what is known about learning and multiple intelligences, on the other, the former doctrine dominates the scene.

One has only to note the reduction in music and art classes to make the point. The sad fact, of course, is that one can learn or reinforce basic skills in any school activity, be it physics or the marching band. The sadder fact is that to pass tests in the "important" subjects, schooling continues to lose the richness of opportunity and skill building vital to well-rounded individuals. "Fill 'em up with facts and move 'em to the next filling station if they pass the test!" is the current political–educational dogma. One suspects that even ardent advocates of this narrow approach know better—based on their own school experiences or those of their children—but they seemingly cannot make a connection to the realities of schooling beyond a get-tough stance.

I am reminded of my first courses in education. I was taught that our system of education was superior to that of other nations because we did not determine a child's life chances solely on the basis of a test. We were taught that the British 11-plus examination, so called because children took it at age 11, was an elitist practice. It determined who went on to what type of secondary schooling and then to universities and higher-status professions. In effect, it was a sorting mechanism and a powerful inhibitor to social mobility.

The civil rights movement and research on racism, gender discrimination, and tracking demonstrated that we in the United States were not as pure as we claimed to be. Despite the evidence, we are now imposing our own system of high-stakes tests culminating in graduation examinations. This is being done on a scale unprecedented in our history. I remain convinced that what I learned as a neophyte served me well. It is wrong to gauge learning and to limit opportunities solely on the results of written tests. Doing so ignores a host of other ways to assess what a person knows and can do. It mocks the richness of life.

I have tried to imagine the type of schooling people have in mind when they insist that tests will determine that standards have been met.

I support the need to raise academic expectations, but the true believers in testing do not seem to see a connection between their advocacy and what has the earmarks of a totalitarian form of schooling. Schooling would seem to be reduced to the following principles: set standards for each subject and grade; insist that each teacher, school, and principal prepare children to meet those standards; reward those that do, punish those that do not. Anything not encompassed by this ideology is a frill or liberal poppycock.

Is this overly simplistic? I certainly do not hear much from testing advocates about alternative ways of organizing for teaching and learning and for ensuring that schooling is more than "fill 'em up and test 'em." There are a variety of possible reasons for their silence on the matter. Are they elitists who accept a permanent underclass in our society as something desirable? Do they really want schools so consumed by testing that all other functions and activities are expendable? Are they so ignorant of the multiple demands on schools that they do not comprehend that most teachers manage to teach content, facts, and the other stuff of testing every day, often in conditions that make it a heroic task?

I do not know what the politicians and testing advocates think about these matters because they dwell on content knowledge as the be-all and end-all of schooling. Perhaps their goals would be more persuasive if they honestly discussed the full range of what goes on in schools and what schools are attempting to accomplish. But that means abiding by my rules for making predictions, and ideological wars have no room for such niceties.

What I do know is that the concerted effort being made by the Republican administration to control education is without parallel. Never before in our nation's history has the federal government attempted to mandate the outcomes of education on the scale now apparent. Never before has an administration determined, as prime examples, how reading shall be taught or how all learning is to be assessed. This administration has even defined what is acceptable as research. The distinctions between state and federal roles in education have become ever more blurred. The line separating public monies from religious education has been crossed. All in all, the agendas of right-wing foundations and other opponents of public education have been adopted by the administration as its platform.

Given this political climate, it is difficult to focus on educational issues that, while important, are at the mercy of powerful political currents. To do so means capitulating to a severely limited and harmful ideology. The profession must continue to work for the best interests of children and public education, especially when problems are of such long standing that the political climate is not a dominant factor. I am thinking here of the rigidity of secondary education. The resistance to change in high schools is far more within the profession. Despite the alternatives demonstrated by the Coalition of Essential Schools and countless other efforts, the American high school remains much as it was a century ago. Most teachers work with about 150 students a day for a semester. Be it literature, history, or math, each teacher must attempt to make each fifty-minute period meaningful day after day, week after week, month after month, year after year.

The grind of this system of organization inexorably works to reduce its effectiveness, taking its toll on all concerned. Many teachers—even those who are well prepared, know their subjects, and are healthy and highly motivated—will adopt standardized presentations, procedures, and materials if only to survive the grinding nature of this form of schooling. Many students will be bored by the endless repetition of the process. We have known this to be the case for decades. And while some high schools are different from the norm, they are anomalies. They are beacons of hope or irritants, depending on one's ideological views.

But if one believes that things can be improved, this scenario offers hope. Stronger preparation programs, stronger induction systems, and better rewards for teacher skill development will strengthen the profession and increase the number of highly capable teachers. Many of the frustrations of teaching and being a student will remain the same, however, because the environments for teaching and learning will remain essentially the same, albeit a bit better.

Many educators and concerned observers acknowledge that changes must be made in schools so that teachers can work more effectively with children. This is a good sign. It is essentially a deferred goal, however, within the profession. It is all too easy to become embroiled in the details of improving some piece of education such as preparation or induction systems. The difficulty in working hard on the details is that it culminates in superficial improvements. It is akin to polishing a stone. No matter how glossy the surface, it remains a stone. In my view, the devil is not in the details. The devil is in the material being polished—in this instance, the way that schools are organized and staffed. This is why I offer a third and most hopeful scenario.

Scenario Three: Teaching Will Be Markedly Different

Scenarios for the future of teaching are commonplace among those who see technology as the key. I am sure there is merit in those predictions, and the uses of technology continue to grow in schools. But as already noted, technology appears to be an add-on rather than something that is transforming the fundamental culture of schooling. It is a part of this third scenario but not a driving force. I put a much higher premium on the encouragement of alternative approaches to organizing schools and to innovative teaching practices.

Over the decades, there have been thousands of efforts to demonstrate different ways of teaching and learning. They can be found in many school systems on a limited scale and at least for a while. The alternative school movement in the 1970s and the current charter school movement are cases in point. There is a major ideological difference between the two, to be sure. The earlier movement challenged the public schools for their failure to better serve minority and poor children. The latter movement uses the same rhetoric, but its supporters come from conservative segments of society that were not part of the earlier effort. While not a blanket condemnation, the altruistic motives of the past have been tainted by religious and profit motives that conspire to weaken public education.

I support selected charter and other alternative schools despite worrisome reservations. I have gone so far as to propose charter colleges of education as a way to accelerate changes in preparation programs. I recognize the danger that some forms of alternatives might deplete resources needed by public education. Again, the explanatory factor here is the ideological warfare that pervades education. Alternative and charter legislation does not have to be slanted to favor anti-public education forces. Those governors and legislators who support that bias can and should be deposed. The legislation can and should be rewritten. I am also aware of the mixed success of alternative programs. Nonetheless, innovation is vital to the future of education. Alternative approaches can provide needed demonstrations of organization and teaching that challenge lockstep, standardized thinking about education. Unfortunately, the term "choice" has been co-opted by some people who are clear threats to public education. And, ironically, some alternative models are less innovative than the public schools they seek to replace.

There are many ways to educate, encourage, and support children. This is why I support smaller schools, schools within schools, magnet schools, and other approaches to encouraging and providing for children. The pluses and minuses of these approaches are not as critical as the need for innovations to be encouraged. My real concern is with the reluctance of many administrators and teachers to be part of innovative approaches. I do not believe that polishing the stone of existent practices will lead to nirvana. New practices are the hope of the future, and they need to be nurtured at every opportunity. My sense of a desirable future embraces efforts to polish some current practices and to use technology. But this view is tempered by the conviction that we are working too hard on polishing existing practices and not hard enough on visions of teaching that would transform schools. Our nuts-and-bolts approach to improving things essentially perpetuates "what is" rather than charting new courses.

As a dean of education, I challenged notions of how a faculty is organized, how content is organized, and how instruction is delivered. I did my best to support and reward groups of faculty willing to change their work with students despite the resistance of their colleagues. I learned, like many others, that changing anything in higher education is difficult—but not impossible. In short, I did what I could to encourage alternatives in a setting where standardization is even more powerful than in K–12 schools. Universities are by and large highly resistant to even minor internal changes, while they preach the desirability of change for other institutions.

Demonstrating alternatives, usually in pilot programs, will not necessarily bring about changes in the mainstream. Defenders of the mainstream have inertia, the law, tradition, established practices, and even the endorsement of those long since graduated in their arsenal. Alternative or pilot programs are allowed to exist as long as they do not threaten the mainstream. Ironically, the mainstream will likely list the alternative as evidence of being *au courant*. Such efforts are often dependent on outside funding, and defenders of the status quo know they will go away in time. Further, the teachers or faculty willing to create alternatives have only so much energy. Their ardor is dissipated by skirmishes with colleagues and administrators who do not provide the nurturance and protection needed by programs built on fresh assumptions.

Because of my involvement in alternative approaches, I came to the conviction that the work of teacher preparation calls for a different kind of faculty from that found in most colleges. Only handfuls of professors are willing or able to devote the intensive time required by clinical, school-based preparation programs. Many more respond to university expectations and other motivating factors, and this is not a condemnation. If experienced teachers are on faculty teams working with interns, the dynamics of what is done changes remarkably. Things simply become more realistic for all concerned. I need not dwell on how difficult forming such teams is, given reward and status differences between schools and colleges. It always takes some remarkable college faculty members, teachers, and principals for anything of this nature to work.

An innovative college of education would not be staffed in the traditional manner since it would not offer the traditional programs now in place. While faculties struggle to improve programs, the same people who offer the old programs will offer the redesigned programs. This means that improving existent programs in schools of education is fine as far as it goes, but the changes made are not at the levels needed. Without the infusion of new people in the process, the ideas and compromises involved will be relatively limited in their efficacy. Neither lawyers nor doctors nor teacher educators can reform themselves by keeping the process within their own ranks. They need the stimulation and challenges presented when outsiders are part of the process and of their work.

In education, evidence abounds that involving teachers, students, and professors from the arts and sciences is vital to any redesign process, and even this listing is insufficient. It is not realistic to expect the mainstream of teaching or teacher preparation to change of its own volition or because positive exemplars of different approaches are available. The institutional conditioning process noted earlier is a powerful detractor. Hence, the change process must bring together people with different perspectives and experiences. It is not an easy process, but learning often takes place among the diverse participants. Equally important, the changes under consideration must be on a scale that will challenge all parts of a highly structured system. The need to crack eggs to make an omelet is an apt aphorism.

These realizations led me to what may be the only way to seriously change the nature of teaching, along with preparation and induction programs. I believe that we need fewer rather than more well-prepared teachers. If I stop at this point, the statement would seem nonsensical. It is contrary to what is heard again and again in education circles. My conviction is based on two fundamental characteristics of the teaching profession.

The first is the "flat" nature of teaching as a profession. Most teachers get the same training and do the same things with only grade and subject variations as they gain in experience. This conception of teaching is no longer the only viable model available. Yet this traditional view of teaching is reinforced with virtually every new teacher licensed and hired. And at the college level, virtually all new professors of education are graduates of doctoral programs only superficially related to alternative visions of teaching and schooling. While the narrowness of graduate programs can be defended as their strength, in the field of education they are often dysfunctional when measured against redesigned preparation programs.

Given present conditions, we will never solve any of the persistent problems to which so many now devote their energies. If the flat nature of teaching is not changed, the quality of the people attracted to teaching and their preparation, their induction, their effectiveness, and everything associated with their work will remain the same, with perhaps only modest improvements. And the colleges preparing teachers will largely remain as they are with only some members of the faculty ready and willing to work closely with colleagues in the schools.

Second, it is doubtful that we can recruit or prepare the two million or more teachers who will be needed over the next twenty-five years, surely not at the levels of expertise needed. We have had roughly a century of trying to strengthen the teaching profession. Only a misanthrope could ignore the strides that have been made in the preparation and work of teachers in ever-more-complex schools. Even so, I believe a reconstituted vision of school staffing is a more realistic way to strengthen the enterprise.

As I read the endless lists of knowledge, skills, and dispositions that should characterize teachers, I wonder about the fundamental premise behind them. It appears to be a belief in human perfectibility that does not mesh with reality. I do not know anyone who has all of the traits described. I do not have them and wonder if those developing the lists might not be deficient as well. These lists serve a heuristic purpose, but they also distract attention from other ways of influencing the future of teaching. If we operate exclusively on the assumption that every classroom will have a highly skilled, motivated teacher, we will not examine other ways in which teachers and other adults can work with children in redesigned schools.

Further, as often as the "best and brightest" mantra is reiterated, only some of the best and brightest will choose teaching. Every profession has the same mantra, and most of them have salaries and other inducements not yet matched by teaching. Happily, we may be seeing a shift in this regard as school systems offer bonuses or favorable mortgages to attract teachers. However, all in all, it is safe to assume that the people attracted to teaching will be much like those of past generations.

What teachers and others will do in schools of the future is more important than concentrating on every single teacher having the same level of preparation, skills, and dispositions. We need to redefine what a teacher can be and will be doing in the future. We also need to involve more adults in schooling rather than assuming that the one-teacher-one-group-of-children model is an inviolate arrangement. I am suggesting that not all people working with the young must be fully trained, career teachers. However, I have two important caveats. First, only highly prepared and effective teachers will be the leaders of the teams working with children. Second, all those who work with children will have appropriate levels of training and licenses. Nothing being offered here is intended to suggest that we flood schools with ill-prepared people in order to cut costs.

We have had demonstrations of differentiated staffing in schools for years, but they have not seriously weakened the bedrock assumption that for every class there must be one qualified teacher. Some teachers have aides, some work in teams, but the standard of the industry remains one classroom, one teacher. This mode of staffing need not disappear, but it should not be the only or prevailing norm.

We already know to a highly accurate degree what the one-teacher-one-classroom model can and cannot attain. We have polished this stone to perfection. Other approaches need to be devised, and the most promising would appear to be schools organized around instructional teams. A team might include one or more teachers, aides, interns, parents, and community members. The size of the team and of the group of children for whom the team is responsible would depend on what is taught, grouping practices, and other variables unique to a given school.

Whatever the numbers, the basic organizational framework for schools would include instructional teams, cohorts of students, and the blending of subject areas. Flexibility in how instruction is delivered and the uses of time would be the norm, again, under the leadership of well-prepared, experienced, and well-paid career teachers. Some already advocate that such leadership might be a role for some National Board-certified teachers.

While interns, aides, parents, and experts from the community would be on teams, their work would always be supervised by lead teachers. This point cannot be overemphasized since it is at the heart of a new conception of teaching and staffing. There is not a fixed formula for the composition of teams, nor should there be. An elementary school of three hundred students now will have about fifteen teachers. Perhaps only half of that number would be needed in the model being proposed, but that number is not the key to the concept. Some troubled schools may need twice the number of career teachers found in a similarly sized successful school. The prime guiding principle must be how best to serve students in a given school utilizing a range of people to support and augment highly skilled career teachers.

Issues such as alternative certification would be fairly easy to resolve using this model. *All* people becoming teachers would serve one- or two-year internships, depending on their prior training or work experience. They would be encouraged to teach at different stages of life, full or part time. Those seeking to become teachers would not receive teaching licenses until they had completed adequate preparation programs and demonstrated their abilities on instructional teams. Colleges of education would no longer, in effect, license their graduates, as is now the case. (Although licensing is a function of the state, and some will argue that colleges only *recommend* people for a license, the reality is quite different.)

The relationship between principals and teachers would be altered, since instructional responsibilities would be shared by them. The preparation of administrators, like that of teachers, would be closely linked to school needs. The traditional curriculum in educational leadership departments, like the curricula of teacher preparation, would be dramatically different from what is now offered. At this juncture, it is difficult to find programs of teacher or administrator preparation that focus on alternate visions of staffing, teaching, or administration.

Five-year teacher preparation programs would be the norm, with the fifth year being a clinical internship. Anything less perpetuates the current practices and expectations of teachers. Every intern would hold a bachelor's degree with a strong content background. The distinctions between elementary and secondary preparation programs would be minimal since expert teachers need pedagogical skills that transcend the usual grade-level distinctions now in place. Partnerships linking colleges and school systems would focus on learning and achievement in the schools in which interns are placed. Specializations in education would require a minimum of a master's degree and additional internships.

Licensing, salaries, and professional development options would be predicated on the assumption that even a five-year preparation program cannot fully prepare a person to be a lead teacher. Career-development activities would offer the path to this goal. The four-year programs offered by most schools of education would be, in this conception, at the paraprofessional level. I am *not* equating competence with the length of time required to prepare people. I *am* advocating higher levels of preparation, however. The content and pedagogical limitations of what can be accomplished in four years are well known, but the majority of schools of education remain trapped in the traditional pattern.

I have only begun to sketch the characteristics of the types of teaching and learning structures that could characterize schools in the future. Changes in preparation programs are only the tip of the iceberg. With well-prepared and well-paid teachers responsible for teams of people at various levels of training and responsibility, differentiated salaries would be required. Indeed, differentiated staffing may be the only way by which the resources devoted to teaching can be utilized in new ways while at the same time raising the salaries of career teachers. Whatever the defects in the model, it offers a way of breaking the gridlock that characterizes debates about teaching.

Not everyone in a school would necessarily be a full-time employee. This change alone would make it possible to attract more people to the educational enterprise, including licensed teachers and paraprofessionals. Some teachers in rural areas could work in two different schools, spending a day or two in one and a day or two in another. This could be a way of dealing with chronic shortages in selected subject areas. I have long advocated that having, for instance, a physics teacher for two days a week would be far better than not having one at all or having someone who is unqualified offer the course. Any number of changes will be required in personnel policies, the assignment of teachers, compensation packages, and certification codes. While the task of changing so many pieces of the puzzle is formidable, the pieces now in place are all based on the premise that there must be a teacher in each classroom. Once that premise is altered, all the other pieces begin to crumble.

Nothing I have proposed is off-the-wall. Actually, it is all off-the-shelf. Everything suggested has been debated or demonstrated over the decades. Is it possible that there has been enough ferment in education so that the next two decades could be characterized by a renaissance of sorts? Not necessarily one of great, flashing changes, but one where innovative ideas are encouraged, revisited, and cobbled together so that who becomes a teacher, the paths to preparation, the induction systems, and the very staffing and organization for learning in schools is a creative rather than a static phenomenon?

Will the public support such changes? Will governors and legislators help? Will the critics of education back off? Will the teacher unions fight the differentiated concept? In my mind, these are premature and not really important questions. One can assume that other visions and goals will be in evidence. Achieving consensus will never be anything but difficult. It is far more critical to determine if we as a profession want to work toward such a future. Convincing others that this is the best path will be as difficult as preserving the status quo.

I believe that new ideas are always the way to go simply because the status quo is a known quantity. It does not take much imagination or gumption to look in the rearview mirror. Are there enough people in the profession who share this conviction? Are we at, as some call it, a tipping point where all the change efforts of the past three decades will come to fruition over the next thirty years?

Or will we continue to polish the stones of our respective subjects and specialties? Will we each remain convinced that if only we can make our program a bit better or get a few more dollars we will have improved education? Will we continue to focus on mentoring new teachers while the conditions of teaching deteriorate further? These are but a few questions that need to be addressed in order to determine the fiber of our convictions as a profession. Our track record with respect to such questions is not encouraging, but it is not hopeless, either.

Some of the answers to these questions are dependent on the priorities set by the teacher unions. Collaboration between teacher educators and the unions remains problematic because of the nature of higher education. While working closely with schools as partners has become acceptable, the idea of working with the unions remains a hurdle for many in teacher education. Some of the fragmented nature of teacher education can be explained by this condition. Many institutions preparing teachers have evaded national accreditation because the National Council for the Accreditation of Teacher Education is strongly supported by the National Education Association. This mechanism for meeting basic standards remains contentious to this day. This situation prompts two observations: (1) the relationship between unity and strength continues to elude many in higher education, and (2) advocating high standards for schools but not meeting them via the accreditation process is blatant hypocrisy.

One reason the Strengthening and Sustaining Teachers initiative is important is the involvement of the teachers unions in the process. SST provides evidence of what can be done when a school system, the local union, and an institution of higher education work in concert. This collaborative pattern may be the key to a better future for teaching despite the opposition of anti-union groups. Over the past three decades, the two teachers unions have become powerful forces. Preserving the status quo while advocating improvements might be an apt descriptor of earlier efforts, but both the NEA and AFT now support serious systemic change. The so-called new unionism may well be the wave of the future.

CLOSING THOUGHTS

The ideas, issues, and concerns on which I have but touched are in the literature and are voiced at conferences. I do not cite sources because these matters are part of the profession's common currency. Instead, I would only paraphrase a gifted musician who said he was indebted to every good piece of music he had ever heard. So it is with this offering. I am indebted to far more people, readings, and debates than I could possibly specify.

I have encouraged thinking about the future as a product of what we do today. I have advocated far more innovation and flexibility in education across the board as a way of breaking through lockstep practices. I have offered a vision of differentiated staffing in schools as a way to change dramatically how teachers can work with children. Although making accurate, long-term predictions is nearly impossible, envisioning the relatively short-term future of teaching is not beyond our abilities. A beach is created one grain of sand at a time. As all of us in education examine what we do as teachers, professors, or administrators to contribute our individual knowledge and skills, we are shaping the future. In general, our actions perpetuate what we already know and can do. They point to a future much like the present. But if we explore and implement new ideas, we open the door to a different future. My scenarios have flaws, and I have not dealt with all of the pros and cons of each choice despite my third rule of offering predictions. Doing so would require a far deeper analysis of many points. The third scenario, however, at least moves our vision to the road ahead, a road different from one we know all too well.

For my part, I continue to be inspired by and salute those demonstrating different approaches to recruiting and preparing teachers and changing the nature of schooling. They offer the best hope for a positive future for teaching. As one who has both gone the route of maintaining the status quo and sought alternatives in the world of teacher preparation, my happiest and most positive memories are of deviations from the norm. Creating or supporting programs that challenged the mainstream was far more interesting than maintaining the status quo. Doing something that goes against the grain and has to prove itself gives one a sense of being a part of the future.

Those who would strengthen schooling and teacher preparation by seeking to invoke even more standardization are often well meaning. They essentially want a world they know, not one with many unknowns. Whichever stance one takes, it is a choice difficult to avoid. Either we help shape the future or we struggle to preserve what is receding ever more quickly in our rearview mirrors. Whatever the choice, all of our yesterdays are today, and all of our todays are tomorrow.

Finally, I return to my friend's decision not to encourage young people to become teachers. Though I share his concerns about what is happening in education, I would still encourage bright and capable men and women to choose teaching as their calling. If the first scenario prevails—that is, more of the same for years to come—it follows that those things that draw people to teaching will also essentially remain the same. It needs to be noted, however, that the variations in funding for education are such that many people recruited to systems now and in the future will be paid relatively well, have good facilities, and experience a high level of professionalism. In other words, the inequities found in education make quite different the experiences that children and teachers alike will have in schools. The teacher shortages and limited resources faced by urban schools in the world's richest nation are the most telling evidence of this fact.

In the second scenario, encouraging people to teach would be easier. The new teacher will come better prepared, will receive mentoring and a graduated induction process, and can look forward to faculty development opportunities and salary gains linked to student achievement. These changes are at the beginning stages in systems across the country and they will make teaching a much more attractive profession. True, the conditions of teaching would not be changed much, but people have taught and survived—and some have even thrived—under those conditions for decades.

My strongest endorsement of teaching is directly related to the positive vision for the profession outlined in the third scenario. Even if that scenario does not come to pass, the struggle over the future of education can and should be a powerful argument for becoming a teacher. Teaching is no longer a way to escape from contentious times—if it ever was. It has become ever more at the core of all of our societal values, aspirations, and problems. Each fall, a new cohort of Americans begins its schooling. Children come to our nation's schools with an increasingly complex set of backgrounds and experiences, and the overwhelming majority of teachers will do all they can to educate them, often under inadequate conditions.

I share my friend's hopes for schools where creativity is nurtured, but teaching has never been a haven for risk-taking individuals. Until the emergence of strong unions, the docility expected of teachers was a pervasive characteristic of the profession. The reasons why people become teachers are well known, as are the demographics of the teaching population. There are, of course, creative teachers, my friend among them, but their number has never been high. They have often struggled to be creative in a culture far more supportive of conformity for students and teachers alike. All institutions expect their inhabitants to conform, to fit in, not to rock the boat, and not to be "too creative." Public schools and higher education are not much different in this respect.

The conditions of schooling and teaching experienced by most teachers do not allow time for reflection or creativity. The relentless nature of the school calendar, grade and subject groupings, testing mandates—the system—encourage conformity with only minor deviations being allowed. The movement toward standardization and routine behaviors is overwhelming. It is even more of a problem given the federal mandates being imposed on schools. Until schools are reorganized and staffed along the lines suggested, the trend toward conformity will only increase. Creative teaching will become more and more rare. The demise of creative teaching and freedom among teachers is bad for children, and it insidiously weakens public education and our democracy. Despite these conditions, teaching continues to attract many people who want to educate and nurture children and perhaps to make the world a bit better. These are desirable and commendable traits. And, contrary to often spurious charges, students in colleges of education compare favorably in academic performance to college students across the disciplines on most campuses.

My encouraging people to teach, then, is not based solely on promises of better pay and teaching conditions. It is a call to fight the good fight for children and for public education—a moral cause, if you will. I view teaching as a calling, something more than simply wanting to work with children or to earn a living. The stakes have always been high in the struggle to develop and preserve public education. It is possible that many teachers have fulfilled their years in the classroom with little thought given to the drama in which they were playing a part. They were happy to know that they helped as many children as they could. The broader struggle has always been evident, however, and it is now virulent. It cannot be ignored or evaded.

Never before have as many well-funded conservative groups focused their energies on attacking public education. Future teachers not only must know their subjects and have pedagogical skills; they also need to be prepared to be strong advocates for educational reform and the preservation of public education. Yet, as I review preparation programs past and present, I see a growing emphasis on the skills aspects of teaching but little emphasis on the broader vision needed by teachers. Preparing people for a different future is not evident in most preparation programs. My years in colleges of education taught me that most teacher educators try to protect their students and themselves from controversial matters rather than grappling with the realities of teaching, which include being prepared to deal with controversy.

Because of my optimistic bent and despite the odds, I argue that there has never been a better time to become a teacher for a person with a strong sense of calling. If one wants to be where the action is, teaching is at the crossroads of what America is becoming. If one wants to reinvent education, this is the era in which to become a teacher. Granted, the newcomer to teaching is at a stage of his or her career when getting "my room and my kids" is a powerful motivator. One of the major weaknesses of preparation programs is that they condition teachers to want and expect this and nothing more. In this day and age, as one example, it is unbelievable that neophytes are not prepared to work with a teacher's aide unless that should occur by chance during student teaching. But more to the point, beyond subject-matter competence and teaching skills, a commitment to being an advocate for children and for public education should be a prime goal of the preparation process.

A successful program like Teach For America has its limitations, but it has demonstrated that many capable college students respond to an idealistic appeal. The same is true of programs such as Teacher Corps, VISTA, AmeriCorps, and the Peace Corps. As differentiated staffing takes hold in more school systems, teaching will be an option for people other than college students. My fondest hope for colleges of education is that they become far more active in recruiting people with strong idealistic aspirations rather than polishing the stone of their traditional programs. This means creating programs that are renewal oriented and open to a larger pool of potential teachers. I have acknowledged changes being made in teacher education, but they remain at a tentative level. The need for alternative paths within colleges based on new conceptions of who and how one becomes a teacher remains great.

I can only urge those concerned with these issues to spend less time trying to polish to perfection the nuts and bolts of preparation, induction, or career development systems. We need to concentrate instead on conceptions of teaching that by their very nature would dramatically facilitate and nurture the levels of teaching and learning desired. The harder we work to improve the system now in place, the more we guarantee that the system will remain essentially the same.

NOTE

1. The title is drawn from a character in a novel by Tom Robbins: *Fierce Invalids Home from Hot Climates* (New York: Bantam Books, 2000).

About the Editors
and the Contributors

John I. Goodlad is president of the Institute for Educational Inquiry, professor emeritus of the University of Washington, and former dean of the Graduate School of Education at UCLA.

Timothy J. McMannon is a senior associate of the Institute for Educational Inquiry and a history instructor at Highline Community College in Des Moines, Washington.

Richard E. Barnes is an associate professor of educational leadership and former dean of the College of Education and Human Development at the University of Southern Maine.

Sheldon Berman has been the superintendent of the Hudson Public Schools since 1993 and is a former president of the Massachusetts Association of School Superintendents.

Sharon Feiman-Nemser is the Mandel Professor of Jewish Education at Brandeis University.

Thomas Gillett is the regional staff director for the Rochester office of the New York State United Teachers (NYSUT/AFT) and a former English teacher.

Paul E. Heckman is director of the Center for Educational Renewal and a research professor at the University of Washington.

Daniel Katz is assistant professor of secondary education at Seton Hall University.

Corinne Mantle-Bromley is executive vice president of the Institute for Educational Inquiry and a research professor at the University of Washington.

Nancy Jean Sahling is a private education consultant specializing in advancing the understanding and improvement of teacher professional development.

Roger Soder is a research professor of education at the University of Washington.

Adam Urbanski is president of the Rochester (NY) Teachers Association, a vice-president of the American Federation of Teachers, and director of the Teacher Union Reform Network.

Patricia A. Wasley is dean of the College of Education at the University of Washington and chair of the Coordinating Council of the Strengthening and Sustaining Teachers initiative.

Betty Lou Whitford is dean of the College of Education and Human Development and professor of education at the University of Southern Maine.

Richard Wisniewski is a professor and dean emeritus at the University of Tennessee and former dean of education at the University of Oklahoma.

Index